MODERN MADNESS

The Hidden Link Between Work and Emotional Conflict

DOUGLAS LaBIER

AN AUTHORS GUILD BACKINPRINT.COM EDITION

Modern Madness:

The Hidden Link Between Work And Emotional Conflict

All Rights Reserved © 1989, 2000 by Douglas Labier

AN AUTHORS GUILD BACKINPRINT.COM EDITION

Published by iUniverse.com, Inc.

For information address:
iUniverse.com, Inc.
620 North 48th Street, Suite 201
Lincoln, NE 68504-3467
www.iuniverse.com

Originally published by Simon & Schuster

ISBN: 0-595-08900-3

Printed in the United States of America

CONTENTS

Can the individual spirit survive the society in which it has to live?
— Nathaniel Hawthorne

An era can be said to end when its basic illusions are exhausted.
— Arthur Miller

ACKNOWLEDGMENTS

Of those who helped in various ways throughout this project and in the writing of this book, I am most indebted and especially grateful to Michael Maccoby, who first encouraged me many years ago to write about cases of people whose emotional problems related to work and career. Since that time, as teacher, colleague, and friend, he has consistently provided support, valuable criticism (sometimes painful, always helpful), clarification, stimulating discussion, fresh ideas, and practical suggestions, all of which made it possible to transform this project into concrete reality.

Others to whom I am grateful for helpful comments and ideas include Mauricio Cortina, Jon Frederickson, and Diana Hanson. Heddy Slatovitch and Jan Shapiro provided helpful assistance as the book took shape, and Anne Buchwald provided useful advice during the book's formative stages. I am also grateful to Linda Sunshine, Doe Coover, and Susan Lee Cohen, who provided encouragement and useful editorial suggestions; to Laura Tracy, who provided challenging criticism and discussion, which strengthened the revisions; to Eric Ashworth, who provided guidance and sound advice during the genesis of the revised edition; to Carole Hall, whose editorial help was valuable in preparing the revised material; to Pearlbea LaBier, who contributed helpful criticism; and to my children, Michael, Sarah, and Peter, who always helped me keep the work on this book in a sane perspective, whether they knew it or not.

And, of course, I am most grateful to all the people who participated in my research, and who must remain anonymous. A note in that regard: to protect the identity of the people I describe in this book, I have disguised all names and potentially identifying information about them. None of these alterations, however, have affected the description or interpretation of case material.

PREFACE

Although I am psychoanalytically oriented, conventional psychoanalytic thinking does not explain to my satisfaction the link between career *success* and emotional problems. Neither do the grab bag of pop-psychology theories which fill the shelves of bookstores. They are too lightweight, simpleminded, and too quick to shift in and out of fashion as people latch on to the latest "how-to" guide to happiness and success, and then quickly abandon it when it fails to have any lasting impact on their lives or behavior.

Questions and observations about how people's emotional lives are affected by the culture of work have been in my mind for several years, since the beginning of my career in the early 1970s. At that time, most practitioners I met had no such interest. In fact, they believed that social, political, economic, and historical forces had nothing whatever to do with understanding or treating emotional problems—and that psychoanalysis had no relation to studying social or moral issues.

Erich Fromm was the only analyst I knew of who dealt with these issues in his writing and teaching, until an article in *The Washington Post* caught my eye, around 1970. Co-authored by Erich Fromm and Michael Maccoby, the article was an excerpt from their study of the character of Mexican peasant villagers under the impact of new technology and the social forces resulting from industrialization and modernization.[1] Though I knew little about Mexican culture, I was struck by how Fromm and Maccoby integrated an analysis of social and political forces with psychoanalytic understanding of the character, values, and unconscious motivations of the villagers.

Their work was guided by the psychoanalytic point of view developed by Fromm through his many writings on the psychoanalysis of materialism, consumerism, and relation to authority. Many of Fromm's books, like *Escape from Freedom, The Sane Society, The Art of Loving,* and

others had been widely read by the general public, but largely ignored
by the mainstream of American therapists and analysts. Yet Fromm had
been practicing psychoanalysis longer than nearly anyone else alive, at
that time, and he had probably influenced the general public's thinking
about psychoanalysis and society more than anyone since Freud.

I noticed that the article described Maccoby, who later achieved
international recognition for his studies of corporate and government
leadership, as an analyst who had just arrived in Washington to be a
Fellow at the Institute for Policy Studies. With Fromm, Maccoby had
developed a method of social-psychoanalytic research for studying the
character development of people in the context of social institutions
and political forces. Fromm had pioneered this method in the early
1930s in Germany, before fleeing Hitler. Directing a group of researchers at the Frankfurt Institute, he studied the likelihood of the German
masses supporting Nazism, should Hitler come to power.

Maccoby had come to Washington to begin a Harvard University–
sponsored project to study the social character of successful corporate
managers in America: people in the advanced technology industries,
like electronics, plastics, and chemicals, whose products and work organizations represented the cutting edge of economic and social change.
Using the methods he had developed with Fromm in Mexico, Maccoby
began researching who becomes successful and why; and what the consequences were for them, intellectually and emotionally, as well as for
the future of American corporations.

Shortly after reading the *Post* article, I heard Maccoby speak at a
professional meeting. He had an open, friendly face, a lively manner,
a sense of humor, and a penetrating gaze. Aside from the latter feature,
he did not seem like a typical analyst. We talked briefly about the Harvard Project and his previous work with Fromm, and shortly after I
made a decision to begin psychoanalytic study with him.

Maccoby's Harvard Project culminated in his popular 1976 book
The Gamesman,[2] which was hailed as a landmark study of the modern
corporate manager. My work with him through that period, combined
with my study of Fromm's contributions to understanding people and
society, affected me in two parallel ways. First, it showed me the value
of expanding the psychoanalytic point of view to include the realm of
adult choices, decisions, and values, which could be influenced by how
we adapt to cultural, political, and economic conditions, not only by hur
early childhood experiences.

This more interpersonal and "here and now" focus had been central
to Fromm's psychoanalytic thinking—he had written about common-
alities between the Zen tradition and psychoanalysis, for example—and
it differed from the direction mainstream psychoanalysis had taken in
the decades since Freud's death. That is, psychoanalysis now tends to
neglect the power of our passions, our impulses, the cutting edge of

Freud that Fromm had emphasized further in his work. Mainstream psychoanalysis has become increasingly caught up in abstract concepts and theories which often have little relationship to the emotional realities and sources of problems for the contemporary person. Orthodox practitioners today tend to reduce everything about adult life to issues of childhood, examining its minutiae ad infinitum, often ad nauseam. The orthodox method can subtly exonerate the patient from facing the reality of adult life and the responsibility for change, all the while maintaining an illusion of "working" on one's problems. The consequence is seen in the tragicomic emotional meanderings of the urban careerists that Woody Allen portrays so well in his movies.

The second way my work during these years affected me was that it forced me to reexamine my patients' lives and struggles in relation to the career culture and the workplace. While many had said they believed that the successive conflicts and trade-offs they had made in their work and career were linked to their conflicts, I had listened with a deaf ear. I had always assumed that these complaints were simply the product of their difficulty adjusting to the realities and demands of work, which is a part of the adult world. And we regularly see cases of this: for example, there are people for whom adult demands trigger problems rooted in unconscious attitudes about authority, about submitting to or rebelling against mother or father, unresolved feelings of competition with brothers and sisters, or in other family issues which family therapists have shown can be reenacted over and over in our adult lives.

But I now began to rethink all this. I began to see that there were more reasons why people become troubled or conflicted than a bad childhood. Guided by Maccoby's work on the social character of corporate executives, I started to look at the emotional consequences of the character traits and attitudes that organizations do—or do not—support among the men and women who work within them. I began to look more closely at the possibility that some of my patients were troubled by problems within the realm of adult adaptation, problems related to our changing culture of work and the standards of success and normal adjustment it has defined for us.

I felt I had stumbled upon a trail, after thrashing around in the woods and underbrush. I didn't know where it would all lead. But one thing had become clear: I needed to get out of my office and immerse myself in the outside world of large organizations, in order to better understand how career experiences affect our emotional lives. I had become comfortably ensconced in my office, treating people individually in a situation that, for the practitioner, is very isolating and encourages a limited, if not grossly distorted view of the world outside. I needed to study people who had never sought professional help, not just the skewed population of those who had; and people who had never reported any problems regarding work as well as those who did

Finally, an opportunity arose. In late 1977 Maccoby suggested that I study these issues as a corollary to a project he had begun to improve the quality of work and leadership within a large federal department, at the beginning of the Carter administration. Because of that department's wide range of work—administrative, policy-making, legal, economic analysis and forecasting, budgetary, scientific, technical, and so on—it represented a good cross-section of government bureaucracy. At the same time, many of its activities were more similar to those found in private-sector organizations, which is not the case for most federal agencies and departments.

I set out to study why certain people developed what looked like clear neurotic symptoms on the job, noticeable to others, whether colleagues, superiors, or subordinates. I questioned why some became outright "troubled employees," as they were known, and whether their troubles might relate to their work or management. Could I learn something that would account for the difference between them and others who were more clearly "career winners" and who also showed evidence of problems on the job? Or still others who were also successful but who had never shown any job-related problems? Would any of them differ from people who sought out professional help for their problems? And what could the organization do to help such people?

I began using the social-psychoanalytic method to interpret the meaning of the symptoms and conflicts troubled people had on the job. This method does not involve psychoanalyzing individuals as one would if they were patients, but rather applying psychoanalytic interpretation to a combination of intensive interviews about personal and work history, personal values, goals and philosophy; analysis of Rorschach tests, which facilitates understanding of unconscious attitudes and passions; and interpretation of dreams, particularly those about work (see Appendix).

I also studied the larger context of people's work and career history; the attitudes they shared with others about career success and what it meant to them; and unconscious motives and attitudes which often appeared only in symbolized form as neurotic symptoms, or in dreams. In addition, I interviewed a range of other people, including managers and nonmanagers at all levels of the hierarchy, as well as union officials, to explore why, from their perspective, some people develop emotional conflict, stress, burnout, and other symptoms on the job. All interviews were voluntary and I kept all material confidential, although I discussed my interpretations with the participants, to generate feedback and clarify understanding.

Over the next seven years I studied and interviewed people between about twenty-five and forty-seven, the age range which, at that time, shared a common core of values, attitudes, motives, and behavior regarding work, career ambitions, and life goals; all of which differed from those of previous generations. For this group, the career drive, despite its many pleasures and rewards, generates many emotional and value conflicts which can remain hidden or disguised. In effect, this is the negative side of normalcy in our culture. I found that the drive for success, and its criteria of money, power, and prestige, exists alongside a parallel, but less visible, drive for increased fulfillment and meaning from work. The tension between these two drives, as they are played out in the arena of the large organizations in which most of us work, and in the political, social, and economic culture of late-twentieth-century America, has unleashed the dark side of successful adaptation.

When I began to study how career success can affect people emotionally, the term "yuppies" had not yet been coined. But over time, I saw that these new-breed careerists steadily populating our organizations and professions were synonymous with what became the public image of the yuppies. What that public image left out, however, was that yuppies are really a caricature of the negative side of the new-breed careerist. The yuppie orientation appears when the drives for achievement and fulfillment fail to merge into a vision of adult life that stimulates creative imagination, passion, and connection with others, and sinks, instead, into an emotional and spiritual dead end of self-indulgence and self-centered preoccupations.

The people I studied came from a wide range of careers in a variety of organizations. Within government, they came from federal, international, state, and local bureaucracies, in the private sector, production and service industries, particularly banking, stock brokerage, real estate development, law, scientific research, universities, advertising, computer companies, journalism, publishing, manufacturing, health care, and hotel management. I was able to broaden the base of my project as a result of the response to several newspaper and magazine articles about it, some that I wrote and others that were written about it in some national publications.[3] The unexpected response to these articles resulted in additional opportunities to interview people from a wide variety of jobs and careers, and in requests to conduct workshops and lectures on my findings with them in different parts of the country. This greatly helped clarify my findings and interpretations through discussion. Also helpful was the feedback from participants in workshops and seminars at the Washington School of Psychiatry, where I presented some of my initial material.

Along the way I also interviewed fellow practitioners about how they perceived and dealt with the possible role of work when helping troubled people—if, in fact, they dealt with it at all. Many refused to talk with me. But of those who did, some were private practitioners, while others worked for clinics or for organizations as a company psychiatrist, psychologist, or counselor. I also interviewed human resource managers, personnel staff, union leaders, and the staff of employee assistance programs and employee health units of organizations. In addition, I studied the kind of training psychiatrists and psychologists receive today at hospitals, clinics, universities, and advanced training institutes.

It was during that first part of my project that I discovered the paradox of people who looked disturbed but were normal, and others who looked normal but were sick. How to make sense of this, and what it meant for career professionals in our business and organizational culture, were the questions that I would pursue for the next several years and the subject of this book.

The reaction to *Modern Madness,* following its initial publication, has made me realize that the urban careerist understands quite well that the culture of work within large organizations and the professions exacts an emotional toll that has been overlooked and misunderstood. What I regularly hear, from feedback when I give lectures and workshops, and from letters and calls I have received from career professionals in all parts of the country, convinces me that there is a growing consciousness about the conflicts and trade-offs facing the careerist. This has, so far, resulted in mostly increased conflict between the desire for success and for greater meaning and fulfillment. Some have been forced to examine what they are searching for by virtue of becoming casualties of reeling economic forces—for example, competent, fast-track executives who find themselves dealing with failure for the first time in their lives, having lost their positions because of cutbacks, mergers, or political changes at the top; or people who lost their positions because of the stock-market crash of October 1987. For many, these crises or simply internal questioning become opportunities to assess, often for the first time in their lives, how their career path, choices, and decisions have affected the overall direction of their lives to date; what they have come to value, in practice, and what kinds of lives they are leading, in terms of their relationships, goals, and overall vision.

In the absence of any clear alternative or solutions, I also see growing desperation regarding how people think of adulthood, judging from how it is portrayed in the popular culture of books, television, and movies. There is a growing theme that being adult is not much fun: a wistful experience of resignation to "realistic" limitations upon creativity, imagination, and love; an experience of longing for adolescent-like enthusiasm for life, our only model, it seems, of passion and excitement. Career conflicts, then, are really part of a larger malaise related to how we envision and practice adulthood in our society. Our modern madness, the emotional downside of career success, is the most acutely experienced form of this malaise today.

In order to find a positive solution to these problems, one must begin by asking the right questions, and learn what the problems really are. This is the only way to create an atmosphere of experimentation and openness which is crucial to arriving at solutions. In contrast, the "how-to" approach found in many popular books clouds over the fact that personal development is a quest that one has to undertake on one's own. This can be hard to accept, especially when a person feels without resources or "tools" to know what to do or how to do it. Examining one's answer to the question "Why do I believe that the solution lies outside of myself, and that I am unable to generate any alternatives of my own?" however, is the first step in the direction of creating new alternatives. One can always learn from alternatives that others have found and the themes that are common to them.

People who become troubled because of their success, as well as those who do not and want to stay that way, are faced with the task of taking responsibility for their own personal development. It helps to know both the real limitations and the opportunities in today's career world. But even more important is having a framework—a vision—of adult life, in which career success is integrated into a larger definition of success in life overall. This perspective helps one to develop a greater sense of trust and reliance in oneself, in one's capacities to face life fully, to see the truth, and develop courage to take action.

HIT THE WALL RUNNING

1

It is not enough to be busy ... the question is: what are we busy about?
                                        —Henry Thoreau

There are two sources of unhappiness in life. One is not getting what you want; the other is getting it.
                                        —George Bernard Shaw

Jacket slung over shoulder, Jim eased through the glass doors into the sauna-bath afternoon waiting for him outside. Retrieving his silver BMW from the parking lot, he glanced once again at the week-old dent on the door: someone's anonymous signature, marring the smooth perfection of the metal. *Damn car only two months old and already ruined by some bastard.* Pulling out into traffic, Jim aimed the air conditioner ducts straight at his face and took a hit of mechanical coolness. He kept the window wide open, hoping to quickly evacuate the heat from the oven that enveloped him. *Running late, Jimmy-boy. Good way to impress the shrink your first session. And the traffic's jammed up, too. Just great. Bet the old blood pressure's already off the scales.* He did a quick maneuver through a few side streets and headed uptown on Connecticut Avenue, a major link between Washington's downtown business core and its uptown neighborhoods. One of several long arteries that seem to radiate outward forever from the heart of the city, it eventually crosses the Maryland border into the tony Chevy Chase neighborhood and heads toward the outer suburbs. *Bet it becomes one of those winding-road countrysides with trees and vegetable stands. One of these days I'll just keep on driving and maybe find something for a good story. But not now. More important things in store today, my friend. And I've put it off long as hell already.* Jim noticed some dark clouds quietly slinking their way across the sky from his right. Suddenly they covered up the sun. Ominous, he thought, with a little smile. Feeling queasy, he loosened his tie and tried to compose what he was going to tell the shrink. Suddenly he was gripped by that anxiety vise that often got him just when he began writing a story. All the material is there; the words just don't come.

Something else did, though: an old recurring fantasy of something snapping and bursting inside his chest. Geysers of blood shoot out his mouth, his ears, and fissures in his chest.

He shoved in a Bruce Springsteen cassette and turned it up loud.

Jim said he had been referred by a colleague who was a former patient of mine, and that he wanted to begin therapy because he had a variety of things "crippling" him. His name seemed familiar; I thought I had seen his byline from time to time in a magazine he wrote for, and in occasional newspaper articles. But I tried to resist making any interpretations about Jim from his socio-political, New Journalism-style writing.

He looked to be somewhere toward the far end of his thirties: trim, sandy-haired, and well dressed, though his Ralph Lauren shirt appeared to be the loser in a battle with the afternoon's tropical humidity.

We shook hands, and he walked across my office looking a tinge weary—or maybe wary. He didn't look around the room as new patients often do, but sat down in the chair opposite me after a short pause in front of the sofa. Then he turned his head and gazed silently out the large window which looks out upon a fenced-in rock garden. He seemed to be studying the rhythmic swaying of the fir trees, which all of a sudden had started taking a beating from one of those quick and violent thunderstorms so typical of Washington summers.

I was curious about why he was interested in therapy. Finally he started talking. Slowly, and in a monotone, he said, "I want to make it clear from the start that I don't think there's very much wrong with me. I had a pretty good childhood. I was always an achiever. I went to the best schools. I think I'm pretty creative. I'm flexible—it was a piece of cake, for example, switching over to the word processor from the typewriter. And I know how to get ahead in my career. I've already proven that. I've always wanted to be the best, have the best. It's just . . . sometimes I feel I don't enjoy any of it. Nothing. I feel listless, like a dead battery. I need something to get me more charged up, but nothing seems to work anymore. Yet I know I've got so much going for me. Recognition, travel, women . . . so I was hoping you could find out what's stopping me from enjoying life more, and fix me up. I need to get more turned-on to life."

Jim turned away from the window and stared directly at me for a moment, looking for something. He flashed a nervous grin, revealing a slightly crooked front tooth. Then he turned back to the window as tears began sliding down his face.

It doesn't take a highly trained psychoanalyst to realize that a person like this is troubled and wants help. The harder task is to understand the meaning of his complaints and know what would really help him.

A conventional approach would be to analyze why Jim seems unable to enjoy the fruits and perks of his success. On the surface it seems like a classic case of some deep-rooted childhood problem interfering with Jim's happiness as an adult. After all, other members of his generation of hard-driving, ambitious careerists are going all out for success without any conflict. At least it seems that way. Is Jim hampered by trying too hard, unconsciously, to please a father who was overly demanding and critical, so that now he can't be satisfied with the success he has achieved? Or perhaps he feels he doesn't deserve to be successful because of some early damage to his sense of self-worth, awareness of which has become repressed. Possibly he is unable to handle the recognition and rewards his work has brought him because it conflicts with an unconscious wish to stay tied to and protected by mother, and that he fears "defeating" his father if he is too successful—a typical Oedipal conflict. Or maybe his narcissistic balloon has been punctured by some failure or disappointment which he cannot face or accept. All plausible explanations. All potentially on target.

Except for one thing: none of these interpretations adequately explains the fact that complaints like Jim's are increasingly shared and voiced by people who, like him, have successful careers in large organizations, and who had relatively normal childhoods. Like an image on a tapestry which can only be seen when you back off a bit and look at the whole instead of the isolated parts, the emotional suffering described by people who are more or less well-adjusted individuals and career winners forms a pattern of conflicts rooted much more in adult decisions, choices, and values than in childhood trauma.

This, then, is the modern madness: the invisible link between careers and emotional conflict. Its victims suffer various disturbances—genuine emotional conflicts—that range from mild distress to feelings of self-betrayal, to stress and burnout, to acute psychiatric symptoms and irrationality. These symptoms, sometimes invisible on the surface, are generated by work and career within today's large organizations. They reveal a pervasive malady that may affect thousands of workers, particularly the new breed of careerist—achievement- and success-oriented men and women, mostly within the 25- to 47-year-old range.

We find that many of these career professionals describe, like Jim, a vague dissatisfaction with their lives that gnaws away at them. They speak of feeling empty and detached, of a lack of meaning, despite career success. Some say that they feel numb emotionally, and that they can't love anyone, that they feel no passion about anything, despite being good in their work. A common theme is the feeling of not being at the helm of things in their lives, despite outward achievement and outwardly comfortable lives. Many have disturbing dreams in which they are trapped inside an airplane or train, careening towards some unknown destination, and terrified of crashing into something sight-unseen. They describe feeling passive and helpless, at the mercy of forces that seem outside themselves and beyond their control, beyond their comprehension, even.

Some critics of mental health treatment describe such people as the "worried well," implying that they suffer from "non-problems" for which "treatment" is but a self-indulgent luxury that lines the pockets of practitioners. While this can always be said about some patients and some practitioners, it would be a serious mistake to dismiss the real and serious emotional impact that work in our culture has upon people.

What is it about work today that can cause such harm? For many career-oriented professionals, most of whom work in large organizations, conflicts have increasingly become a product of the values, roles, and behavior needed to succeed within the organization. Conventional thinking holds that normalcy is equivalent to adjustment, and that a person without conflict or psychiatric symptoms is, by definition, emotionally healthy and well-adjusted. But there is a relationship between career adaptation, normal adjustment, and emotional conflict which has been overlooked and misunderstood. Successful adjustment in life has come to be defined more and more in our era by how we work, particularly within an increasingly bureaucratized society of larger and more complex organizations. How we adapt to work in today's organizations determines whether we develop overt problems or not, more so than whether irrational passions, the kind that usually arise in childhood and result in a neurotic personality, dominate us. Work and career pursuits affect people emotionally in ways that cause some people to become more emotionally damaged by their career and value conflicts than others, independent of how disturbed or balanced they might be inside.

While adaptation to the organization allows us to get ahead and develop our intellectual abilities with enjoyable material reward, it also has a downside. It can bring out the *negative side of normalcy*, like feelings of guilt over self-betrayal or of trading off too much. These feelings underlie the rage, depression, anxiety, and escapism found among many otherwise successful careerists. All of these are psychiatric symptoms. But when found among people who do not have neurotic personalities, these symptoms represent the emotional effects of too much compromising and trading-off to get ahead, even though we do those very things to succeed and therefore be considered "normal."

The mainstream of psychoanalysts and psychotherapists—the very people to whom today's troubled career winners turn for help in dealing with these conflicts—are less equipped than ever to adequately understand or provide help that works. The mental health mainstream knows very little about the significant role of work upon the emotional lives of adults in our society: how careers, the culture of organizations, and bureaucratic layering affect people emotionally. Moreover, practitioners are working with an obsolete view of normalcy, and therefore can't distinguish between problems that are internal, whether based in child-hood or brain biochemistry, and those that are situational: the downside of successful attitudes, values, and strategies developed by career professionals today.

Changes in the modern, ever-larger organization bear directly upon how and why we become emotionally troubled. But because the role of work and career in our emotional conflicts and suffering has been relatively neglected or misunderstood, in contrast to childhood issues, the methods of the analytically influenced mainstream help an increasingly small minority of people who seek help.

Contemporary work-related conflicts have two sources. One is the downside of adapting to the values, attitudes, and behavior that are necessary for successful career development in the large organization. But there is also a range of conflicts generated by the transformation in work from a production-oriented economy, with its bureaucratic-hierarchy form of organization, to a techno-service economy. The latter requires teamwork, participation, flexibility of job competencies, and integration of new technology, to create successful business strategies within highly competitive markets. The new-breed careerist wants more personal development at work, less dependency on old-style authority, and more self-fulfillment in general. But large organizations have been slow to accommodate the new realities. This sets the stage for conflict.

I began my attempt to understand the relationship between careerism and emotional conflicts by looking at some implications of the pioneering effort to understand individual and social adaptation to the modern organization, Michael Maccoby's 1976 book, *The Gamesman*.[1] I found that Maccoby's work provided a link to the questions I had been trying to understand. In *The Gamesman* Maccoby had described four main types of successful corporate managers. He called them the craftsman, the jungle fighter, the company man, and—the most adaptive and successful at that time—the gamesman. The gamesman character tended to be dominated by intellectual traits, such as systems-like thinking, intellectual innovation, teamwork, and flexibility. In contrast to these qualities of the "head," Maccoby found that qualities of the "heart" weren't needed and therefore remained underdeveloped. These included, for example, compassion, generosity, idealism, courage, reason, and the capacity to love.

He found that people who move up the ladder have to be highly motivated to do what the organization wants and needs them to do. An internal selection process occurs in which personal traits and attitudes that are most useful to the work and the roles at any given level get supported and reinforced. Those that are not as useful, or which are unnecessary, are discouraged, thwarted, unused, and are gradually weakened. So the result is a selection and gradual molding of certain kinds of orientations for different kinds of work, a congruent fit between what is required by the work and the character of those who do the work.

The managers Maccoby studied were mostly normal, well-adjusted people. Few showed any signs of disturbance. For example, most were not overly destructive, overly dependent, or grandiose. Most of them were not exceptionally greedy or hungry for power. But from the standpoint of the "heart"—in contrast to the "head"—they were underdeveloped human beings, limited by such attitudes as dependency, power-seeking, and, most importantly, careerism.

These attitudes were not pathological, but they did limit the executives' human development. For example, despite successful careers, they were not particularly happy people. Some complained of an inability to love, which they had never confided to anyone. Most lacked compassion, were emotionally cool, and protected themselves against intense emotional experience.

How does a normal, if "underdeveloped," careerist differ from someone who is truly emotionally disturbed? Generally, a neurotic person is unable to develop his or her heart not because of a lack of opportunity, support, education, or will, but because of irrational, unconscious passions which conflict with—or pervert—development. Underdeveloped people can be troubled and have psychiatric symptoms, but are not necessarily neurotic, in this sense.

Therapists sometimes see patients who are quite emotionally troubled, but who also appear, in some ways, to be more developed than some other patients who have fewer overt symptoms. For example, some have greater capacity for emotional expression and enjoyment of life, a sense of humor about themselves—always a good prognostic sign— or a healthy attraction to beauty and pleasure.

The experience of work can arouse troubles and conflicts because, in some organizations, qualities of the heart aren't needed and supported, and therefore are maladaptive. Then, emotional conflict results within otherwise normal people. And in other situations, explicitly sick attitudes might actually be supported and even adaptive to success. The SS, the paramilitary organization in Nazi Germany, would be an extreme example of the latter. There, one could say, the organization "required" sadistic and destructive attitudes from the people who worked within it. The more sadistic and destructive, the better one could perform the work of the SS and function smoothly within it without conscious conflict. Such passions had to be more adaptive and successful in terms of the activities and mission of the SS than, say, compassion or love of life. So there was an organization in which people dominated by sick attitudes were well adapted to sick work. Yet, within the context of the SS organization, they would have appeared "normal," as long as they remained detached, efficient, functioned well, and showed no conflict.

This framework of thinking allows us to see that actual disturbance, defined in terms of internal, irrational passions, does not necessarily lead to observable symptoms. Put the other way around, symptoms don't necessarily result from unconscious pathological attitudes.[2] So the meaning of symptoms, when they do appear, has to be understood in terms of both what is inside the person and what the situation requires: whether the symptoms reflect unconscious, irrational motives and passions, rooted in childhood experience, or the response of a normal person to threat, stress, or something humanly damaging about the work situation itself.

Either way, for an adult, work plays a major role in determining one's level of development, by either stimulating life-affirming attitudes and supporting development, or, through frustration and oppression stimulating regressive attitudes. For some people, the experience of work can push them over the edge into regressive behavior and unproductive attitudes, or into the acquisition of values which generate feelings of self-contempt, emptiness, and malaise.

These conditions often create a twin paradox, which is a feature of our modern madness. Some people who are very disturbed inside are well-adapted winners in their work. They show no symptoms or outward signs of their sickness in their daily working lives because their career environment, in effect, requires disturbed attitudes and passions for success. And others who do show overt conflicts and troubles, which emerge on the job and can harm their lives outside it, and who appear to have neurotic personalities, are nevertheless within the normal range of adjustment.

I unexpectedly discovered this paradox when I began interviewing career professionals from various organizations who were generally successful and ambitious but who also showed the kinds of problems that usually point to a neurotic personality. Symptoms like anxiety, depression, unexplained physical ailments, escapism, rebelliousness, chronic indecisiveness, passive-aggressiveness, and rage, or problems like burnout, stress, and values conflict, eating and sleeping problems, and overusage of drugs and alcohol. Yet despite their problems, I found them to be within the normal range, though underdeveloped, like most careerists. When I analyzed their interviews, Rorschach tests, and dreams, I found that they lacked significant underlying irrational attitudes and passions. In fact, some were healthier than other people I interviewed who appeared better adjusted to the workplace and who breezed along without experiencing any conflict or difficulties.

Relatively trouble-free in their intimate relationships, outside of work, and relatively conflict-free in their inner emotional world, they nevertheless had noticeable troubles at work. As I studied them further, including their work situations and career histories, and compared them with patients of mine who had similar kinds of emotional conflicts on the job, I began to realize that these were people who showed a range of emotional problems and conflicts, but were not particularly troubled inside. Of course they had some irrational tendencies, like all of us, and some more so than others. But not enough to account for the overt problems and symptoms they showed at work.

To make better sense of this, I began interviewing another group of people, fast-track career winners who had risen high in their careers and who had never shown or complained about conflicts or problems on the job. I hoped to learn something about them that would shed light on the others who did show psychiatric symptoms.

What I discovered was that within this group were people who were very sick. Some were dominated by unconscious, irrational passions of power-lust, conquest, grandiosity, and destructiveness, or conversely by cravings for humiliation and domination. Yet their pathology did not seep into the arena of their daily working lives and on-the-job behavior. They appeared very well-adapted to their work, very competent, and intellectually skilled. From the outside, perfectly "normal."

People who appear sick but are normal. People who appear normal but are sick. To make sense of this paradox and what it means for people who are or may become troubled requires moving beyond the one-dimensional thinking that has characterized our understanding about work and mental health. The kinds of problems related to careers which I have found in my research are different from and more complex than those problems we typically think of as being work-related.

For example, both the typical careerist and mental health practitioner tend to think of work-related disturbance as having one form: a person has a problem because of some internal disorder and it shows itself at work (usually by interfering with the employee's performance). If the person didn't have an internal problem, he or she would have been able to adjust to the workplace without any problems to begin with. This kind of thinking usually recognizes two kinds of work-related problems: severe psychotic disturbance, or the burnout-stress syndrome.

When I first began interviewing careerists in large organizations, I was generally directed to these kinds of people. What was interesting, from the standpoint of the management and organizational culture, was that many of the people who had serious and long-standing disturbances, which did interfere with their ability to perform, had somehow managed to hold on to their jobs. This was often achieved with the help of managers who, out of sympathy or fear, would reassign them from one supervisor to another, or assign their work to other people.[3]

Even with such seriously disturbed workers, the experience of work itself can affect their disturbance. The management philosophy of an organization can reinforce a person's existing disturbance. The demands of work, the behavior of superiors, and other situational factors can combine to trigger new outbreaks of psychotic, bizarre behavior.

And when we think of work-related disturbance in terms of problems like stress and burnout, we again equate adaptiveness with health. We have all seen the articles and "how-to" books that have flooded the marketplace in the last several years, advising people how to deal with the "stress" of fast-paced careers, the dangers of "workaholism," the problems of "burnout" or "situational anxiety" we encounter while coping with career demands in the high-tech fast lane, and the multiple pressures on members of the modern dual career family. Unfortunately, these theories and how-to approaches all uncritically equate the values of careerism with emotional health. They fail to distinguish the positive potential of career success from the negative, and end up equating adaptiveness with healthy functioning. For example, stress and burnout tend to be described as something which is lurking "out there" and can floor us quicker than a classic Sugar Ray Leonard combination. Therefore the "healthy" person should be able to "adjust" to it by using the right techniques or coping skills. Sort of like strengthening your resistance to a powerful flu virus that's going around. The aim is to carry on, but with little insight into what we are carrying on with, and what the effects of *that* are upon us.

The values and culture of the organizations in which we work including the sea-change occurring within them, can stimulate or mask emotional problems, independent of any childhood conflicts which we might have repressed. This is the one area in which none of the stress-management, burnout-avoidance, or workaholism-control experts have much to say. Their prescription is flawed by assuming that successful personal adjustment, which means for most of us career and material success, is necessarily the same as fulfillment and sanity. The stress management and burnout-control experts view emotional conflicts as simply a reflection of some internal weakness or deficit, which prevents us from becoming winners. Their solution is to develop a hardened shell, become more adept at self-promotion and putting down others, and finely hone our techniques for gaining control over the situations which make us feel weak, frightened, and angry. In short, their message is get yours before the Bomb drops, the economy collapses, or you become too old.

Many are seduced by this argument, which has received nourishment from the ideology of the times. The seduction is understandable, because in our present historical period we feel increasingly helpless, passive, and victimized by forces that seem beyond our control. Weighted down by frustration, impotence, and anger, many want solutions, and will opt for the only goals that seem attainable—money and material possessions. If that's the name of the game, no savvy person wants to end up a loser. The result is the media caricature of the yuppie.

TROUBLED WINNERS

The people who experience conflict today and who seek help from therapists and analysts tend to be, by and large, fairly well-adjusted middleclass successes: educated and ambitious people like corporate managers and administrators, businessmen and -women, lawyers, media professionals, journalists, doctors, professors, government workers, scientists, bankers, and others from various fields requiring professional and technical expertise. They are mostly white-collar workers, both men and women, and of increasingly varied racial and ethnic backgrounds. In short, they are career and professionally oriented people who have apparently made it. Outwardly successful, and yet emotionally troubled.

It's a tough world out there, they recognize. Everyone wants to be a survivor. So to cope with their conflicts many absorb what they hear in the media or read in pop psychology books about stress management, how to deal with burnout, or control their anxiety and depression. Yet in the same breath many say they think it is their very coping and "controlled functioning" which somehow relates to their stress and conflict. From some of the very people who have adapted the most successfully we hear that not only the tremendous pressure of our fast-paced lives in our high-tech world troubles them, but that the values, the behavior, and the attitudes molded in us by our careers in big organizations are in themselves emotionally debilitating and destructive. That the conditions of work in large organizations generate conflict over our values and emotions. As one man put it, "I want to control my own environment more, rather than function well within a controlled environment."

The pursuit of career success occurs within a context of major transformations in the world of work. A sea-change, spearheaded by rapid advances in technology and computerization, and by changes in the attitudes and desires of a new breed of careerist, converges upon us most sharply in our daily experience of work, the major source of influence upon us as adults. We are now living in a countdown era toward the twenty-first century that many popular magazines of the 1950s predicted would be a time of amazing and positive technological advances. I recall, growing up back then, that magazines like *Fortune* and *Life* published articles which confidently described a future in which technology and science would emerge as a new patent medicine guaranteed to cure all ills and make life easy and worry-free (at least materially). As any intelligent reader could see, we had gotten a monopoly on the good life, and there would be no stopping our growing prosperity, technological progress, nor, of course, our happiness.

The stories overflowed with prediction about the astounding technological and material marvels that would appear as we picked up steam toward the twenty-first century. Some provided drawings of gigantic glass domes covering futuristic cities, connected together by gleaming monorails; hydroponic gardens sprouting giant vegetables without need of soil; futuristic-looking houses with rooms that looked like the insides of space ships; and smiling people zooming around in personal rocket ship-cars, presumably headed to stores to buy new things with lots of money. It was a vision of Eisenhower-fueled prosperity for all: everyone a winner, happy and excited about life in the new age.

Tremendous advances in technology and our material living have, of course, occurred. And it is in the workplace that these changes converge upon us and have the most impact. They profoundly affect our values, our motivations, and what we find fulfilling and stimulating or frustrating and demoralizing, as well as our potential for either emotional fulfillment or conflict. They do this, in part, by setting the standard for what we hold to be a successful life. For example, if asked for a definition of success, the average person on the street would probably respond by talking about career achievement. For most adults today, success has become synonymous with career achievement. And as we have seen, successful career means successful adaptation. Fitting in. A gradual molding of attitudes, traits, and desires—one's basic life orientation—into those for which there is a payoff at work. This is especially true for careers within the larger bureaucratic organizations, which, we must remember, increasingly characterize the public and private sectors of industrialized nations. Despite all the talk in recent years about entrepreneurialism being the wave of the future, the reality of our era is that our economic and social system is, and will continue to be, dominated by increasingly large, and increasingly service-oriented, white-collar organizations. Increasing numbers of jobs are found within such organizations, not in factories, farms, or small businesses.

Most of us spend the bulk of our waking hours within such a world. In the 40 years since the end of World War II there has been continuous, unrelenting growth of large organizations throughout our society. This includes corporations, government, and unions. Over 50% of the labor force in America work for organizations that employ over 100 people. And 33% work for organizations of over 500 people.[4] Both the size of our organizations and the percentage of the work force working within them is growing; though many creative but bored careerists will be seeking entrepreneurial activity in the years ahead, hoping for a challenging alternative to feelings of entrapment and stifled creativity. But even the new, successful entrepreneurial companies find that success means growth in size as well as profit, growth which inevitably means increased organizational structure staffed by growing cadres of professional managers.[5]

In addition to the increasing size of organizations, we perform our work and pursue our careers within an environment of rapid technological, social, and economic change. This is a new age of computerization and robotization, competitive international markets, shrinking career opportunities in some fields, and rapid growth in others. But that's not all. We are also in the midst of major changes in people's attitudes about work and how they want to be managed, changes found among workers at all levels, from people who sweep floors to people that run multinational corporations. And we are also living in a new age of increasing and irreversible entry of women and racial-ethnic minorities into the professions and into management levels of business organizations and public-sector bureaucracies. Finally, we are in the midst of a major transformation from an industrial-bureaucratic economy to a techno-service economy. Careers increasingly exist within organizations which emphasize service, information, and cooperation rather than industrial production and hierarchy. This change carries with it the requirements of decentralized authority systems, participation, flexibility, teamwork, and opportunity to develop new skills. In contrast, the old hierarchical, segmented-role, bureaucratically structured organization no longer works. It fits a disappearing world. And there lies a bind for the careerist: changes in worker attitudes about authority, the desire for increased opportunities for personal development and fulfillment, and the changing nature of the work itself all require more participation and decentralization and less hierarchy in order to increase productivity and quality.[6] But most large organizations have been slow to accommodate the new realities. This evolution has stirred up a negative side to careerism.

Problems experienced by today's careerists represent an evolution in their own right. Contemporary emotional conflicts are different, in many ways, from those that Freud tried to untangle early in this century. In fact, the kinds of problems that people have had in the decades since Freud, and their link to careers, have continuously evolved.

INTERWOVEN THEMES

The emotional impact of the transformations in the workplace and the evolution in the kinds of problems people experience have taken on concrete expression in the form of two different but interwoven themes that have emerged in our public consciousness over the last few years. The first is a theme of increasing dissatisfaction with and often outright hatred of work. Particularly among the baby-boomers and yuppies who appear so career-oriented and hell-bent on "having it all," we increasingly hear and read about the lack of pleasure and fulfillment from work. Many people would think it was a joke if they were asked whether they really enjoy their work.

When I began interviewing people in large organizations I quickly discovered that the reality of job-related emotional problems is well known among career professionals themselves, if not to therapists and analysts. It is something that most people can identify with. For example, we are all familiar with the common office jokes about needing to take a "mental health day"—calling in sick when there is no physical prob-lem—now and then, in order to maintain one's sanity. Or the comment "you have to be crazy in order to work in this organization," which most of us have heard (or said) at some time. National surveys report dramatic drops of job satisfaction occurring among all age groups, in every oc-cupation, in every social class, and in every part of the country, despite the simultaneous increase of commitment to career in the mid-20s to mid-40s age range.[7] The complaints include a lack of meaning in work, a lack of connection with the products of work (whether on the assembly line or in the corporate suite), lack of opportunity for participation and development of new competencies, and pervasive dissatisfaction with management and supervision.

Rising from this pool of complaints is increasing evidence about the emotional effect of our work and careers upon us, in terms of actual psychiatric symptoms (depression, chronic anxiety, paranoia, debilitat-ing indecisiveness, and uncontrollable hostility on the job) and a range of stress, burnout, and debilitating trade-offs. A current study by the National Institute of Mental Health estimates that almost 20% of all Americans have a diagnosed mental disorder, with anxiety, substance abuse, and depression heading the list.[8] This is an underestimate, since it only takes into account those who have entered the traditional mental health system. Estimates of people who suffer from work-related prob-lems like stress, burnout, acute psychiatric symptoms, as well as from a broad range of work-related values conflict, malaise, and feelings of compromise, which don't take the form of an acute psychiatric symptom yet take a serious emotional toll on the individual, range as high as 45%.[9] Approximately 25% of all employer-paid medical claims are for emotional problems, and the percentage is growing each year. And the most severely affected by the lack of opportunities for development and fulfillment at work are the younger, highly-educated, ambitious ca-reerists.[10]

An understandable reaction to troubles related to the workplace is found in the example of some career-oriented people who try searching out some substitute pleasure or fulfillment from alternative activities or interests, while opting for all the money and material benefit they can get by performing work that they don't enjoy very much. But this is an end-run strategy which is ultimately doomed because it can't substitute for satisfying work, and only feeds debilitating feelings of self-betrayal.

Many others are upfront about wanting more from their career, yet feel passive, hopeless, and helpless about the prospect of improving their working lives. And there are others who report feelings of estrangement from their commitment to success. For example, recent classes of MBA students at the Harvard Business School have openly raised concerns about the costs and trade-offs of molding themselves to corporate career values in order to become winners. They question the meaning and worth of it all.[11]

Some become so troubled by personal conflicts related to work that they seek professional help from psychotherapists and psychoanalysts—whether out of hope or desperation. I had observed this over the years in my own patients, and had found a similar picture from discussions with colleagues who also recognized that increasing numbers of patients were seeking help for problems that seemed related to work. More than one had expressed feelings like Ted's. He was a preppy-looking professional who also did wildlife photography on the side, as a hobby. He sat down one day, pulled off his glasses, and began crying. He finally looked up at me and said, "You know what I was thinking about on the way over here? When I was a little boy I used to have a lot of fun. I was interested in everything, trying anything, learning anything. If someone had told me then that my life would be like this today I would never have believed them. I used to feel excited about lots of things when I was a kid, but no more. I hate my work. I spend hours and hours doing things that are totally uninteresting, totally meaningless. I can't stand it any more. The routines, the schedules, the bullshit meetings, squeezing things in, doing this, doing that, living life according to all the programs and formulas. If I were no good at it, that would be easier, in a way. But I am good; it's just that I can't stand it anymore."

Ted felt his life was moving down an increasingly narrow tunnel. He imagined himself looking through the wrong end of a telescope, with his future being that little speck of light at the end. He reminded me a bit of the title character in Thomas Mann's classic short story "Tonio Kröger."[12] Always feeling on the outside, looking through a window into a world that others seemed to accept and enjoy without complaint or distress. Torn between bohemian and bourgeois values, yet not fully a part of either world.

Many younger careerists today describe, like Ted, feelings of self-betrayal. Life has played a big joke on them, a joke that only began to dawn on them after they finished their education and began the career climb. Their subsequent lives constitute the punch line. They long to recapture the spirit of adventure and interest and the expansive excitement about new pleasures and new competencies they had felt as a child. Buying expensive pasta makers or new clothing they seldom wear isn't enough. But when they become so troubled that they seek help they are told by their analysts that they must learn to accept reality and adult responsibility. In effect, accept your success and stop complaining.

And this brings us to the second theme building in the public consciousness over the last few years: a resurgence of interest in psychoanalysis. Both as a way of helping us make sense of the problems and frustrations we experience in today's world, our passions and human dilemmas, and as a method of treatment which just might, after all, help us overcome our problems better than any other that has been devised. Throughout contemporary culture, as seen in all the books and articles that have appeared over the last several years about psychoanalysis,[13] there is a growing consensus that there is no way to deal with emotional issues without facing and making sense of what we experience inside. Namely, the passions that can enslave us, the hidden motives that can pervert us, and the illusions that can blind us.

In part, this refocus on inner experience represents a swing of the pendulum away from the quasi-therapy fads of recent years like est, assertiveness training, "growth" experiences, and "behavior change" strategies, which advocated putting on new "behaviors" or attitudes as though it was as easy as slipping on a new coat. Like most fads, they have now run their course, and are being seen for the banality and foolishness that most of them are. For example, people are realizing that the so-called self-actualization programs inevitably lead into a morass of self-indulgence and self-centeredness. In fact, they are out of sync with the more positive traits of the 1980s new-breed careerist, like commitment, teamwork, flexibility, and practicality, which exist alongside the tendencies toward egotism, selfishness, and materialism that characterize the public image of the yuppie.

There is an ironic twist to this resurgence of interest in psychoanalysis, however. As we will see, mainstream psychoanalysis, including the related psychotherapies it has spawned, has rendered itself almost totally impotent to deal with the kinds of problems that trouble people in the 1980s. Why this is becomes clear as we understand the connection between the twin themes of dissatisfaction with work and renewed interest in psychoanalysis. Conflicts generated by work, including successful work, are either ignored or grossly misunderstood by the mainstream of practitioners, who are not trained to understand the world of work, or how people develop within or are affected by the culture, values, and behavior within large organizations in the business and professional world.

Freud was right on target when he defined mental health in terms of both love *and* work. But experts in psychiatry and psychology throughout our century have focused almost exclusively on problems in the love category. And with good reason: a person's intimate relations with mother and father or other parent figures, as well as with siblings, through early infancy, childhood, and adolescence strongly affect the kinds of adults we become—our conflicts in relationships and behavior.

our level of self-esteem, how we deal with separation, loss, rejection, or disappointment, as well as with the strength of our emotional passions which may frighten or twist us.

We are, of course, products of our development. This affects our overall adjustment, character, and functioning in society. Many people discover this only when they enter adult roles, as workers who must support themselves and deal with issues of authority, independence, and values; as partners in love relationships, who must deal with mutuality, intimacy, and respect; or as parents, dealing with responsibility, moral values, and balanced nurturance. There are troubled people who have failed somewhere along the way to master the successful passage into adulthood because of unresolved childhood conflicts which only erupted when they became faced with the demands of adult responsibilities. The stress of these experiences can trigger unresolved conflicts that have been lurking within us and produce conscious emotional problems where none had been apparent before. Irrational attitudes and passions which develop because of childhood or biological reasons, or some combination of the two, are the root of emotional problems for many troubled people.

Our attention to how work and career in adulthood affect mental health—the other half of Freud's equation—has been blunted by the fact that, as therapists and analysts, we are trained to interpret problems in relationships or social adjustment primarily in terms of childhood origins. We therefore home in on buried early memories, wishes, guilty feelings, impulses, and fantasies. The aim is to help the person reexperience and emotionally face these early memories, and to develop emotional awareness about what he or she is doing in the present that reenacts or maintains old conflicts and results in suffering. This is really the core of all the "talking" therapies that originated with Freud's discoveries at the turn of the century.

There are many people who suffer from problems that are childhood-based, for whom the above treatment is necessary and appropriate. There are others, as well, whose conflicts are likely to be rooted in a defect of brain biochemistry, whose suffering can be curbed or minimized by the proper medication.

But mounting evidence now requires us to expand and enlarge our understanding of people's problems. Our conflicts—mental, emotional, and, in particular, conflicts over values—as well as our attempts to deal with them, are affected by our work as adults to a much greater extent than we have realized.

Conflicts in the realm of adult experience and adaptation have a direct connection to psychiatric problems. In fact, for many of us, the external situation of work plays a greater role in the development of emotional conflict, including repressed attitudes and awareness, than any internal problems. And even when we are troubled because of serious internal problems, whether unresolved, buried childhood conflicts or biochemical problems within the brain (reasons which have nothing to do with work per se), the severity and outcome of our emotional problems are nevertheless affected by our work, including its purpose, atmosphere, values, and the kind of management we receive.

Either way, the consequence can be a loss of contact with our experience of reality and the passions that motivate us.

Passions at Work. In our eagerness to apply high technology to our personal lives and career pursuits by grafting on "new behaviors" and plugging in "strategies for success"—like slipping some new software into the computer—we have forgotten that our lives are often driven by hidden passions. We may hide or mask our passions to ourselves, even without realizing it, but they are nevertheless expressed through our lives, like themes that unfold in a Shakespearean drama or Balzac novel. The intense demands of the heart, which have been better understood and described by novelists than by most analysts, resist the pleadings and demands of reason. As Pascal said, "The Heart has reasons of its own that Reason is unaware of."

Passions, in this sense, are forces within us which we may not comprehend or be aware of. They have been described since antiquity, and often with more understanding than contemporary mental health experts. For example, the seventeenth-century philosopher Spinoza described passions with acute psychoanalytic insight. He distinguished the "active" or positive emotions, based on awareness and guided by reason, from destructive and pathological passions, which, when irrational and unconscious, dominate us and can lead to insanity. Other writers, both ancient and modern, have similarly described how the demands of the heart resist the pleadings and demands of reason, and create gaps between how we would like to be and who we really are.[14]

These gaps take several forms, in relation to our problems. There are people for whom terrible problems in personal relationships contrast sharply with apparently successful careers. And for others it is the other way around; they have significant problems at work but little difficulty or unhappiness in intimate relationships outside the office. Then there are those who seem to be able to develop themselves emotionally and intellectually from their work, even in large, impersonal, bureaucratic organizations.

It is these gaps that *Modern Madness* addresses, for today's successful careerists are feeling the costs and limitations of their successful adaptation, and no longer want to pay. They want to remain successful, but also want more from life. These younger careerists, whose motives and conflicts are setting the standards for career behavior for the remaining years of this century, want and expect more personal fulfillment, more fun and pleasure, and meaning from life, in addition to a successful career and all its perks.

While they want success, they don't want to be such slaves to career and achievement. In contrast, careerists above the age of about 47—the rough dividing line I have found in my research—have grown up within a career environment in which they more readily accept the limitations, traditional hierarchy, and trade-offs of careers in large organizations. They privately admit to sharing many of the same yearnings that the younger careerists have, but are more resigned to living with conflicts and less fulfillment. For both the younger and older groups, however, serious emotional and value conflicts can develop. This often takes the form of valid, though sometimes unconscious, criticisms of their work, their values, as well as of social and political situations which concern them. These people are troubled because of their situation, because of their normalcy, but not necessarily because of childhood problems, as therapists who are locked into a view of normalcy thirty years out-of-date continue to assume.

When the twin drives of success and fulfillment slam against the brick wall of organizations that have not yet adapted to the new technological, economic, and psychosocial realities, a range of problems and conflicts results. Without understanding the meaning of what one is experiencing, and with national leadership that supports escapism through rationalized self-indulgence, it is no surprise that the younger careerist is duped into pursuing escapist materialism in the form of high-priced cars, expensive cappuccino makers, and cocaine highs, as compensation for the emptiness of values and spirit that keeps bobbing up to the surface.

More broadly, the conflicts of the younger careerists reflect a clash between the values of love versus career ambition. The reports of lack of fulfillment, lack of love, entrapment, and loss of a sense of spirit which I have found paralleling the career drive are themes that increasingly resonate throughout our culture. It has been portrayed, for example, in popular movies of the mid-'80s like *The Big Chill* and *Desperately Seeking Susan*. Some roots of this theme can be found in popular literature from earlier decades of the present century, in the premonitory sense of the emotional impact of careerism and of a society dominated by big organizations.[15] Today, this creeping yuppie malaise is fast becoming the central emotional dilemma of the late 1980s. There are those who have become casualties of the conflict between the values of success versus fulfillment that has become the legacy of the '60s and '70s. These are people who tend to live in fantasy or the past rather than to struggle with the present. They resist reconciling what they experience in reality with what they had hoped to see and feel. Caught up in emotional ambiguities that have paralyzed them, they are people who try to connect but without any intimacy.[16]

The chapters that follow explain what the specific problems are, both within the person and the situation, that develop during the pursuit of careers today. How and why career adaptation can disguise emotional problems of very troubled people, or—more insidiously—create emotional problems and value conflicts in people who are normal. They will also describe the major changes now occurring in the world of work and in what we think of as "normal," and how these affect our emotions and values.

Later chapters will explain our much-discussed contemporary problems like stress, burnout, and situational anxiety in a way that provides a new understanding of what causes them, as well as other, more serious, emotional problems. Specifically, how they relate to the values and attitudes adults develop while seeking successful adaptation to careers in today's world of large organizations.

Further, we will learn how to tell the difference between troubles that develop because of actual internal conflict and those caused by the situation, and what we can do to better deal with it all. And why the typical analyst or therapist is unable to adequately comprehend or deal with the problems people have today. How the training and experiences of practitioners result in ignorance about the world of work, and in the knee-jerk reaction of uncritically equating successful adjustment to one's situation with emotional health, while ignoring what it is we are adjusting to in the first place, and how that affects us, positively or negatively.

A later chapter will evaluate what helps and what doesn't when trying to deal with conflicts, either on our own or when getting professional help. It shows how to evaluate—as an educated consumer—the kinds of help one is likely to receive from the mental health mainstream, as well as from organizational and management consultants.

All of this is important to know if you are troubled yourself, know or work with someone who is, manage or are managed by someone who is. Or, if you are not troubled, and would like to know how to stay that way as we rollercoast toward the twenty-first century.

FAST-TRACK BLUES

2

Even when you feel you are displaying insensitivity to the point of being inhuman, you have to hang tough. Even when you feel that you are doing something disgusting, or merely in bad taste, you have to follow through. Like sticking a mike under the nose of an old woman whose grandson has been stabbed to death. If I fail to do it, and a competing station did, my boss would ask me "where were you when the other channel was getting the good stuff?"

— A TV news reporter

It is very difficult for people to admit that they do not enjoy what they are doing. Too many people try to tell themselves their job is great when, deep down, they do not enjoy it and refuse to face reality.

— Bjorn Borg

Let's listen to what troubled people say and think about their conflicts—how and why they think their careers affect them emotionally. But first, a warning: it makes good psychoanalytic sense to retain some skepticism about what people say they think troubles them. There is resistance in all of us to seeing the truth about our motives, attitudes, and our passions, which are often unconscious and covered over with illusions we weave to protect ourselves from pain. Such resistance has provided rich material for novelists and dramatists for centuries. But on the other hand, a person's own interpretation of his or her experience should not be dismissed out of hand, which therapists are so often prone to do under the assumption that whatever a person says is, by definition, warped and distorted by unconscious attitudes. Distinguishing what may be distorted by unconscious attitudes from what is not will not be jeopardized by learning first-hand about the effect of large organizations upon our emotional problems from careerists within those organizations.

Some echo the words of Richard, a youthful looking man with a slight paunch, who is a highly successful consultant. During an interview he told me, "I've just spent a couple of hours telling you how important my work is. But you know something? I've been holding back something the whole time. I really feel I'm just a high-paid prostitute, nothing more. And I don't see any way out." Similarly, a successful lawyer confided to me that he has never liked his work at all, even though he is recognized as one of the best in his area of law. And that his personal life is empty and meaningless. He summed up his career as "depressing comfortableness." He has tried to deal with it by buying new things he doesn't really need—a new sport coat he won't wear much and a new car that's not much different from what he already has. But he gets less and less cranked up each time he buys something new. "I feel like an object junkie," he laughed.

Martin, at 38 a salt-and-pepper-haired executive with a large paper manufacturing industry, described a similar dilemma and its emotional impact by saying, "I think after a while you cease to aspire for anything. You top out, you see new pay packages, and you think 'so what?' Initially, like in your 20s, I think there is a lot of idealism, of what you can learn, what you can do, then you become motivated to work hard and move up through your 30s. Then, when you reach 40, you begin to feel that what you are doing isn't worth anything. The money, the position, are the only things. What can you do? See a shrink? He'll just tell you to cope better and stop complaining, or give you some valium. I'd rather spend the money on a VCR or Club Med. The sad thing is, I don't see any solution. We're all caught up in this, really."

Another person, a 46-year-old accountant, heads a very successful firm that he built from scratch in a southwestern city. He told me he was depressed about his work. He said he hated "all the bullshit" associated with the business, like courting clients and attending affairs he wasn't interested in. Similarly, another person, who directs a trade association, said he was depressed about his successful career because, in the final analysis, his work was "inconsequential." He added, "I can get wrapped up in it all right, during the day, if I try hard, but at the end of the day if I take a good look at it all, it really means nothing. It's boring. There's no challenge. And I'm not qualified to do much else. I know I'm not about to take a big risk or sacrifice my life-style, or go back to school." This person, like many other career men and women I interviewed, also expressed the feeling of having gotten "off track" at some earlier point in life, having had ideals and a desire to contribute something which was useful and engaged their abilities. A number of people who expressed these complaints had served in the Peace Corps, and described it as the most meaningful, "connected" period of their lives, in terms of a sense of service and work grounded in ideals. But for reasons they say they do not understand, it had all dissolved. And they were left holding on to the money and the ancillary perks because that was all they had left.

I have found variants of these themes throughout my research with men and women from a wide range of career experiences. Take the case of Ann, for example. An outspoken, slightly built woman in her late 30s, she told me that she had worked for a variety of companies while "determined to improve" her position by always going for training courses and seminars in her field. Not just to make herself more marketable, she said, but to become better educated, because she valued that for its own sake. Ann was raised in a small northeastern city, in an ethnic family which valued learning, but which was financially poor. She told me: "I started out working as a clerk-typist to help put myself through school. I eventually earned two master's degrees, but I developed a lot of feelings of worthlessness, rage, insecurity, constant bitchiness, and unhappiness. It took me a long time to realize that these feelings were not natural attributes of my own being. I was responding to what I found in many organizations, which was that the values are very ego-oriented and what I would even call 'fascist,' mainly because the work is done to glorify a higher-up, or because it is routine and meaningless. At one point I searched for some help and understanding from a therapist, but was told, in effect, 'How can you ask for anything more? After all, other people are starving.' I have a good career now, but I feel pretty cynical about it all. At this point I'm just in it for the money."

We could dismiss Ann's comments as the sour attitude of a person who feels sorry for herself or resentful because she wasn't given the breaks, and had to pull herself up. But I found her to have a basically positive, down-to-earth quality about her, and an inner grittiness and resilience that contradicts the sour grapes interpretation, but which underscores her point: that she has reacted negatively to what she perceives to be concern for glory and pressure to accept the lack of meaning in work.

Tom, who is now trying to make a go of it as the owner of a small business, described another kind of conflict which he experienced while working for several years in a big firm. He calls it the "looking-good mentality." He said: "I've come to the conclusion that there are people who are as intelligent and capable as anyone else, but who can't stomach the 'looking-good-moving-up' attitude at all. I'm talented and well educated, but got sick of hearing people tell me that I could really 'do something' with my life, defined as an empty job with no tangible product. I tried several corporate jobs, and it became nothing more than a question of how much money I could put away before my nerves snapped. At present," he continued, "I have to spend more time counting my change, but I have far less of a feeling that I'm wasting my life."

Not everyone would want to try Tom's entrepreneurial alternative, nor should they. Most say they want a successful career within an organization. And perhaps Tom became too jaded about his experiences, in which case both he and the corporate world have lost out. But many would nod their heads in recognition of his comment, "I don't see how any real human being can put up with the petty backbiting, the competition to beat out the guy next to you, the empty facades, and complete futility of a so-called 'good career.' Too much of the career world is all show and no substance. Who wants to adapt to a world where people take themselves seriously to the point of pompousness, but really accomplish nothing?"

Suzanne is a 40-year-old editor who has worked for a variety of companies which publish trade newspapers and technical publications. She observed that "the problems are not always the fault of the company itself. Sometimes bosses use the 'good of the company' as an excuse for their own cruelty, when actually the company, that is, top management, wouldn't condone their behavior outright, but may be promoting it by ignoring the situation or being unaware of the personality problems of their managers.

"I've worked in a number of large organizations in several cities, and also abroad. At times I've either been fired or chose to leave because of various nutty situations I wouldn't put up with. One company fired me for what they called 'failure to adapt to the work environment.' I considered that a compliment, given the work environment."

Another kind of experience some people describe is found in the remarks of Lisa, a 32-year-old Ph.D., who heads a research unit of about 15 people in her organization. She said to me, "I consider myself an achievement-oriented person, and have found the road to promotion and advancement fairly smooth. I was pretty young when I earned my Ph.D., and have had what most would call an extremely successful experience. Until recently, I've felt quite satisfied with my career.

"My position as a manager places me squarely between researchers and administrators. I'm required to respond to the different and often conflicting needs of both of these groups. And actually, I find I'm able to empathize with both. I know some would find this commendable, but it makes me feel like a Jekyll and Hyde. It gives me a clear impression of two different perspectives, and I feel I'm teetering on a rickety fence between them.

"My staff is very productive, but they're laid back kinds of people. They rarely have to take work home. They don't feel compelled to take their jobs home with them, so to speak. They've got no reason to feel guilty if they spend more than their allotted thirty minutes each day eating lunch. I used to be in their position, so I know what it's like. But on the other hand, the managers above me rarely eat lunch anywhere but at their desks, in conjunction with their work. Each person seems to feel that he carries the weight of the company on his shoulders alone. They act like everything is so important! To me, they're old before their time, very anxious, burned out, or at least on the verge of a 'creativity collapse.'

"Frequently I'm asked to help some of them carry their weight, and I act as administrator during their vacations and business trips. I understand how easy it is to get caught up in that role. But in spite of my empathy it's very hard to swallow some of the things the role requires. The problem for me is that I have a terrible fear of becoming one of those tired, worried, overcompromised bureaucratic managers. From an emotional standpoint I'd much prefer to drop to a lower salary at a research position level. But I can't bring myself to ask for a demotion. I know I'm headed in the opposite direction.

"And few people understand this. My family and friends all think I should be wildly happy with my so-called success, and so they're not very sympathetic to what I've lately begun to realize is a troubling problem. I've become acutely aware that I've made some emotional trade-offs to achieve advancement, and that if I decide or am subtly coerced into continued advancement, the emotional toll could be considerable. And I don't know what can be done about it."

Weaving through all the thoughts and feelings of these and many other troubled career professionals are recurring themes: *"I've made a lot of compromises,"* and *"I've had to make constant trade-offs."* The feelings are of entrapment, guilt, and self-betrayal, which leave the person feeling out of kilter, off-balance, and unfulfilled, despite his or her success.

Across the board, every person who pursues a career in today's world experiences these conflicts to some degree. They are an inevitable part of today's careerist orientation; a by-product of the culture, values, attitudes, behavior, and management to which people must adapt in order to advance within the modern organization.

In this and subsequent chapters we will see what these conflicts consist of and discover that people are affected by and deal with them in different ways. But to help understand that the ways in which we adapt determine whether or not we become overtly troubled, let's examine what the careerist orientation is, and its impact upon us.

The Good and Bad of Careerism.   Careerism has become the main work ethic of our times. At root, careerism is an attitude, a life orientation in which a person views career as the primary and most important aim of life. An extreme but not uncommon expression of this is found in the comment of a man who told me that he feared dying mainly because it would mean the end of his career. Successful career development means feeling motivated by the prospect of upward movement within a large organization to positions of increasing responsibility or managerial authority. Because it has been the dominant work ethic throughout most of our century, we all subscribe to it, adapt to it, and are influenced by it to some degree.[1]

The extent to which the norm of career motivation has blurred our capacity to distinguish its positive from its negative potential can be seen in the way the definition of "career" has increasingly broadened in our culture to now include virtually all of life. People talk of their children's "career" at school, one's "career" in interpersonal relationships, and the "outside career" one may develop, i.e., interests outside of work. What used to be defined as the sequence of roles that marks our progress in an occupation, career is now viewed in terms of our progress through life itself: "the link between the individual and society," as one consultant grandly put it.[2]

The implication is that our career should be equivalent with our identity. A progression of self-definitions that we evolve and shed like a series of cocoons while we are moving through the occupation of life. So it's no surprise that our careers and career development have become a hot topic for managers and workers alike, who have created a growing market for professional career counselors and consultants. They tell us that career now includes even the non-work aspects of life. They speak of assessing a person's progress, achievement, and position regarding his or her entire life, as the basis for determining "success." Some even describe phases and developmental tasks of adult life in terms of career development. That one needs to think of managing life as though it is all one big career. One's funeral, presumably, would be the ultimate retirement party.

We all absorb this thinking. For example, a study of 44 male alumni of MIT's Sloan School of Management, conducted ten to twelve years after they graduated,[3] found that after a period of five to ten years they tended to define themselves as individuals totally around their career. According to organizational psychologist Edgar Schein this gives the person what he calls the "career anchor."[4] This is a set of driving and constraining forces on a person's decisions and choices. A composite of a person's needs, values, attitudes, and abilities that tie the person to a certain kind of work and career development. It all sounds like a neat and tidy package. Except for one thing: how do we deal with a situation in which we do not want to do, or in which we feel conflict over, what we may be good at? In other words, when we feel that our "career anchor" is pulling us under? Of course, a person often desires to do what he or she does well. But as Maccoby's research has shown, people can also learn to do well what he or she is pressured to adapt to. Viewing life as one big career means constant stifling of feelings of self-betrayal which occur from constantly making oneself accept and ignore the limitations, values, and motives that seem best geared for coming out a winner.

Like most things in life, careerism has good and bad potential for us, particularly in its effects on our mental health. For example, a person who develops a successful career is continuously supported for developing and utilizing complex intellectual skills. These are positive benefits for the person as well as for the organization, which depends upon such skills in order to function effectively and competitively in the market-place. We value and enjoy careers which are interesting, challenge us to expand our capacities, provide the opportunity to accomplish something tangible, increase our self-esteem, and reward us for it, materially and socially.

But now for the bad news: careerism also has a dark side, which is not so good. Upward movement on the career ladder has come to be equated more and more with one's self-worth and identity. In large organizations the individual tends to feel subordinated to the interests of the organization itself, which is usually concerned with its own perpetuation. As ambitious careerists, we tend to silently assess each other's worth as a person according to the kind of work we do and how high up we are in our organization, relative to where we "should" be, given our age and years of experience. For many of us, careerism brings with it a gradual loss of self, integrity, or inner core, independent of and apart from our career position or worth to the organization. The tragedy this can lead to is seen in the newspaper stories written periodically about someone who commits suicide because of career frustration or demotion. One senior executive jumped off the roof of his building when he walked into work one morning and discovered that his desk had been moved. A chemist who failed to receive a grant for a research project returned to his lab one night, concocted a poison and drank it, dying where he felt most at home. And most betrayed.

People also express the downside of careerism through semiconscious attitudes of self-betrayal, despair, and unfocused self-criticism. The price of successful careerism is feeling trapped and caught as they navigate upward through layers of hierarchy, fueled by visions of recognition, power, and position that lie just ahead. But smack in the midst of their career steeplechase they find themselves semiconscious of criticisms about themselves and what they do in their work. Particularly, values which disturb them and leave them feeling uncertain and anxious about what to do that would help.

Take Peter, for example. Originally trained as an engineer, he works on contracts regarding missile guidance systems for a big corporation. He said to me, "All this talk going on about the nuclear freeze makes me nervous. I know they're right. I've always felt, inside, that we're flirting with total destruction. It's madness. But for me to do my job successfully, I've got to detach myself from thoughts like that. They would interfere too much. But it's getting harder and harder, and it's pulling at me more and more. I feel guilty about doing work that's connected to . . . let's face it—the bottom line is death and destruction."

Or Tom, who was brought into an agency of the federal government by the Reagan administration, mostly as a political payoff. Towards the end of our interview he suddenly said, "If I play my cards right, this is my ticket to the top. I can feel it. But sometimes I'm really bothered by what I'm doing here." He paused, as though debating whether to retract his words. I asked him to go on.

"Well," he continued, "in actuality I'm helping to destroy the work of this agency." [He was brought in to limit or non-enforce activity of the agency which the Reagan administration was opposed to.] "To make it worse, I don't agree with that much of what the administration is doing. I know I want more from life than an important career. Life is too short. But I really like having power, too. So you see the conflict?"

For many people like Peter and Tom, career success carries with it a gradual chipping away of integrity, and fueling too much concern for power, domination, and greed, as compensation.

Other people describe feelings of having sold out for position and comfort over time, without realizing the psychic cost until it is too late. Judy, a 35-year-old corporate manager, illustrates this. At the time I interviewed her she had been divorced for several years, and had few interests outside her career and young daughter. She said to me, "Lately I keep having this dream in which I'm running in a marathon race, and all the other runners are people I recognize from my office. Then all of a sudden I realize that I don't know why we are all in the race, or where the finish line is."

Our dreams and nightmares can reveal inner struggles or insights which may be completely unconscious or exist in a kind of netherworld of semi-awareness. An example of this is seen in Erik, an investment banker in his early 30s. Beneath his polished manner and appearance I sensed an attitude of coarseness and contempt towards clients and colleagues alike. When exploring this with him I asked if he ever had any dreams related to work. He immediately said no, but then added that, in fact, he did have a recent dream which disturbed him. In it, he is yanked out of bed by an external force and pushed into the bathroom, facing the mirror. He stares into it and realizes that he sees nothing where his face should be, just the outline of his skull. At that point he woke up screaming. Though Erik had never been in analysis, he said he was convinced that his dream symbolized the "inner emptiness" he felt from an accumulation of systematic self-betrayals throughout his career. He also said that he's "too aware" of things for his own good, and that he secretly feels self-contempt, which, he added, "I deal with by dishing it out to others in generous portions."

The successful careerist can also end up performing work which is unstimulating or deadening, particularly in the larger, more impersonal bureaucratic organizations, in which working one's way up frequently involves doing work which is thin and empty, with little visible connection to a specific product or result. The frustration of this, which, among other things, is an assault on the person's dignity, leads many people to battle for power, puff up their importance beyond what they know it is, or go all out for money. The career environment feeds a sense of emptiness about our personal values as well, which can lead us to seek applause for appearance and actions as compensation. We are left with trading off for the higher pay and position that go with career advancement. Of course we usually deny all this, to avoid facing threatening or hopeless feelings. But more and more people are conscious of it. And it sows the seeds of emotional disturbance.

Interviews conducted by the *Wall Street Journal* with several top students from the Harvard Business School, twenty years later, reveals some of these feelings and conflicts.[5] Though they were all top students of their graduating class, and most were doing well financially, their attitudes and reflections about themselves at midlife revealed a pattern of frustrations and heartbreaks, which the report acknowledged as common to many ambitious executives today.

One had topped out as an assistant general manager at Ford, and another became so disillusioned that he dropped out and moved to a New Mexico commune, where he works with an ecology organization. Another was squeezed out of his post as financial vice president when his company brought in new people with marketing and consumer backgrounds. He eventually became an independent consultant, working out of his basement, with all the perks of corporate life in the past. He said "We're all water bugs on a wave; we can scamper around to get to the top of the wave but the wave must be there. Then the wave breaks and a lot of people get tossed around. There's a time to get on the wave and a time to get off."

Another said his education was really a test of glibness, a question of whether you can wing it in front of the others in your class. He said being a business executive is not intellectually fascinating. "It's action oriented. Your satisfactions are power and money. They aren't humanistic or intellectual. The basis is competitiveness. You have to have this tremendous need to win." But if he could do it all over again, would he? No. He said he would go to medical school instead.

Adding to these conflicts over successful careers is the fact that upward mobility in large organizations is gradually becoming less of a possibility in our changing economy and job market, which has fewer jobs at the top for people to aspire to. Right now there is a numbers crunch of people entering midlife and older categories from the postwar baby boom. Massive numbers of people now moving into their 30s and 40s are entering a plateau stage of their career. Since the early '70s there has been an explosion in the 25–44-year-old group, one in which there is usually the most rapid career growth. But with the economy and the job market having become more competitive, the feelings of blockage and frustration are deepening. It has been estimated that tens of thousands of managers now in their late 30s have received, or are about to receive, their last promotion, because there is no more room at the top. And it's going to get worse: a boom in the 45–64-year-old category is expected in the early 1990s. By 1989 the first wave of the baby-boomers will be forty and the young executive of today will be middle-aged. Big organizations will find themselves with large numbers of people still young who, after rapid promotions, find themselves at a dead end.

The conflicts that result are not limited to careerists in our own society, either. For example, the same pattern of complaints is seen in a study of mid-level managers and professional workers in their 30's and 40's, half French and half British, who attended programs at INSEAD (The European Institute of Business Administration) in Fontainebleau, France.[6]

Many careerists who have started to privately question the values, attitudes, and behavior they have taken on in order to move up don't know how to change, or how to shift the balance. They see no alternatives which might be more fulfilling but also realistic. This underlies much of the joylessness and semi-depression that has become so rampant in our society. The feeling that no one can really win; that there is no way out. Though well-adapted to our high-tech, fast-track culture, many feel emotionally numb and without a sense of purpose or overall framework for guiding their lives.

The yearning for release from feelings of passive entrapment is seen in the pleasure some describe when they do something daring and risky, such as the white-water rafting trips which the Menninger Foundation conducts as part of a leadership training program for top executives. Being on the edge, having to do something that requires reaching down into one's reservoir of strength and independence, and finding what is— or isn't—there provides them a kind of antidote to the helplessness and passivity that so many successful careerists privately acknowledge.

SYMPTOMS OF OUR TIMES

For some, the conflicts exist as a kind of chronic, low-grade fever. Whether for reasons of the person's character orientation or particular career environment, only a mild toll is taken. For others, more serious psychiatric problems result. The symptoms that more acutely troubled people describe include both the physical and the emotional. They describe physical symptoms of fatigue, gastrointestinal disturbances, high blood pressure, under- or overeating, drinking and drug-taking, chronic headaches, and sleep disturbances. The emotional symptoms include anxiety (ranging from mild to incapacitating), stress, pervasive depression, helplessness, malaise, passivity, chronic indecisiveness, and explosive rage.

When asked about what they think are the sources of anger in the workplace, many say they think it comes from feeling uncreative, blocked, or controlled by bosses whom they hate. One psychotherapist who works for an employee assistance consulting firm told me of several cases of executives who were all generally successful in their careers but who had entered therapy because they were brimming with anger and hated their jobs. A common theme, the therapist said, was that they felt they had reached a level in their careers at which they didn't have anything else, and experienced tremendous rage. He described several cases in which the person blew up, screaming and throwing furniture around the office. Rage and anger are widespread throughout our organizations, and are the sources of many other problems, as well. For example, employee counselors report that many of the absentee and disciplinary cases they encounter reflect tremendous anger and frustration with work at all levels. But they are uncertain if those feelings are justified or not.

No one would disagree that some people who boil over with rage are very disturbed to begin with, and may routinely threaten violence when they are told to do something. Often such people have noticeable problems across the board. For example, there are people who are always filing grievances or lawsuits, or paranoid people who erupt easily when they feel threatened. Some practically make a second career out of it. They write documents, send letters to the Board of Directors, to government officials, hire and fire lawyers. One manager told me of an encounter with a subordinate on the street, while walking to lunch. The subordinate walked up to him and, jabbing a finger in his face, shouted "I'll see you in court, you son-of-a-bitch." Then he walked away. The manager was dumbfounded; he had no idea what the person was talking about.[7]

But it would be a mistake to dismiss all anger and rage that erupts or threatens to erupt at work as nothing more than the product of an emotionally sick person. Too many people who are otherwise well-adjusted contend that the entrapment and conflict they experience during the career climb gives rise to anger, which often has no outlet.

For every person that "loses it" and blows up, there are several others who keep the anger within, where it simmers like a low-grade pressure cooker. In such cases, the toll it takes may be known only to the person or to family and friends. Many speak of burning anger at the office as one of the most distressing problems, particularly when there are no productive outlets or constructive actions that can be taken. Often, women suffer the most. One editor for a major publishing house told me that she and her friends frequently talk about the difficulty handling and expressing work-related anger. This difficulty is enhanced by the fear of breaking down and crying in the work situation, something which some male bosses encourage, because they feel that they can then control a woman more easily.

Anger at the workplace is often masked by other behavior or symptoms, like violence, depression, physical problems, passivity, or sabotage. And there is no question that it has tremendously destructive effects on the person, emotionally and physically. For example, anger has been linked with cancer, chronic headaches, and heart disease. There is some evidence that chemicals released into the body during the experience of anger and rage can literally wear down the system. Some people can be described as "anger junkies" because they know it is destructive, yet they can't stop it. They feel addicted to it.

Unfortunately, psychiatric symptoms which reflect conflicts over values and situations are often dealt with by practitioners in terms of "controlling" or "coping" with the symptom, rather than by facing what in the situation generates it in the first place, and what can be done about that. Such is the case with anger. For example, some therapists and consultants conduct programs of "anger coping" strategy or "assertiveness training," which too often results in teaching people how to be angry without feeling bad about it. "I'll be as rude or obnoxious as I feel like, and if you don't like it, that's your problem," is the message.

Psychologists and psychiatrists often ignore or don't understand how anger relates to the situations and values we adapt to at work. For example, social psychologist Carol Tavris in her book *Anger: The Misunderstood Emotion*,[8] advocates trying to change "mistaken ideas" rather than deal with the emotions involved. While making a valid point that bad behavior is often excused by claiming it is better to let anger out than keep it in, she neglects the roots of the experience of anger. To say simply that we should control our anger or that we feel anger because the culture allows us to get away with it is misleading. Anger can reflect serious self-criticisms or accurate perceptions about our situation, but about which we feel impotent. And anger can be turned inward, masked by depression, or even lead to suicide. Dealing with anger is not a cognitive or intellectual process, though we may use our intellect to rationalize it or disguise it. Anger is frequently unconscious, particularly when the experience of it at work threatens our security or career advancement. When that is the case, a person needs help to become aware of feeling the fury, frightening as it may be, as a prior step to exploring its meaning and what can be done about it.

We tend to assume that the attitudes and behavior which are largely shared by others and therefore "normal," are unrelated to emotional troubles. The latter, we prefer to think, belong to a special category of people, who cannot "adjust" as well as us. Yet there is a range of emotional and value conflicts which are a product of our well-adjusted attitudes. For example, feelings or criticisms about one's career or the value of one's work can be a handicap to successful advancement if one is too aware of them. So one may repress or ignore those feelings—like anger, self-disgust, boredom, or self-betrayal—if they conflict too much with fitting in and moving up.

An example of how this can affect a person is seen in Bob, a man in his mid-30s whose poker face and monotone leaves you wondering what lurks behind the facade. While talking with me about an issue at work in which his recommendation had been rejected by his superiors, he said, "I have to believe that I agree with them all the way on that decision. I can't allow any questions to creep into my thoughts about it. If I did, it would open up Pandora's box for me. My career could get derailed. And," he added with a little smirk, "I might end up hating myself even more than I do now."

Feelings like these can occur for many reasons. Some sell themselves constantly to others, violating their principles and ethics in order to promote themselves. Others are submissive, unconsciously seeking to gain favor and approval. Still others try to achieve domination over others. There are people who constantly opt for the easy path, the easy choice. What inevitably results is emotional detachment and feeling like a fraud. For some this may remain unconscious and break through only in the form of acute psychiatric symptoms or disturbing dreams. But for most, the price of molding oneself too much to "fit in" or "look good" is a normal but troubled feeling of being centerless, of having no self. Many well-adapted but troubled careerists therefore feel depressed, lonely, and alienated, vaguely anxious and passionless, and dissatisfied with life and success.

Reports from counselors within organizations, such as employee assistance staff, human resource managers, psychiatrists, psychologists, and social workers employed by organizations to help troubled employees, underscore the above pattern. The symptoms of people who are referred or refer themselves to their organization's health clinic or employee assistance program are often a blend of physical and emotional. For example, binge-style drinking, absenteeism, psychosomatic complaints, insomnia, along with significant, noticeable anxiety, depression, passive or avoidant behavior. An example of the latter was a person who was very obese, and whose manager complained that he wouldn't produce work and wouldn't meet deadlines. He was known to get sick when pressed to do work, always had elaborate excuses, and appeared to be noticeably depressed.

I have found that the number of cases referred to employee health clinics or employee assistance programs that involve a fairly clear cut emotional or mental problem tend to average around 80% of the total. Within this, the largest single category—about 25%—concerns dissatisfaction or conflict over one's career, job functions, or manager. The balance consists of cases of severe depression, anxiety, alcoholism, situational crisis, or psychosis. Other estimates from a variety of companies indicate that about 60% of diagnoses of new cases in employee assistance programs represent psychiatric or stress symptoms.[9]

In the opinion of one human resources manager, noticeable psychiatric problems often "result from the fact that principles are not very important to a lot of people." I asked him to explain.

"I think people are all too willing to compromise too much," he went on. "They don't see they can maybe make a contribution somewhere else, if their situation is bad, or that they can try harder to maintain their principles. From what I've seen, the problem for some people today is that they sell out too much, or are engaged in graft, corruption, and so on. I don't mean in an illegal sense, necessarily, but often in terms of themselves. Some people are always conning themselves and others. There's no question it all takes a toll, in terms of real emotional problems. You don't have to be a psychiatrist to recognize that. You see it all the time.

"I recall one high-level guy who had a breakdown. He was always compromising, and it was a real conflict for him. I knew the guy; he wasn't really screwy. He was just always being asked to do a 'dirty job,' and it would have been bad for his career if he didn't go along. Or so he thought. On the other hand, maybe he could have taken a stronger stand. Maybe he was just too weak; it's hard for me to tell. But I've seen a lot of psychiatric-type problems resulting from selling out your principles too much. So there's got to be some connection."

Others describe acute psychiatric problems that they link to playing for ever-higher stakes and risks, particularly those on the fast track. Some self-described casualties told me that they were aware of the need to develop other parts of their lives more, but for too long they made themselves believe that their job was where it's at, only to find out that it wasn't so. Sometimes they were jarred awake by the discovery that their spouse had been having an affair right in front of their eyes, or that they couldn't remember the last time they experienced any real pleasure. But they didn't know what to do about it. One person described this in terms of an increasing level of frustration over limitations versus aspirations. He said that he has observed that many of his colleagues are creative people who became disillusioned. They felt stifled when they found they had to fit into a mold if they wanted to move up. They had expected total fulfillment from work, know they don't have it, but don't know what to do about it. They may try to cope with it by ignoring it, and suffering is the result.

A psychiatric nurse who works in an employee health unit told me that she has seen many cases of people who had become immobile and had to be practically forced to act. "I often try to get them to do something for themselves. They have a trapped feeling. Maybe the reality is that they are trapped by the perks and realistically can't change careers. But they need to resolve their feelings of pressure, somehow. Trying to please, for example, can be a positive value if you work at it. I've seen so many people who feel beaten down, discouraged; that nobody cares. They feel trapped, that they're being screwed and don't know what to do about it. A lot of the problem is that they see themselves as their job. They can't see themselves outside of their career in the organization. There is a feeling of 'Why me? I've done all this and have gotten this far, then I'm knocked down.'"

Many give up and seek escapes that are really blind alleys, like opting for greed and selfishness, haute consumerism, or escape through alcohol and drugs. Typical, now, among some fast-track careerists is the extensive use of cocaine, particularly among people in high-pressured careers, such as financial areas like securities, commodities, and the financial service industries. In a survey by a national drug treatment service, 75% of the workers reported using drugs at work, of whom 83% use cocaine. Twenty-five percent reported using drugs every day.[10] The survey also found that corporate executives and other high-paid professionals use twice as much cocaine as those who make less. In fact, alcohol and cocaine have become the twin escape routes of the '80s, providing artificial aliveness to the inner dead, and mellowed-out numbness to the self-betrayed.

Another acute symptom increasingly shared by careerists in big organizations is severe loneliness. A woman journalist said, looking back, "My ambition is wholly personal now. I can't understand people pursuing worldly success. All I want to do is fall in love." And the other side of the coin: a banking executive in a large southwestern city said, "I've become a workaholic because I'm so lonely." Some psychiatrists interpret this as a person's disappointing recognition that career success is an insufficient barrier against loneliness.[11] But this makes it sound as though the loneliness is a natural part of life. It doesn't separate the recognition of being alone as a reality of life—in the sense that we are individually responsible for our fate—from loneliness as an emotional problem, a product of conflict. Within the context of careers, loneliness and the resulting despair which can lead to alcoholism, drugs, or suicide is one product of our contemporary values of success run amok; a personal and spiritual isolation that results from the career culture's overemphasis on possessions, status, and position as illusory compensation for boring work and insufficient opportunity to develop oneself at the workplace.

Loneliness, then, results from the lack of attention paid to forming and maintaining relationships that often characterizes the personal lives of yuppies and baby boomers. The fall-out is seen in data like the 25% of the population that lives alone, and the 50% of all marriages that fail. And the 20% of all children who now live with only one parent. Like our contemporary novelists describe, many people don't feel connected to anything, family or community. And at the workplace itself, success increasingly precludes opportunities for companionship and relatedness, particularly in big organizations. Thomas J. Peters, coauthor of *In Search of Excellence*,[12] has described this, using the example of the auto industry. He points out that at Ford, for example, there are 17 layers between the first line worker and the chairman. "The middle manager really has no job. He sits there manipulating figures, computer displays, abstractions about profits and writing reports to ace out the people next to you. It's a lonely existence."[13]

When a person crosses the threshold into acute problems and symptoms, how can we tell if it is because he or she is a victim of the situation or is truly disturbed inside? When is a person's conflict a normal, adaptive response to a bad situation, or overadaptation to careerist values, and when is it that of a neurotic personality responding in ways that are unrelated to how normal people deal with the downside of career success? How can we tell the difference?

"IS IT ME OR THE SITUATION?"

A social worker I interviewed put it best. She was an intense-looking woman, with bright blue eyes. Her jet-black hair was streaked with gray, and a little disheveled, which somehow gave her an appealing look. She worked for a large service-type organization, where she counseled troubled employees who were either self-referred or referred by their immediate superiors. Most were mid- and upper-level careerists. While describing the kinds of cases she sees, she hit upon both an observation and a dilemma. She had been telling me that she sees a lot of marital problems, affairs, and all sorts of relationship problems that affect work. One man, for example, kept four or five relationships going all at once. He told her he was always trying to please everybody and be a "perfect man." He was very depressed, and it was affecting his work. "But at the same time," she went on, "there were real problems in his job, too. His work was not very rewarding. It wasn't enough to keep him challenged, and I think this played a big role in his depression and behavior. I see a lot of troubled people who have feelings of guilt, as a result. They feel something is wrong with them but they don't know what's causing it—or what to do about it."

She paused to blow out a cloud of cigarette smoke that she watched drift up and hover around the fluorescent lights on the ceiling, giving them a hazy glow. "The point is," she said, "I'm convinced that a lot of emotional problems are being prompted by conflicts about work. But I just don't know how to tell when it's the job and the career values that cause a person to be that way, or if it's that some people just can't accept the organization as it is, because they're neurotic and can't accept adult reality. This question is almost always raised by people who talk about how their work affects them emotionally. At some point they question if there is something wrong with them for feeling conflicted. Or whether it is "normal" to develop conflicts in their situations; that perhaps their situations are emotionally unhealthy in some way. Counselors, human resource managers, consulting psychiatrists, and others who deal with emotional conflicts of people in large organizations often say that they suspect personal problems are intertwined with work, but they don't know how to separate it out. This, in turn, limits their ability to help people. And as we saw in Chapter 1, we have had very little understanding of how career adaptation and values affect us emotionally.

Some people develop problems while others do not when coping with the negative side of normalcy. No one would disagree with that observation. The question is whether those who do develop problems necessarily have some emotional weakness or deficit—a neurotic personality—to begin with. What has made it hard to answer that question is that the mainstream of mental health practitioners doesn't realize that if we look only at external symptoms or outward behavior, in relation to how a person deals with careerism, we don't get the whole picture. We are forced to fit our observations into one of two usual explanations, both of which are limited and incomplete.

One of these viewpoints is that of the mental health mainstream, which assumes that all problems are rooted in an internal defect. The other, more sociopolitical, assumes that conflicts are "caused" by bad situations. As we will see, each point of view can marshal convincing evidence to support it, but in doing so ignores a chunk of reality. The result is that the issue of what is in the person vs. the external situation is further mystified.

"It's All in Your Head." This explanation is provided by mainstream psychoanalysis and the many varieties of psychotherapy it has influenced. Although most analysts do not deal at all with "external" issues like work, some have tried to understand emotional problems in terms of the person's work organization. Let's look at some typical problems they would interpret in this way. One example is the success-driven workaholic, characterized by the statement of a man who said he had always believed that if he worked and sacrificed hard enough, his reward would come. Provided, of course, that he never took time off to enjoy his accomplishments. He expected that he would eventually receive enough money, fame, power, and peace of mind that his family would forgive him for years of neglect. He said, "I thought life was like sex. You build up to a great orgasm at the end. But what you do at the end of life is die. I did not think I had any choices. I had to sacrifice everything to be a success."[14]

People like this are often obsessed with status and money, and chronically feel they are not working hard enough. They often operate in a high-stakes career game with no room for failure. Understandably, they measure their success by how far they are ahead or behind their colleagues, and often have a nagging feeling that they haven't achieved enough. Others say their success means nothing to them; that they feel empty and hollow inside.

A conventional psychoanalytic explanation of all this would be Oedipal: that there is an unconscious attitude that if I outachieve my father, I will have taken his place with mother, which is taboo (although it may be unconsciously desired). Any conflicts over success—whether fear of success or failure—are therefore interpreted in these terms, as variations of this theme. In recent years some analysts have broadened their interpretation of work-related problems by arguing that emotional and value conflicts over careers reflect social forces, like the rapid change and growth of technology, as well as the growth of bureaucracy. But the impacts of these forces are not studied in their own right, in terms of their effect upon adult development. Rather, in the view of these analysts, such forces have stimulated regression to less rational, more primitive and infantile attitudes and behavior—regression to an early stage of life, before the Oedipal period. There, the argument goes, "splitting" occurs in a person's perceptions between "good" and "bad" objects in the environment. The result is a combination of primitive fear of danger coupled with desire for protection and nurturance from mother-substitutes. Some analysts argue that all this gets displayed in the workplace because of the authority and parental symbols of both managers and the institution.

Other mental health practitioners who are less analytically-oriented interpret feelings of being trapped, giving all the time but never getting anything, of anger and depression as problems of communication, of insufficient awareness of feelings, and the style of interacting. But like the more explicitly psychoanalytic practitioners, these therapists pay little or no attention to the role of the situation itself upon adult values and motives.

For example, problems a successful male careerist might experience, such as marital problems, conflicts over behavior at work, alcohol, drug, or psychosomatic problems, are interpreted as the product of suffering from unmet dependency needs, the desire for more closeness, or from the need to feel needed. The therapist here often tends to agree with the male: that he is a successful person doing a lot of things to benefit the family, and is not appreciated for his hard work. So understandably he devotes himself more and more to his career, where he can get some reward and boost to his self-esteem. Because men are taught that it's not OK to have emotions and express them, and that they are supposed to be strong and competent, the argument goes, males must become more aware of their feelings. Therapists who take this position attribute work-related symptoms to not having the male's "dependency needs" met, which leads to disappointment, anger, guilt, withdrawal, and despair.

While it is important to help the male careerist recognize the reality of his emotional life, to interpret all this as internal conflict, whether a fear of defeating father, primitive splitting of objects into good and bad, or lack of awareness of feelings and needs, is a limited and partial understanding, because the traditional psychoanalytic and more general psychological explanations are unable to see beyond the person, to understand how the values, pressures, and culture within an organization emotionally affect the broad range of normal people who don't suffer from internal conflict. Moreover, my research finds that women careerists suffer from the same kinds of conflicts, and sometimes more so, than men, as we will see in Chapters 4 and 5.

What makes it hard to see beyond the person is that the traditional psychoanalytic view is right on target in many cases. That is, there are people who are disturbed internally, and whose criticisms of the work situation may be simply an expression of their disturbance, and not a product of a normal person to overadaptation, values conflict, or the stress of a bad situation. In such cases, the work and career environment provide the stage upon which the neurotic plot unfolds.

Usually, when there is a neurotic problem it stands out. For example, most people can recognize extreme examples of people who bury their emotional needs and live too much by the values of the company, because they are driven by some internal conflict. Successful business people who are troubled inside frequently rationalize the time spent away from their families. They use their work to avoid the explosion of inner conflict that would probably erupt if there were too much intimate and personal interaction.

Some people who are neurotic or psychotic to begin with perceive the workplace as responsible for their problems. Others are wedded to a paranoid, anti-organization ideology, and need to see themselves as victims of an oppressive environment. They often have a valid criticism or observation about the workplace, but because they are also very neurotic they are ineffective and unproductive in terms of doing anything about it. One man I interviewed was constantly raising charges of corruption regarding contracts—cost overruns, poor accounting procedures, and mismanagement—and in several cases he was found correct. However, he was also so paranoid and grandiose about his self-created role of crusader that he was not taken very seriously by higher management. His potentially positive contribution was lost because of his neurotic character. Another person, a mid-level manager, raised many valid criticisms about poor management practices, lack of support from above, and so on. But she was also very troubled inside. She could not channel her criticisms into constructive efforts. Histrionic, abrasive, and hysterical, she frequently shouted at co-workers and bosses, and eventually got herself fired.

Mental health practitioners are trained to recognize internal emotional problems that are acted out and displayed in relationships and through behavior. They can recognize, as one psychiatric consultant to a large organization put it, "people who are paranoid, or very manipulative or defensive, who often see nothing wrong with themselves. Everything is the fault of the organization, the system. And the person's superior doesn't know what to do with them." One employee counselor told me of a particular manager who kept asking why there was such a turnover of secretaries in his office. "He couldn't see that he was driving them away because of his own craziness."

People with neurotic personalities are often unable to see that their own problems are the source of their complaints about the organization. Or that their problems may prevent them from any kind of productive action in dealing with what may be a legitimate complaint about the workplace. As one counselor put it, "There are a lot of psychotics around here. It skews the sense of reality. Makes you wonder how the person has functioned over the last twenty years. I have to tell them, 'reality ain't what you think it is, Jack.'"

"Organizations Do Bad Things to You." The other conventional, but equally limited, explanation for overt conflicts at work is the "organizations-are-bad" point of view, popular among some academic Marxists and liberal intellectuals. Unless you are speaking of government organizations, in which case it is also popular among conservatives. Just as there are themes to the kinds of conflicts which are truly internal, there are also common threads to the situations at work that are emotionally damaging. As we will see, they concern problems that trickle down from higher levels, poor management and communication systems, and under-utilization of talent. But to understand these problems that are, in fact, rooted in the situation and negatively affect normal people, we must first filter out the alleged problems of organizations that are really an ideological broadside attack upon organizations, per se.

The "organizations-are-bad" explanation is the other side of the coin of the psychoanalytic, and suffers from the reverse limitation: while the psychological explanation fails to see beyond the person, the organizational doesn't recognize that individual pathology may be present. It ignores the fact that some people are disturbed for reasons that have nothing whatsoever to do with the organization. Theories that come from outside the mental health realm, which do try to understand how the outside environment affects us, are limited by a lack of clinical understanding of the individual.

Such theories, which are more sociological or politically based, usually blame external forces like destructive and oppressive socioeconomic systems, racism, bureaucracy, too much or too little government regulation, etc. External forces are seen as the causes of all conflict. So mental health practitioners tend to be ignorant of the influence of the outside world; social critics, of the inner.

And like the psychoanalytic, the limitation of the "organizations-are-bad" view can be hard to see because it happens to be on target in many cases. Anyone looking for evidence that large organizations breed destructive values, alienation, and emotional conflict can find it, because there are situations in organizations which, all by themselves, create emotional victims. Sometimes, too, the organization can make it difficult to recognize emotional problems that have nothing to do with the situation. For example, American families stationed abroad in the Foreign Service often can't get psychological help prior to a moment of crisis that leads to medical evacuation. One person said that "bureaucratic paranoia" gets in the way of a rational perspective on emotional problems, because such problems are viewed politically—they will stand in the way of a career officer's promotion. Yet the constant change and adjustment required of a Foreign Service officer's family often generate pressures which show themselves in symptoms that include paranoia, apathy, alcohol and drug abuse, depression, and schizophrenia.

Another kind of evidence of the "badness" of organizations cited by some critics is corporate corruption, including bribes of officials or government contractors, embezzlement, and other kinds of cheating for personal gain. This can be interpreted as evidence that large organizations support greed and lead to personal corruption. As evidence, anti-organization critics point to statements of managers who accept illegal practices as commonplace. For example, a survey of 531 top and middle managers by the Opinion Research Corporation found almost 50% agreeing that foreign bribes should be paid if such practices are prevalent in that foreign country—even if illegal.[15] Their rationalization is that payoffs are common practice, they do it for their shareholders, that the illegality is not all that serious, and that there are too many laws anyhow.

Periodically one reads about pillars of the community who are discovered to be corrupt—like a man indicted over scams involving foreign currency speculation; a lumber products conglomerate that was found accepting illegal discounts from furniture manufacturers; an oil venture investment by bank officials which were a conflict of interest with the bank's loan activities; a banker who embezzled almost a half million from kickbacks on loans and failed to file federal currency reports. The list goes on; just pick up the newspaper.

A survey conducted by the *Wall Street Journal*[16] shows that the public gives low ratings for honesty and ethical standards to executives. A huge share of the public has cynical views of the ethics of business executives, seeing them as much more dishonest than do the business execs themselves. Sixty-four percent think they cheat on taxes, 74% think they pad their expense accounts, and nearly 30% think they give bribes.

A destructive social and economic consequence of this, as Ralph Nader has accurately pointed out, is that executive criminals exact tribute in the form of higher prices, death and injury due to pollution and hazardous products, and corrupted government.[17] They violate public trust and inspire mistrust. But people who have anti-organization paranoia tend to appropriate sound criticisms like Nader's for their own purposes: to support an ideology that organizations are inherently bad and destructive.

For example, it is a common theme within this point of view that organizational life will eventually do you in, or turn you into a robot. A popular view is that the modern organization inevitably demeans and destroys people's spirit because the authoritarian, pyramidal structure breeds alienation, domination, and submission. Earl Shorris' book *The Oppressed Middle*[18] presents evidence for this point of view. He presents some very moving examples of how the modern corporation can dehumanize and destroy its members in tragic ways. He contends that power resides in mysterious corners or layers, and that one never knows whom or what to believe. That large organizations are Kafkaesque worlds which transmit self-contradictory whims and caprices to its members, who must always assume they are in error.

In the organizational world Shorris portrays you can never be certain if you've made a correct move. You must either live in fear or obedience. Incompetence is rewarded, competence is punished, and confidences are betrayed. He gives evidence of broken spirits and lives which result from this totalitarian world which, he claims, characterizes our organizations today. He says people put up with it because they accept the organization's definition of happiness as materialism, and so they engage in a trade-off of autonomy for the illusion of security. This frees them, they think, from making hard moral and intellectual choices. His point is that if the worker identifies self-interest with that of the company, he won't be alienated. He will be loyal and unquestioning. The end result, he says, is pervasive fear in the middle levels.

Variations on this theme have been expressed by many writers. For example, Joseph Heller's novel *Something Happened*[19] typifies the view of the organization as a place in which everyone fears everyone else, with corruption and degeneracy rampant. His character Bob Slocum is comfortable within it, though his personal life is a failure. He is popular and successful, plotting his way to the top. This vision of the modern organization tends to be accepted by many novelists and social critics. The organization is blamed for a whole range of symptoms, like alcoholism, anxiety, impotence, and even the lack of conversation.[20]

HOW THE SITUATION AFFECTS US

If we separate out anti-organization paranoia from the reality of problems which are caused by the large organization, we find that the latter cluster around emotional problems of upper-level managers which trickle down to lower levels and cause problems for others; problems rooted in inadequate or poor communication and management systems; and problems resulting from underutilization of human resources. All of these undermine self-esteem, morale, and self-confidence, at best, and create crippling psychiatric symptoms at worst.

Trickle-Down Problems From Above.   Many problems for career professionals people are generated by working for higher level managers who
are, themselves, emotionally disturbed. Or from, as one human resources
manager said, an "overall management philosophy which robs people of
their ambition and their capacity to be productive. The result devastates
the person emotionally."

For example, a personnel manager with 25 years of experience with
different companies told me about a person who said he couldn't stand
looking at the computer's VDT all day long. The employee claimed that
he had developed a "handicap," and tried to get a disability retirement.
What came out was that his supervisor was known to feel very insecure
and inadequate, and was extremely critical of his subordinates. The employee couldn't stand it any more, saw no alternative, and wanted out.
"The truth is," the personnel manager added, "lots of people have terrible
problems because there are lots of terrible managers around. Some people who are power-mad or nuts in some way express it through making
their programs and people suffer."

In another organization I consulted to, a manager was very uptight,
intimidating, and known to have a lot of personal problems, which he
took out on his subordinates. An ex-military officer, he was rigid, compulsive, and couldn't adapt either to subordinates who had more relaxed
attitudes about their work, or to the nature of the work itself, which
required teamwork and group problem solving rather than autocratic
decisions from above.

Stress, anxiety, and clear-cut psychiatric problems among upper-
level managers trickle down to affect workers at lower levels in various
ways. In one company a mid-level manager was reassigned to a different
part of the organization and given new work. Managers there had a
reputation for treating people like replaceable parts in a machine. They
liked to joke that they were the company's "S.O.B.-Team." Soon they
began complaining about her slowness and initiated steps to get rid of
her. They saw a poor fit, and knew the situation was not bringing out
her best, but they wanted a person who could produce, and didn't care
about helping her develop. She became anxious and depressed, and
started popping valium to get her through the day.

An executive in his late 30's told me his personal experience included
working ". . . for a manager who was completely paranoid. She hated all
men and took it out on her subordinates, who happened to be all men.
The first year I was there she praised my work and supported two trips
to Europe. Then she, herself, got a new boss who disliked women managers, and suddenly I became the fall guy."

Another person, an upper-level executive in a federal government
agency, said, "I ended up in a mental hospital for two months while
working for Uncle Sam. Four of my fellow patients held good government jobs, intelligent people. It wasn't the ass-kicking or cracking the

whip that got me down, in itself. It was the constant fending off of these people. From what I've seen," he added, "certain agencies are more likely than others to produce this. Some are mixed up and uncertain while others are efficient and well-run organizations. The current of friction is unnerving. Whip-cracking comes from up high and for the sheer joy of it. It was surprising to see both men and women in high positions behaving like this. There are many good and honest people in government, but some bureaucrats crave power and behave in ways that ruin people."

Pathological or incompetent managers create tremendous insecurity and mental health problems for subordinates. A frequently heard complaint is that many managers are either so grossly unskilled in managing people, or so disturbed, that they make others sick and maladjusted. Or that bad managers are promoted when they shouldn't be, which then creates tremendous pressure upon lower-level employees. Problems can suddenly erupt when a person transfers from one part of the organization to another, in which the working environment or manager creates tremendous stress and conflict for the employee, who then feels trapped.

One psychiatrist who consults to a large organization told me that whenever he gets a number of cases of "troubled employees" referred to him from a particular division of the organization, he invariably finds that the source of the problems is the situation: usually a manager who is, in effect, causing problems for the people beneath him. The latter, in his view, are usually normal people who have become troubled because of the situation.

Poor Communication and Management Philosophy.   There are also situations in which poor or inadequate communication systems and philosophy of management can arouse emotional problems. One mid-level individual expressed the view that "It has to do with the organizational structure here, a lack of cooperation and communication, poor work organization, poor planning, too much uncertainty because of inadequate or misleading information. There's nothing wrong with the people, per se." Another said, "In my experience" (he was an upper level business executive) "big organizations have depressing environments. Jobs often go nowhere. It's as simple as that. You have to learn to ignore it, develop a 'take the money and run' attitude, but it takes a tremendous toll on you."

In some situations the overall management philosophy generates emotional stress which can overwhelm the person. For example, an editor at a large East-Coast newspaper told me that his organization doesn't care about the problems its writers and editors may develop as long as sufficient work is getting done in their department. Those who are most competitive, aggressive, and intense win; the others get shunted off to the side. If someone is too sensitive about having a story that they have sweated blood on get edited down to practically nothing, it's tough. One could argue that at least these values are out in the open, like them or not, and that people can choose to try to become a winner within that system if they wish.

The real problem, however, as the editor pointed out, is that the management philosophy is maintained at great expense to the human resources of the organization, both to the individual "losers" who suffer emotionally because they can't adapt, and to the newspaper itself, which loses the talents of the "losers." Many people suffer such damage to their self-esteem that they don't realize that if they are not good in that kind of environment, or good at selling ideas to their editor, they might be more productive and effective journalists in a different kind of environment.

Problems within management and communication systems which create emotional conflicts are also reflected in surveys of men and women careerists' attitudes about the organizations they work for. One study, of 250,000 workers by Opinion Research Corporation in Princeton, found that only 57% of middle managers viewed their companies favorably. This figure dropped from 73% five years prior to the survey.[21] Middle managers increasingly question with cynicism and negativism what's going on in the company. A 1983 report of a three-year study of worker attitudes found that most American workers said they want to do high-quality work, but believe that their desire to do so is constantly undermined by management practices.[22] The report concluded that management within large organizations blunts rather than stimulates or reinforces people's desire to work productively.

Interestingly, it also found a distinction between what people said would make jobs more satisfying versus what would make them more motivating. For example, workers said they would be more motivated by the potential for advancement, by opportunities to develop their abilities, and meaningful job challenges. But most said they did not believe that employers really wanted high quality or optimum performance. It is becoming clear that new ways of organizing work and new management systems that emphasize participation are not only more efficient economically, but are necessary steps toward changing the emotional climate of our career culture, as well.

Coming from a different angle, Paul Solman and Thomas Friedman say that most of the responsibility for poor performance in the economy is in the executive suites. In *Life and Death on the Corporate Battlefield*[23] they contend that the Harvard Business School model of teaching is more likely to damage than improve the efficiency of American capitalism. U.S. companies focus on a company culture that looks for quick profit and shirks from risks. Successful managers are loyal mostly to themselves and their careers. Their own success may or may not coincide with success for the company. Since chief executive officers have an average tenure of seven years, they feel they would be foolish to risk their future on a risky product or process that would take years to develop. Also, American managers are removed from the manufacturing process. They manipulate things on paper, such as financial estimates, strategic plans, advertising and marketing ploys.

Possibly the most blatant examples of the effects of poor management philosophy and poor communication systems are seen in large government organizations. The prime example is the federal government, in which one often finds, as one person observed, "Presidential appointees who have a nagging fear of losing their high-power, high-prestige jobs. This creates a degenerate and vicious state of affairs which results in a sick and unhealthy environment for the rest of us."

Managers and career employees of federal and state government organizations who have suffered career-related emotional conflicts frequently point to a severe lack of constructive management philosophy at the root, often because much government time is wasted dealing with frustration and the lack of clearly identified goals. A common view is that if government service were made more psychologically rewarding, efficiency and productivity would increase. The public perception of government bureaucrats, together with the internal politics generated whenever new political administrations enter office can cause many otherwise normal people to develop emotional problems. For example, the Reagan administration brought in many appointees who tried, in effect, to change the government without changing the laws, by intimidating huge numbers of career bureaucrats through the threat of putting their jobs on the chopping block. Policy changes were made with little regard for Congress or existing regulations. What resulted was both a sharp drop in morale throughout many federal offices and severe emotional problems, which often caused work to come to a standstill.

Underutilization of Talent. The third source of emotional conflict, underutilization of talent, is illustrated by the comments of one woman who said, "A big source of depression for me is the lack of interest in my advanced education and training. It gave me very useful skills which are not utilized as much as they could be by my company. And I don't think I'm unique in this situation. This began to bother me so much that I finally went to see a therapist—I was feeling so depressed—but he didn't want to talk about the reality of what it's really like every day, just my mother and father. I don't think he had the slightest idea or interest in what it's like out there in the big world."

Underutilization of human resources can exist in any organization, but it is most visible in the larger bureaucracies. For example, in some parts of the federal bureaucracy and in some international bureaucracies there are situations which cause the most talented to "top out" at a high salary and position by the time they are around thirty years old. They cannot go further up the career ladder in the foreseeable future. This blockage has become even more severe in this era of government cutbacks, and it feeds an attitude of paranoid competitiveness for the "good" or choice assignments among people whose work really requires cooperation. Those who remain in such situations very long develop destructive, suspicious, cynical, and undermining attitudes, or passivity and laziness.

People with government careers, including federal, state, local, and international bureaucracies, are faced with this constantly. One man who resigned a high-level job in a federal department after seven years to take a position with a United Nations organization, said, "I think there is an incredible number of federal workers who are seeing a psychiatrist as a result of working in the government. It's a fact of life. Most workers don't take risks and are afraid of losing their jobs. Productivity is often nil. As a Ph.D. in management I can see that it's not the workers, but the managers. They aren't trained worth a shit in understanding people. They're nonprofessional, and couldn't even pull down 30K on the outside. They'd be fired in private industry if they tried to pull their crap on the morale of the workers. But they try to get away with it because it's the in thing in government."

Underutilization often goes hand-in-hand with lack of recognition, which is also emotionally damaging. One example would be research scientists who may feel they are insufficiently appreciated by their organization if they can't get the laboratory, staffing, or equipment they need for their research. Some become depressed, mildly paranoid, and unproductive as a result.

UNRAVELING THE KNOT

There are people, however, who are more adept than others at dealing with the system so as to get more of what they want. And there are others who feel secure enough to leave and go elsewhere rather than accept too much loss or lowering of status. They know when to stop throwing good money after bad. Taking into account how disturbed upper managers, a poor communication system or management philosophy which creates more problems than it solves, and underutilization of talent can all generate emotional conflicts in some people, how do we distinguish a "normal" response to a situation from that of a neurotic personality?

Without a framework of understanding how a person's orientation, including both conscious and unconscious motives and attitudes, affect and are affected by the reality of organizational roles, politics, and culture, it is not possible. And this is the dilemma of both the mental health mainstream and organizational consultants. They are faced with what looks like a hopelessly intertwined tangle of person and situation, to which the only response is forcing an ideology or theory to fit what they observe.

To an extent this is understandable, because there are examples in which the person and the situation seem to be woven together, such as that of a woman who resumed her career after taking time out to begin a family. She found that she had conflicts about her work. It was not as fulfilling as when she was more eager to move up. To make matters worse, she had a disturbed boss and was sexually harassed. She began having dreams of falling, and acknowledged to me that she had some personal problems which prevented her from dealing with the work situation better, or, perhaps, from enjoying the work more. But, as she astutely pointed out, "Some situations and managers combine to make it very hard if there are some things troubling you to begin with. And if you can't hack it, you're crushed." She was a woman who was basically rational but had some problems which got in the way.

There are examples of the opposite. For example, I was a consultant to a case of a man who was disturbed but was also responding to a bad situation in his career. He was paranoid. But there was more to it than that. A personnel staffer I talked with said, "I think his problem was also a by-product of his career. His situation and his manager, who is a very insensitive person, made him more crazy; it added to whatever tendencies he already had in that direction. His manager simply told him to do what he was assigned to do; that he—the manager—was not about to change. The problem for me is how to separate out what the reality is. It all seems so intertwined."

"Most mental health professionals," he added, "emphasize only childhood, so they are no help." He tries as best he can to figure out if it looks like a situation reaction. If it does, he tries to work out a solution at the level of the work problem and the manager, but he won't refer the person to a therapist.

Why he and others make that decision can be understood when we listen to the comments of one psychiatrist. He told me, "I don't need to know anything about the work situation. The problem with a lot of [careerists who are troubled] is simply that they have had their lives structured for them too much since childhood. They've had it too easy. Now, when they have to do things for themselves, it's too much for them. They get frustrated, anxious, rebellious." He acknowledged that some environments may be "a little more stressful" than others, but maintained that the healthy adult can "deal with whatever is dished out."

His problem, like many practitioners', is that neither his training nor his experiences have helped him develop a framework of understanding how different kinds of people can be affected by the situations they adapt to. So he understandably has retreated to the explanation he knows best: It's all pathology; childhood-based conflict.

So we must unravel the tangled threads of the neurotic personality vs. the external situation. The kind of tangled web raised by Henry James in his questions, "What is character but the determination of incident? What is incident but the illustration of character?" And we must also enlarge our understanding of emotional problems beyond the limitations of both the "person is disturbed" and the "organizations are bad" points of view. Doing this requires, first, an understanding that how and where problems originate is a different issue from how and where they are expressed. There is a dividing line between what is bearable and what isn't. There is a point at which a work environment becomes so uncomfortable that any normal person will feel troubled and perhaps seek help. To distinguish these situations from those in which symptoms mean that a person is disturbed inside requires knowing how different people adapt to the work, its culture, values, and attitudes, in terms both of the person's character orientation—including the healthiness of his or her passions—and the external requirements for career success.

To properly understand symptoms requires understanding both the person and the situation. One must explore whether the symptoms do, in fact, reflect unconscious, irrational motives and passions, rooted in childhood experiences, or whether the symptoms are a response of a person within the normal range to threat, stress, disturbed working environments, or overadaptation to the values of the career culture.

Clarifying all this is aided by understanding the process of social selection that Maccoby described as occurring within the organization, once the person enters it.[24] A molding occurs, which explains how different people adapt to different situations, and with what consequences. For people to move upward on the career path they have to feel or become motivated to do what the organization requires them to do. This includes not only actual behavior, but also values, attitudes, and a general orientation which meshes with organizational needs. What happens is that traits and attitudes that are useful to the work and the role the person is in are stimulated and reinforced. Those that are unnecessary or impede work are thwarted, suppressed, unused, and gradually weaken.

We can look at any organization as a "psychostructure," which selects and molds certain kinds of orientation in order to achieve a congruent fit between the requirements of the work and the character of those who do the work. The result is to select particular types of orientation for different kinds of work. Maccoby found that the process of selection of different orientations of people for different roles resolves the argument between the more sociologically minded, who claim that the role determines behavior, and the more psychologically minded, who claim that personality determines behavior. Of course, he also pointed out, there is leeway in any role for differences in style, intelligence, and character, but, as one moves up within a competitive and selective organization, the variations become less important. The individual's orientation becomes molded in the process of upward movement to fit the needs of the role and the organization as a whole.

The upshot of this is that it is possible for the psychostructure of an organization to stimulate, support, and make adaptive disturbed attitudes. The latter are then, in effect, "required" for success and upward movement. Or, an organization may create conflict for normal people because of the values and attitudes required by the organization for career success.

People within the normal range who feel conflict over the values they have adapted to—or overadapted to—in the course of their career development require help to understand and effectively deal with the conflicts that result between careerism and self-fulfillment, and how these differ from repressed emotions from childhood. Help may require change in either the person, the work situation, or both. Ironically, Freud always maintained a broad view of how the larger environment, of social and cultural circumstances, can contribute to problems. But this view has gotten lost. For many practitioners today, social adjustment per se is so synonymous with mental health that any questions about what it is the person is adjusting to in the first place gets ignored.

So while we all deal with, to some degree, compromises, trade-offs, and anger, they lead to different emotional solutions and different consequences for different people. Some attempt the solution of trying to hit the wall, working even harder, keeping one's nose clean, and assuming everything will be all right. Others rebel, consciously or unconsciously. Some suffer overtly, and others severely, though not visibly. These differences, how and why they occur within different kinds of large organizations, and how we can make sense of the different passions and symptoms that people experience as a result is the subject of the next two chapters.

Specifically, we will see that some careerists who are very sick inside show a surface sanity. They function well on their jobs because their career environment and organization support and reward their sickness. Then, in Chapter 4, we will learn about the broader range of troubled careerists who are within the normal range—not particularly neurotic, and with relatively minor irrational tendencies—who nevertheless suffer from a variety of problems and conflicts *because* of their normalcy: the Working Wounded.

SURFACE SANITY

3

Gary is a 39-year-old executive moving on the fast-track. He has just entered his nearly barren apartment after another long day at the office. Lanky-tall, with graying hair and Robert Mitchum eyes, he closes the door behind him and leans against it in the darkness for a moment, eyes shut. Lots of busy hours behind him.

Then, striding across the living room he flicks on the TV to catch what's left of the 11 o'clock news. He peels off his jacket and tie, grabs a cold bottle of Molson's from the near-empty refrigerator, and sprawls across the sofa, pushing aside some newspapers.

Relaxing now for the first time that day, Gary takes a look around the room and reminds himself—again—that he'd better get some more furniture and fix the place up. Divorced for almost a year, his apartment still has a warehouse flavor, cluttered with stacked and half-opened cartons.

> But what the hell. Too much excitement at work right
> now. Just don't have the time. I've got the opportunity
> of a lifetime and I'm not about to get sidetracked and
> blow it.

A smirk comes over Gary's face. He's thinking about his successful put-down and humiliation of an office rival earlier that day at a meeting with top executives of his division. He can do it good all right. And with finesse; like a knife through butter. Nothing crude about this guy.

They know him at the office as hard-working and very aggressive. Savvy about the ins and outs of the system, and always ready to lunge for the next project or opportunity that comes along. A real go-for-it man. But that's only part of the picture. He is playing a high-stakes game in an organization that has a destructively competitive environment at the top, where everyone is constantly maneuvering to do each other in as they try to climb higher and higher.

Soon the sound of the TV anchorman fades as Gary drifts into sleep, where he encounters an old companion: a recurring dream of walking down a long empty corridor in his office building. As he walks along he feels mounting tension, and each time he passes an office doorway he strikes a karate pose, anticipating some unseen attacker. Eventually he passes a door to a stairway. It springs open. Standing there is a person wearing a frogman's suit and mask. The figure points a speargun at Gary. Without saying a word, he fires it at Gary's heart. In slow motion, Gary watches it penetrate his chest and feels it tearing into his beating heart, which pours forth great torrents of blood. And then he wakes up screaming.

THE POWER LOVERS

Gary is deeply troubled inside, but he doesn't realize it. Nor is he alone. Within our organizations and institutions are many people who are very successful in their careers, yet sick inside. Their upward movement has strengthened emotionally disturbed attitudes which had been lurking, dormant, within them. Their disturbance has been supported by their work, but in ways which don't appear very noticeable on the job. So to the observer they appear "normal." But what goes on in their interior lives, in the passions motivating them behind the scenes, tells a different story.

Some of them do show little quirks or bizarre behavior on the job, which a few people notice. Like one high-level executive who is known to urinate into his wastebasket before leaving the office at the end of the day. One might think that most of these sick people would regularly show some extreme or bizarre behavior at the office. But in fact, most are like Gary: highly successful at work and seemingly normal to others. What they say and how they act are not too different from other people in their situations; at least in their organizations. They have adapted themselves to their workplaces in ways which have been great for their career advancement but disastrous for their emotional health. And ultimately, for their organizations as well.

People like Gary are dominated inside by irrational passions like power-lust, sado-masochism, fantasies of conquest and domination, narcissism and grandiosity, glory seeking, and desires for subjugating and destroying others. In extreme cases, these can extend to cannibal lust, dismemberment, and drinking the blood of defeated enemies. What looks like normalcy and successful adjustment for these people is actually adaptive sickness.

The passions of the power-lovers (we will see later that there are two kinds) get rewarded by their organizations, sometimes to such an extent that their sickness bursts out like from a broken water pipe, and floods everyone around them, as we will see later in this chapter. But usually, they get ahead and succeed to the extent that their sick attitudes "fit," and their sickness is therefore masked because it is adaptive. Sick people well adapted to a sick work environment, they don't show overt psychiatric symptoms. At least not on the job. Some do, of course, in their intimate relationships, which are often chronically and noticeably troubled. But I have found others who arrange their lives so that there is little intimacy to threaten the eruption of their inner conflicts. Gary, who rationalizes his failed marriage and spartan existence, is an example of that. He says he's "too busy to get involved" with anyone right now, but periodically picks up "some bimbo" when he feels the need. Which is not too often, because, as he told me with a smirk, "At this point in my life I get more pleasure screwing my work than screwing women."

Another man I interviewed has a different solution. He has a wife and children who live in a small town a few hundred miles away from the city in which he works. He sees them on the weekend, and during the work week lives in a motel room. He talks to them once a night over a short-wave radio he keeps there. He rationalizes this as being better for his family, because of the advantages of small-town living, and that anyway his work is so demanding that he must keep long hours. So, he assured me, his solution was completely "rational."

The economist Albert Hirschman, who has studied the underpinnings of capitalism as it emerged in the seventeenth and eighteenth centuries, found that passions then like glory-seeking and power-lust were recognized as human and real, but potentially dangerous to the person and society, because they knew no bounds.[1] If fed to an extreme, it was believed, these passions could drive a person into madness or evil. Therefore a political and social philosophy evolved, according to Hirschman, which held that these passions could only be held in check by the power of a countervailing passion: economic self-interest. This created the philosophical, religious, and political basis for the development of capitalism in Western society. Back then, the reality and danger of the human passions, particularly power and greed, were well recognized and accepted. But today these same irrational passions can be so adaptice that we can become alienated from them. We lose touch with how they can become masked by circumstances that support them, and which make them appear "normal" to us.

Take the case of Ellen. She began her career with the federal government after graduating from a well-known West Coast university. Now in her late 30s, she has moved rapidly up the career ladder, working in the executive office of the President during the Nixon and Ford administrations, after which she joined a private corporation. When I started interviewing her she was still in the government, working in policy analysis and formulation. Her work kept her in regular contact with top, Presidentially appointed officials of her agency as a special assistant to the high-level administrators, who wielded great power.

Ellen's co-workers described her as an aggressive and competent person, who was good at "fire-fighting." She was also seen as someone who could be alternately sexy and seductive, or hardened and tough as nails. In the interviews I found her mostly the former, but I also picked up an undercurrent of calculating coldness lurking within her. If I worked with her, I would not want to become her enemy. Some other women managers told me that they resented her because she was known to use her femininity and attractiveness to get what she wanted, including sleeping with men who are powerful in order to promote herself. Ellen told me that she enjoys being close to people who wield great power and assisting them because that is "where the action is." She prefers working for strong managers who are not afraid to take decisive action. She also said she likes to get specific results to specific problems by using power, and that she enjoys "cracking the whip" once in a while just for the fun of it. "It can be better than sex," she laughed. She said she has begun to call herself a "power groupie." She enjoys living alone in an expensively furnished townhouse. She had been married, but, she said, her ambition and pursuit of a "high-powered career" helped break up her marriage a few years ago. Fortunately, she added, there were no children. "I never really wanted any, but I don't understand why. I don't think about it much."

She told me that her work environment was "very intoxicating," and that she was looking forward to her new position in a private, entrepreneurial-type firm, in which she would have a similar role, but would be making a lot more money working for an old boss from the Nixon White House days.

Ellen told me she was happy. But on the inside is a different story. Unconsciously she experiences a consuming lust for power and a burning hatred of male authority. Deep within her, she knows all is not well. For example, on her Rorschach* test I found themes of inner fury and pursuit of power as a magical solution to vulnerability and helplessness. She uses her emotional sensitivity, which is considerable, as a tool to get more power for herself.

She is a person who will do anything to get more power, which is her real motive, rather than an interest in dealing with administrative and policy problems per se. Ellen is in conflict, though it is mostly un-

*See Appendix for explanation of the Rorschach test and how it is used.

conscious. Within her are deep feelings of self-betrayal and guilt that gnaw away at her incessantly. For example, on one of the Rorschach cards she sees a flaming skull, which she described as a scene of someone who was damned and burning in hell. She also saw images which she called scenes from purgatory, and images of destroyed and deformed embryos on a card which tends to evoke one's sense of femininity. When I discussed her Rorschach with her, she was silent for a moment, and then told me that she had had herself sterilized after she divorced her husband, but had never told anyone. Not that she felt guilty, she assured me, but she never understood completely why she wanted to have it done.

Like Gary, Ellen has a recurring dream. She is all alone in her office building, walking down endless empty corridors. All she hears is the sound of her own footsteps. She finally enters her office, which is also empty. Once inside, she feels a mixture of smug satisfaction and vague terror, and then wakes up, feeling anxious and unsettled. Ellen's dream reveals her inner sense of emptiness and emotional isolation that has become the price, spiritually and emotionally, for her pathological lust for power. It is likely, given the work environments she has sought out, that she will become more hardened, and lose more contact with emotional reality as time goes on, all the while becoming more successful— more adaptive—to her pursuit of power.

Another power-lover, but different from Ellen, is Bob. He had been very active in the student protest and anti-war movements during college and law school in the late '60s and early '70s. After a brief stint with a public interest law firm, working on health issues, he was offered a staff position on an important committee on Capitol Hill, and came to Washington. He told me he had been intrigued by the possibilities of getting things done from within the "seat of power." And he has done well for himself. He is viewed as a "rising star" in his committee, and has become very much drawn into the pursuit of the glamour and power that goes with his position. He told me his earlier lack of confidence about his abilities had faded, though he still feels, sometimes, like a little boy in a man's world who may be told at any moment that he is trespassing where he shouldn't be. But he tosses these feelings aside with a joke, and says that he knows how competent he is, and how important he is to the legislative process. He says it is "tremendously exciting" to do good work and have a "major impact" as well.

For Bob, the success and recognition he received for his high quality work has occurred in an environment which constantly feeds concern for glamour and glitter. This quickly fanned the flames of his underlying self-love—his narcissism. The importance of what he does in shaping legislation is grossly exaggerated in his mind. Before long, he began plotting his way to the top, and ruthlessly planning the demise of those who stood in his path. For example, he successfully undermined the work and reputation of his superior, which contributed to that person's departure. This cleared the way for Bob's successful pursuit of that position, which gave him even more recognition and "visibility."

Inwardly, Bob feels like a little boy who deeply needs to be loved and appreciated. All his life he has been driven by a demanding and possessive mother. She pushed him to develop considerable intellectual powers, which, combined with his significant creative imagination, have become the tools of his success. But this has not come cheaply. The price is that he unconsciously feels driven to always do other people's bidding, that he must perform and show off to win applause, and that he is really an impotent fraud and has no freedom. His needs for glory and recognition are fed by hidden desires for love and protection from mother.

These themes show up in his dreams. For example, he told me about one in which he presents a memo he has written to a powerful senator, and hopes that the senator won't notice that it is filled with blank pages. In another, his mother sends him on countless, trivial errands, to which he responds automatically, like a robot.

Unlike Ellen, Bob had begun to feel increasingly unhappy with his life outside of work. From the interviews he became more aware that his very success at work was feeding his inflated sense of himself. He realized that this was sick, and he didn't want it to continue. He felt empty inside. Moreover, he confided that he didn't love his wife, and, in fact, had never been able to love anyone. He said that he often thought he would never be free until his mother died, a thought which terrified him. A few weeks after we concluded the interviews, he called me and said that he had decided to begin psychoanalysis. This raises the hope, at least, that Bob may begin to face and struggle with his unhealthy passions, which have been so adaptive to his career environment. But will his analyst be able to understand how his workplace supports his sickness? Will Bob have to change his career in order to stop feeding his emotional problems? Or is there a less drastic alternative?

Unlike Bob or Ellen, some power-lovers are dominated by unconscious attraction to submit themselves to sadistic control. Like the first type, they too are highly adaptive to their particular situations of work, and they are functional on the surface. But they are driven by needs on the other side of the coin: masochistic humiliation and subjugation, often by a literal desire to return to the womb. They are people who also lust for power, but with a different twist. They want to submit themselves to it, rather than acquire and use it to dominate others. Behind their backs I have sometimes heard them called the "ass kissers" of the organization—crude, but not inaccurate, because they are pathologically dependent and submissive rather than grandiose and power hungry. They tend to be found more within the middle levels of their organizations, where their passions are most adaptive to career success.

In effect, the first kind of power-lover needs the second. This is because the work roles and relationships with superiors of this second type require, in effect, submission to irrational authority in combination with loyalty to superiors and the organization. So they submit themselves to a kind of psychic torture to those who wield sadistic power, in the unconscious hope of being loved and approved of. Because of their loyalty and adaptability to the middle rungs of the hierarchy, they are the counterpoint to the "ass kickers." And, like the latter, they show no symptoms at work.

David is an example. He has enjoyed fairly rapid promotion and received awards in his corporate career, working in the area of marketing. Like the narcissistic and grandiose passions of people at the top levels of some organizations, David's are also adaptive to work. At his middle level the environment supports the acceptance of humiliation from, and servile submission to, one's manager. David does what his bosses want, and does it well. He told me that he works best when he has "good leadership." Which, he said, means someone who can "guide and direct" what is to be done.

He is attractive and likable, and appears sensitive and compassionate. In his personal life, though, he told me that he feels lonely, anxious, and depressed. In his early 30s, he remains unmarried. Not that he wants it that way. He told me that he tends to find flaws in all the new women he dates, and then withdraws from them in search of someone new. But, he says, he really hopes to find someone to love, though he doesn't feel quite as confident about this as he did when he was in his 20s.

David's problem is that unconsciously he is deeply dependent, and mother-fixated. In the workplace he submits himself to humiliation in order to obtain mother-like love and protection. Like Paul, the character in D. H. Lawrence's *Sons and Lovers*,[2] David suffers from the claustrophobic imprisonment of his need for mother, which limits a fulfilling relationship with a woman in the real life of adulthood. Without help, such imprisonment can continue indefinitely, even after his mother is long dead. As Lawrence wrote about Paul, "His soul could not leave her ... Now she has gone abroad into the night, and he was with her still."

David has considerable emotional sensitivity and compassion. Yet he has sought out bosses who gladly subject him to their sadistic control, telling him what to do and how to do it. He has little opportunity for participation or development of his capacities on the job. Though he told me he seeks out "good leadership," unconsciously he is resentful and hostile toward rational leadership when he experiences it. He craves and seeks out irrational control and domination from a mother.

Often a person has an inner sense of the truth about their "hidden plots," even if deeply buried. They are often revealed through dreams, Rorschach tests, or psychoanalytic treatment. Such is the case with David. Inwardly he knows that he is driven by desires which pull him away from health and independence, and which are ultimately destructive to himself. He told me about some dreams which illustrate this. One of them occurred during a period of his treatment in which he was analyzing his relationship with his father, toward whom, he said, he had never felt anything but "great respect." In his dream he sees his father floating down a river in a casket-like boat, which is loaded with dynamite. David looks down and discovers that he is holding the detonator device in his hands. At that point he awoke in a cold sweat.

In another dream he is riding around and around on a Ferris wheel. It deposits him, finally, on the ground, next to a long, dark tunnel. He finds himself drawn into the tunnel, pulled along by some mysterious force. As he walks deeper into it he can hear the sound of the ocean beckoning him, at the other end. At that point he woke up, feeling terrified. I asked him what he thought the dream meant. He said that he thought the Ferris wheel represented his career, because he often feels that his work is just a lot of activity that goes 'round and 'round and ends up nowhere. When I asked him what he thought the dark tunnel symbolized, he leaned forward in his chair and said in a low voice that it scared him because he thought it meant that there was something he was doing with his career that was sucking him in to some terrible end, and that there was no escape.

Psychoanalytically, this dream symbolizes David's deep attraction to crawling back into the womb, which provides the illusion of complete safety and blissful security. Unconsciously, he knows that this attraction is regressive and self-destructive. But it is also supported every day by his work and management. In fact, his successful career has made it hard for him to face the truth about himself and struggle against his irrational passions. If he did, he might have to alter his work situation, how he deals with it, or start confronting his boss in order to help himself gain freedom.[3]

A TICKET TO RIDE

For both types of power-lovers, irrational passions—whether for power and glory or for submission and humiliation—provide the road to success within many organizations today, public or private. What is it about these environments that makes emotional sickness adaptive? Take government organizations, for example. They are a prototype of the kind of impersonal bureaucracy that all large organizations have the potential for becoming, a Kafkaesque nightmare come true. Certain roles there are more likely to target and support the development of irrational attitudes. These include the various "power positions" found in the organization, such as policy formulation, strategic planning, high administrative positions, or positions of assistant to presidentially appointed administrators in the federal government

Pathological passions like power-lust, grandiosity, or servile submission lend themselves to political purposes. Examples of this have been attested to by several veterans of the quintessential power environment, the Office of the President. People in that environment are often affected in pathological ways by the tremendous power before them. They begin to believe that it is their intelligence, charm, or insights that gave them power. And as their arrogance grows, it is fed by stories and pictures of themselves in national newsmagazines and newspapers, which all convey the same message of how important they are. They say the environment is so blinding and dazzling that it is easy to forget that the power is transitory. Some even described it like mainlining heroin; that a chemical change seems to come over them. They point out that a lot of these assistants and aides are young and without administrative experience, so they fuel themselves with tremendous ambition, risk taking, and self-promotion.

The danger of environments which breed pathological lust for power is that they disguise the sick passions that drive the person to reach the top. One woman who headed a federal agency during the Reagan administration said in an interview that "I always wanted to be the best, the top, that's all I cared about, that's all that was important, that I be successful." Yet she was described as having inadequate credentials for her position, other than her marketing and self-promotion skills. Some colleagues said that the agency's mission seemed to be almost an annoyance to her, something that gets in the way of her self-promotion and lust for perks, such as spending $10,000 on carpets, curtains, and a new doorway so that she wouldn't have to share a reception area with another official. Unlike many, however, she openly acknowledged her burning drive and ambition.[4] Of course, "blind ambition," as John Dean described it, is commonplace in Washington, and is found to a more extreme degree within its glamour and power-charged environment than elsewhere in the country, or within private-sector organizations.

Within any large organization in either sector in which sado-masochistic attitudes are adaptive to getting ahead, people who don't fit in will tend to think that something is wrong with them. In part, this is because the irrational system of dominance and submission in those organizations acts upon the person through a constant series of small, but accumulating humiliations. It is the kind of experience that Norman Mailer described in The Naked and the Dead[5] as the "fear ladder" which, he predicted, would characterize life in America in the second half of our century.

People who have strong pathological tendencies to begin with are, of course, more adaptive to these roles. Whether these tendencies at-

tracted them to their roles or were strengthened once within the environment, they experience, inside themselves, lust for power and glory,
desire to subjugate and/or destroy others, and greed for personal gain,
all of which gradually come to dominate the person to a pathological
degree, although it all may remain unconscious. Their attitudes are sys-
tematically rewarded, strengthened, and supported by career advancement and increasing influence within the organization. So, although the
passions of these people are very sick, they are also very functional. And
they contribute to the person's success at work, particularly if the person
is bright and competent.

The de facto goal of these roles is often to dominate, scare, or
intimidate subordinates and push programs through quickly. What is
highly valued is the ability to look, sound, and act tough, to put others
down and humiliate them, to "get" your enemies and constantly test
others. In short, as one high-level manager put it, to "kick ass."[6] The
ability to produce a flurry of activity—a memo, an urgent meeting, "fire-
fighting"—upon demand from above, is also a valued trait. There is
always a very busy, demanding, highly charged atmosphere of doing,
talking, analyzing, and report writing, to create an aura of tremendous
importance. It is largely fed by those at the top who are under tremendous pressure to get programs through as soon as possible; to satisfy the
government's equivalent of the market—political forces.

Some of this whirlwind activity results in real action which does affect
people or policies. For example, a directive to eliminate a certain number
of positions in a part of the organization, or to reorganize it. But much
of the work—some critics say most—has little real significance or substance. It simply provides an opportunity for irrational passions for power-
and glory-seeking to blossom to a pathological degree. So paradoxically,
career success in this kind of environment can actually deepen emotional
sickness, and make the person believe, more and more, his or her own
image of importance and power. The overriding goal is to appear like
you are doing something important and powerful. This was underscored
by former Treasury Secretary Blumenthal's comment in a *Fortune* magazine interview[7] that the bottom line in government is not profit, as in
private industry, but appearance and prestige. In today's conglomerate,
this is often the case as well. The situation encourages one to lose touch
with a more realistic view of oneself.

For careerists within government or international organizations in
which this kind of work environment prevails their positive motives wither
away. The work does not call forth their sense of public service, caring
about people, or interest in creating rational and useful programs, all of
which was important in drawing many of them into public service to
begin with. In effect, it starves the good motives, and feeds sadism,
grandiose self-love, and power-lust. So the ideal of looking out for the
public interest, or serving the taxpayer, goes right out the window. The

pathological tendencies compete with and gradually overwhelm other healthier tendencies, like attitudes of service and cooperation, which have become little needed and unused at work, and so have withered away. This kind of environment often requires the pathological extreme of the "jungle fighter" orientation,[8] characterized by power-seeking, domination, and manipulation; and by narcissistic and sadistic tendencies, all of which can be within a "normal," non-neurotic range of adjustment.

Any work environment which requires the more extreme traits of the jungle fighter for success carries with it the danger of feeding deeply irrational, yet adaptive, passions: the modern madness which can push a person over the edge. Even though these passions might be masked by their adaptiveness to work, most of these people do not experience a great deal of conscious conflict, at least not in the work setting. But often they sense that something is grossly wrong, or they feel vaguely guilty and don't know why. In their Rorschach tests and dreams are themes of eroticized power-lust, narcissism, as well as feelings of fraudulence, inner emptiness, terror, and self-disgust.

The "ass-kicker" type of power-lover, whether in business or government, is usually found at or moving into the upper levels of management. Their passions get rewarded, strengthened, and supported as the person's career advances and as he or she obtains increasing influence and authority. The organizations in which we find the power-lovers support, in effect, the development of exploitative, sadistic tendencies, and the methods of manipulation, betrayal, or seduction, in order to reach the top and get power. In this process, deeply irrational passions are gradually strengthened, while at the same time they are masked by being adaptive. A surface sanity, part of our modern madness.

What complicates this picture is that the power-lovers are productive and often very bright people, with talents for strategic thinking, planning and plotting options, and mounting offensives. Talents necessary for their roles but which are inevitably put in the service of getting more power and glory, for their own sake. Zbigniew Brzeszinski, during the Carter administration, described the lusts of many of these people when he referred to the strong "aphrodisiac of power" at the upper levels of government.

One lawyer who worked within such a setting for several years told me, "The place is very seductive, because they appeal to your desire to be professional and competent and all that. They tell you that you are going to have an important 'impact' on things if you stick with it, that you will become well recognized, and at the same time you will be doing good, professional work. This is all very enticing, and the next thing you know you're working 24 hours a day, sleeping on the couch in your office, feeling very important, that you're a 'rising star.' But when you take a good look at things, you see that the work is really not all that important, and that what you're really after is power—exciting power. And it's all crazy, but if you try to talk about it, they think *you're* crazy."

Madness Old and New.   The people I have described represent a modern form of disturbance: surface sanity. It stands in sharp contrast to what has historically been called insane. In previous centuries the insane were people who were perceived as "crazy" or "lunatics," because their behavior and thoughts were noticeably irrational and deviant from those of the ordinary person in society. They were roughly equivalent to what we call "psychotic" today: people with serious delusions, confused thought and speech, hallucinations, and bizarre behavior. They were people who suffered from major internal problems, whether from some psychological trauma in their early development, some defect in their brain biochemistry, inability to adapt to changes occurring in their society at the time, or from too much glory-seeking and lust for blood which drove them over the edge of rationality. Whatever the origin, their problems seriously interfered with their ability to comprehend and deal with reality. For some, that meant becoming the "village idiot," or being locked up, and often tortured or put on exhibition in cages like animals in a zoo, until more humane treatments were introduced in the late eighteenth century.

Locking up people who were "mad" became popular in the nineteenth century, particularly in England and France, which led the way in developing huge state-supported institutions. People who were both insane and dangerous had been locked up in cages since at least the Middle Ages. But large numbers of the insane began to be locked up only with the beginning of the nineteenth century.

Gradually, this kind of treatment changed, probably because sensitivity to cruelty grew as the belief in possession and witchcraft declined. Some scholars have argued that the gradual decline of religious faith in the late seventeenth and eighteenth centuries and the growth of a more rational religion paved the way to early modern science.[9] And among the beneficiaries were the insane, because the loss of reason was now seen as neither irreparable nor a cause for treating people like animals. Imprisonment became a preferable substitute for torture, mutilation, and death. The shift to what was called "moral treatment" of the insane was, in this view, an attempt to be more humane.

In the context of today's world of increasingly large organizations, insanity has, in a sense, taken a different twist: no longer does it stand out as lunacy, gross disturbance clearly deviant from the norm, and reflecting the total absence of reason and rationality. Instead, it is reason gone amok, in the sense that it serves an irrational master, passions of sadistic control, power addiction, and its twin, masochistic submission and humiliation. Some recent research on rationality adds to this picture, by showing that destructive or bad social outcomes to actions can result from rational, i.e., instrumental, behavior in situations where individuals have an incentive to act in an antisocial or humanly destructive way.[10] In this sense, one can be highly rational, purposeful . . . and also sick.

POWER-LUST AND MENTAL HEALTH

Interestingly, most of the research and clinical study done on the destructive and debilitating conditions of work as it relates to power ignores what the authority structure and the values within the workplace do to people—both those who fit in and those who don't. The aim of much of the research, explicitly or implicitly, is getting the employee to fit into and accept the values of the workplace with a minimum of complaint.

The vapidness of contemporary psychoanalysis in particular, when it comes to understanding, let alone dealing with, how sick environments can feed yet mask irrationality is seen in the open and uncritical admiration many analysts express for people who are driven by power-lust. Many automatically assume that power has, by definition, positive effects on people. That because the individual who gains power will say he or she loves it (one called it a "long delayed fulfillment" that he strived for all his life) analysts blithely conclude that people who wield great power are, by definition, mentally healthy. For example, one analyst contended in a *New York Times* interview[11] that some of his patients who wielded power, like military officers, high government officials, or top corporate executives were, by definition, mentally healthy. Why? Simple: the patients told him so. They said that they greatly loved and enjoyed their power. The analyst then concluded that because power made them feel good, sexually potent, and so on, they were therefore trouble-free. (He failed to say why they were in treatment to begin with, if they were so mentally healthy.)

Such claims are nothing new. Except, perhaps, to therapists who are ignorant of history. Conquistadors and dictators from the beginning of civilization have always felt energized by power. What is absent from most practitioners' thinking is an analysis of their patients' power: how they obtained it, whether the ends to which they employed it were rational or irrational, and what the effects were on them, emotionally and morally.

The problem is that many practitioners secretly admire and vicariously enjoy their patients' power-lust, which then prevents them from analyzing it with an open and scientific attitude. For example, one has said that people who have less power are the ones who are more likely to be depressed and suffer from mental problems. That it is actually powerlessness that corrupts people. Another psychiatrist called power-lust a "heroin high" which provides a "great psychic lift." And another called it the most effective short-range antidepressant in the world, because of the thrill of having eyes riveted on you as you enter the room, and the fact that the powerful are spared the "mundane problems" of living, transportation, and so on, while enjoying increased sexual attractiveness.

But without understanding the meaning of a person's attraction to power, we are left with a contradiction: equating power-lust with mental health on the one hand, and on the other, describing it as a "heroin high," an "antidepressant," and an "aphrodisiac." One psychiatrist who praised power-lust admitted that several of his patients became "burnt-out" cases, unable even to function, when they ultimately lost their power. And this is mental health?

Under the guise of expert psychiatric knowledge, the many examples from history and literature of what happens when power becomes an addiction are ignored. For example, Aristotle's refusal to continue teaching the young Alexander the Great when he realized that Alexander's power-lust had perverted his heart and led to monomania; Ivan the Terrible's reign of torture and sadism; Shakespeare's portrayal of the effects of ruthless power seeking in *Coriolanus, Macbeth,* and other plays; the 19th century writings of British historian and statesman Lord Acton on the moral and ethical disintegration that results from power-lust. The list goes on.[12]

In our large organizations are high-level seekers and wielders of power and control who are, as we have seen, driven by pathological grandiosity, by desires to conquer and destroy the "enemy," and by extreme self-aggrandizement, none of which is visible on the surface if it is adaptive to the work and to being successful. And, as we have also seen, the dominance of such passions ends up perverting the heart and reducing the person's ability to see reality or use judgment.

The sociologist Richard Sennett, who has written about the problems of power and authority in modern culture, argues that we used to pay homage to authority in religion and government which we perceived as legitimate, but that today we focus on the person as his or her own authority, a law unto oneself.[13] In our present age in which we are chronically seeking acknowledgment for our existence we can end up ennobling suffering and constantly searching for some injury or affliction to justify suffering. He cites Sartre's view that the oppression of workers under capitalism gives them "special knowledge."

This seems to describe the power-lovers who unconsciously seek out the suffering of masochistic enslavement within their careers. Sennett argues that the rise of marketplace ideology did not adequately replace preindustrial forms of personal authority. Both rulers and the ruled need a substitute, and so fall prey to domination and enslavement. Beneath the illusion of independence are forms of dependence and illegitimate authority, which can provide the basis of pathology being adaptive to the workplace.

Similarly, the economist John Kenneth Galbraith contends that the source of power in today's world is not the individual, or property, as in early mercantile capitalism, but in organizations: the large bureaucracies, management-controlled corporations, the modern bureaucratic state, unions, trade associations and lobbies.[14] Sources of power in previous times were the personality and property. Today, he argues, the power to change beliefs is central to the functioning of the modern economy in both capitalist and socialist countries.

Analysts who are either ignorant of history or secretly lust for power themselves will assume that acquisition of power in one's career is equivalent to mental health, and will fail to analyze it as much as they would the patient's childhood. Consequently they fail to distinguish between normal needs for self-esteem and the desire for one's efforts to result in something useful and meaningful, on the one hand, and the perverted passions for conquest and domination on the other. They also fail to recognize that there is a range of power usage, from the more pathological extreme of acquiring and using it to destroy and conquer others; to using it to build a base of security and protection for oneself and others, such as a successful entrepreneur might do in developing a company; to using power in a pragmatic way, guided by principles that have some greater benefit for the larger society, not just one's personal domain. There is a gradient along which both the degree of rationality guiding the use of power and the principles to which it is put can vary.

When Passions Overflow. The lives of the power-lovers I have described so far show us the importance of understanding the passionate forces within us—as distinguished from how we might act or behave in a given situation—as well as the effects of the career work environment, its values and roles we encounter and adapt to while moving up the ladder. Someone may present an outward appearance of normalcy and success even though he or she is very sick by human criteria, as contrasted with the criteria of being functional within the milieu of the workplace.

A person who is adaptive to a disturbed work environment tends to be maladaptive to a healthier organizational culture. The sick but adaptive person maintains a kind of balance between himself and the situation that keeps pathological passions from erupting into noticeable psychiatric symptoms on the job. But as I indicated at the beginning of this chapter, that can be undone. Change within either the person or the situation is a threat to that balance. For example, if the person's career situation changes, for better or worse, it can trigger overt symptoms where previously there were none. What happened to the following two people illustrates this.

Frank, a pudgy, soft-fleshed man in his late 40s who chain smokes

Tiparillos, once had a flourishing, rapidly rising career as a "hatchet man" under a sadistic upper-level boss who had a reputation of being very hard to work for. He didn't originate, but certainly personified the line, "I don't *have* ulcers, I *give* them."

Frank was on a roll. But then it all collapsed. A change of leadership in Frank's part of the organization gradually occurred. The new leadership began to establish a more participative and team-oriented organizational structure. And Frank couldn't handle it. He started openly undermining his new superior and placing obstacles in the path of cooperative work efforts. He began demanding recognition for his "vast experience and knowledge." He also disrupted meetings, and avoided carrying out directives from his superiors.

Frank's history and his Rorschach test reveal that he has always been dominated by strong sado-masochistic tendencies. In the past his unconscious passions had been adaptive to his work and helped make him a career success. But no longer. Now they have, in a sense, broken loose. They no longer "fit" what the situation requires. Unconsciously, he seeks a godfather figure to control and protect him. And he had such a person, during the earlier, more successful part of his career when he attached himself to the sadistic, vindictive, but protective boss. This had allowed Frank to function successfully within his company. Successfully, that is, for his career development.

His Rorschach test shows that he is dominated by infantile and narcissistic attitudes, and by sado-masochistic tendencies. Unconsciously he feels resentful and rebellious, but needy of affection, which he seeks through submission to strong figures. He told me that when he began college he had to major in a field that he hated, but which his father ordered him to do. After a year he flunked out, but eventually returned and majored in a different field, feeling great conflict over his father's obvious displeasure. He financed his remaining college years himself, and after graduation Frank repaid his father "every last red cent" he had spent on his tuition for that first year.

His sado-masochistic relationship with his father was replicated in his adult relationships with bosses at work. As a result, Frank is limited in his ability to deal with any kind of work that stimulates emotional aliveness or requires independence of thought. He told me that he has deep moral concerns regarding some political–religious issues, and he is very active in some of these issues within his community. But I found that these concerns are not really rooted in any particular principles or deep convictions. Rather, they are largely motivated by unconscious resentment of authority and a need to rebel against it, which he is unable to do in a productive way. Consequently, he is always fighting and opposing, without it leading to anything.

Given Frank's character, he functions best doing colorless, detailed work under a benign godfather-type boss. This is why his previously masked irrational passions erupted under improved leadership and a work structure which made cooperation and participation the new norm. He is now viewed as a very troubled person by those who work with him, and top management is considering firing him. People like Frank will inevitably show symptoms of their underlying pathology whenever their work environment undergoes a healthy improvement, which shakes up the previous balance they had enjoyed.

Frank's balance collapsed because of a healthy change in his situation. But that balance can also be disrupted by a change within the person, apart from the situation. For example, the career environment might support and reinforce irrational passions so much that they "overflow." They become so overwhelming that they disrupt the balance that had existed and the person's underlying sickness is suddenly—and often tragically—exposed.

And that is what happened with Tony. Energized by yearnings for power and glory, and quite brilliant intellectually, he had achieved a senior position at a young age in a part of an international organization that deals with economic development. Inflated and intoxicated by his success, recognition, and proximity to glamour and power, Tony became increasingly arrogant and frequently humiliated his co-workers. Par for the course, you might say. But then something happened. After a period in which he had been spouting off wild exaggerations about how important his work was to international affairs, he was challenged one day by a colleague on an interpretation of a relatively minor point in a report they were working on.

Tony decked his colleague. He had to be forcibly subdued by three other co-workers. He was carried out of his office literally kicking and screaming, and shortly thereafter entered the psychiatric ward of a hospital. His colleague told me that he had considered pressing charges, but then decided not to. Instead, he told me in a cold, even voice, he was going to find a way to "retaliate in a fitting manner."

Is it possible that Tony had been suffering from some prior emotional problem and that what happened was the result of some mounting stress or difficulty in his life outside of work? Of course. But we should not ignore, as mental health experts are prone to do, the major contribution to emotional breakdown by work environments which emphasize and reward excessive pursuit of power and grandiosity, make them the standard of normalcy. and thereby pervert the meaning of sanity.

THE WORKING WOUNDED

4

Without work all life goes rotten. But when work is soulless, life stifles and dies.

— Albert Camus

Life is what happens to you when you're busy making other plans.

— John Lennon

In an interview shortly before he was murdered, John Lennon commented on the reasons behind his five years of "retirement," during which he was a househusband and the primary caretaker of his and Yoko Ono's son Sean. He said that he realized that he had become caught, in effect, in a career trap: always having to produce something, keep the career going, churn out product, and that this commitment and expectation was preventing him from clarifying what was really important in life. He came to see, he added, the danger of a person's career becoming so important that it blocked out everything else, especially the development of love relationships and values that have deeper meaning than what one is left with after sacrificing everything for getting ahead.[1]

His comments highlight a theme found in the troubled careerists I have studied that concerns the effect of over-devotion to career success upon a person's values, satisfactions, and, ultimately, emotional health. In the last chapter we saw that people can be very disturbed inside, yet appear well-adjusted in terms of their outward behavior and career progression in today's large organizations and bureaucracies. This chapter is about a second apparent paradox, the other side of the coin: people who feel and act troubled in various ways, and to various degrees, and yet are basically normal inside. Their conflicts and troubles are not the product of a neurotic personality, though they do have some irrational tendencies, like everyone. Rather, their problems are rooted in their adjustment and adaptation to their work environment and the career culture which has enabled them to become successful. They are the Working Wounded.

THE NEGATIVE SIDE OF NORMALCY

When I first met Diane she was a 34-year-old Mercedes-clad wife and careerist, juggling home and work, yet bored and dissatisfied with both. So she had begun looking for some Faustian adventure. Which she found. She consulted me for therapy as an end run around Mephistopheles, who, to her surprise, had come around to collect his end of the deal.

She said she had been feeling troubled in recent months because she wasn't "holding it all together" the way she used to. I soon learned that she thought therapy would be a convenient way to rationalize her life and assuage her guilt. Though she wasn't fully aware of it at the time, she had been feeling guilty over having become a talented user of people, which helped in her profession, in the financial services area. Her husband was an ambitious lawyer who traveled a lot. She had begun filling the vacuum with new furniture, house renovations, clothes, and, finally, affairs. Mostly short-lived, but longer than one-night stands; she felt she had her dignity to maintain.

She was feeling anxious and depressed, which was often more acute in the evenings. What emerged was that she felt a sense of self-betrayal over the life she was leading and the values she had increasingly come to live by. She was the product of a middle-class East-Coast family, a middle child, who graduated as an English lit major from one of the Seven-Sister colleges. After college she travelled for a time before studying business and economics in graduate school. Her early childhood and family relations were characteristic of people in her suburban milieu during the late '50s and early '60s. Like her fictional counterparts in the movie *The Big Chill*, she had traded in her earlier concern for social and political ideals for money and the good life.

Problem was, she wasn't very happy. She gradually acknowledged that her work lacked meaning and challenge, and that she felt her life was basically empty. Nothing seemed to have much purpose or meaning beyond the immediate moment. She had no values that transcended the experience of daily life. Yet I could not describe her as neurotic. Like many of the Working Wounded, neither extensive interviews nor the Rorschach test revealed much in the way of neurotic conflict. Her Rorschach showed some tendency to retreat when strong passions are aroused, but she also showed creative spontaneity, capacity for solid human relatedness, and attraction to beauty and aliveness.

Based on my seven years of study of people who are the new breed of career professionals in our large organizations, I find that adaptation to the values, behavior, and mentality best suited for successful career development has a hidden downside that takes the form of a range of conflicts. They may look neurotic, like Diane, because people who suffer from this downside can develop psychological problems like anxiety, depression, rebelliousness, chronic indecisiveness, diminished produc-

tiveness, dissatisfaction, feelings of guilt, and various unexplained physical ailments. But ultimately we find that these people are within the
range of normal mental health.

The Working Wounded are men and women in the career professional class who suffer from and try to deal with this psychological fallout
from success. Most therapists would interpret such symptoms as reflecting childhood-based difficulty because they occur within work and career
situations with which a "normal" person, they assume, would not have
difficulty. Because it is accepted as a given that the name of the game is
to work hard, be well-rewarded, acquire possessions of high quality, and
be able to feel tranquilized by them, it is assumed that if the person
experiences a problem, it must be rooted in some internal conflict that
prevents the person from functioning smoothly, without complaint, in
his or her adult environment. However, though they may seek out psychotherapy, stress management, or quasi-therapy "growth" experiences,
they do not have neurotic personalities. Contrary to what conventional
thinking within the mental health mainstream assumes, they are relatively
healthy people who have adjusted and adapted themselves to the workplace—its values, behavior, organizational structure, communication systems, management, and culture—at an emotional and spiritual cost. The
result looks like the product of childhood-based neurosis because the
person is openly troubled. But internally we see a different picture: no
greater irrational tendencies than we would expect to see in most anyone.
They don't show the kinds or degree of unconscious conflict and
disturbed passions which form the nucleus of true psychological
disturbance.

My study of these new careerists shows that contemporary work
within large organizations and institutions can generate crises and conflicts as the person adapts to values or conditions within the organization
that are good for advancement but impoverishing to the spirit and sense
of identity. Based on this research, my contention is that a person's overall
orientation that he or she develops regarding values and meaning can
result in feelings of inner emptiness: a spiritual vacuum, which is a legitimate form of emotional disturbance. It generates conflicts and troubles, some conscious and others unconscious, even though from a psychoanalytic standpoint, when we examine the motives, attitudes, and
passions that drive the person from within, we must conclude that the
person is within the normal range of adjustment and does not have a
neurotic personality.

The Downside of Success. For ease of understanding, we can describe
the kinds of problems that normal careerists suffer from as symptoms
of either values conflict, overadaptation, or negative coping. These are
reflected in problems that normal, adaptive, careerists can develop while
pursuing successful careers.

Some careerists suffer from a conflict of values regarding what their work and career culture requires from them in order to become successful. Others develop problems from overadapting too much or too well to the organization and their career. And some struggle to respond and deal with destructive or negative situations in their work and/or management, which results in negative coping. All of these conflicts underlie a variety of emotional problems. There is a range, of course, of how severely or acutely they suffer. For example, some show mostly frozen or unproductive development as the price of adjustment. Others suffer more acute conflicts. For others, adaptation may stimulate and strengthen whatever latent, irrational tendencies exist within them that otherwise would have remained dormant. They move closer to the edge of more serious disturbance.

Understanding values conflict, overadaptation, and negative coping, together with their roots in the New Age of work described in the next chapter, sheds new light on the meaning of both neurotic-looking psychiatric symptoms and the burnout/stress syndrome affecting so many successful careerists today. These problems have developed in the context of changing motivations, attitudes, and goals of the new careerist, who works in an increasingly service-oriented economy and who seeks greater participation, opportunity to develop, and greater meaning from work. In later chapters we will see that dealing with and overcoming these conflicts of the career steeplechase are intertwined with creating more relevant and effective strategies within organizations, to accommodate the needs and values of the new careerist. Companies are gradually learning that this both improves competitive ability in the marketplace and stimulates the positive motivations of the new breed of the career professionals.

How can we explain the paradox that successful career professionals can develop psychiatric symptoms in their daily working lives and yet have emotional attitudes and a character orientation that is within the normal range? The Working Wounded have developed overt problems in the absence of actual inner disturbance because features of the work environments in their organizations, in combination with the life orientation they have developed as they have become successful career professionals, have combined to produce a downside to successful adjustment.

Typically, we don't think of the norms of our workplace and the career culture, which we take for granted and to which we all have to adapt to some degree, as a source of emotional problems. We tend to assume that there must be some defect within us if we become conflicted. Otherwise, we assume, we wouldn't be having problems in the first place. And when this message gets reinforced by the therapists or other merchants of change to whom the Working Wounded turn for help, the person ends up being led down blind alleys of false explanations and snake-oil cures of the latest in-vogue therapy, stress management techniques, meditation, and other "treatments" touted as emotional cure-alls for smoothing off the rough edges along the fast track.

Without understanding that the process of adaptation to careers in big organizations can generate ersatz neurosis, it is difficult to distinguish the problems of the Working Wounded from those of neurotic characters. It's something like the old folk tale about the frog and the fish, in which the fish cannot conceive of what life could be outside of the water. Our adaptation to the environment of work, including our acceptance of its values and our experiences in it as "normal," makes it difficult to see how we can become troubled despite being normal inside.

Yet evidence is mounting, both from clinical treatment of troubled careerists and from research, that work can create a variety of psychiatric problems. For example, a massive, two-decade study of 3100 men who worked in large organizations conducted by National Institute of Mental Health researchers Melvin L. Kohn and Carmi Schooler,[2] documents how the conditions of the job and the experience of work profoundly affect the adult, particularly in molding values and in developing or undermining intellectual functioning. They found that boring, bureau-cratized work causes feelings of powerlessness and distress for even the most well-adjusted of individuals. People with stimulating work develop a fuller life outside of work, while those in dead-end, unstimulating careers gravitate toward passive, escapist activities. These findings are consistent with what we observe in the three forms of the Working Wounded.

All of the Working Wounded suffer, to some degree, from lack of development. Even those with fairly mild conflict are people whose development remains dormant or becomes frozen. While remaining successful, they experience such symptoms as malaise, alienation, boredom, or dissatisfaction. They go after and accept as normal and well-adjusted a desire for high success, recognition, and reward. But their career and work experiences have failed to support their personal development beyond the traits and attitudes that are useful for career adaptation. Because of their inner longing for a fuller emotional life, they suffer. They have capacity for greater love of life, concern for others, creative spontaneity, affirmation of truth, and so on. But these have not been stimulated or developed by their career experiences. They remain dormant, as though in suspended animation. When careerists' development becomes frozen, they become locked into a cycle, in which they are productive as workers, but less productive and alive as people. And in response to recognition of this, which is often semiconscious, they often work and adapt even harder to their career. Many of the stereotyped yuppies fit this description.

To help understand the dominant motives and attitudes of these people, we can think of a range of productive to unproductive attitudes. By productiveness I don't mean more busy or doing more, per se. It is more of an attitude or way of relating to others and to the world rather than a person's capacity for producing work or material success. It refers to the use of human powers like reason, imagination, love, and the ability (and interest) to penetrate beneath the surface of things in order to deeply understand reality. It is related to Aristotle's concept of the "good man" who, because of his activeness and reason, brings to life one's full powers. It is also similar to the philosopher Spinoza's concept of "virtue" as synonymous with the full use of human powers.

Productive and unproductive tendencies always exist as a range of possibilities in a person. Fromm described the person in whom a more productive orientation exists as experiencing him or herself more as the "actor," not alienated from his or her human powers.[3] He or she is at the helm, in the driver's seat. People with conflicts in this area sometimes have dreams of travelling in a train or bus, in which they are conscious of not being the driver, but of riding passively to some unknown destination. The productive orientation is based upon freedom and independence, guided by reason. Within any character-based attitude, one may find a range of unproductiveness–productiveness. For example, from practicality to unimaginativeness, from open-mindedness to lack of principles.

As a group, careerists who have become relatively frozen in their development have productive attitudes about work, and they possess a wide range of intellectual talents. They are stimulated and turned-on by their careers, usually more so than by their intimate relations. Certain intellectual traits have been rewarded and strengthened in them by their success and career development within their organizations. They look for stimulation from their work, and the more flexible ones will leave a position if it becomes too deadening. But their personal development, as well as their potential contribution to improving the organization, is limited by their coping with their situations in the organization which do not support continued development. So their capacities remain locked up, or become deadened, by their adaptation.

Dan is an example. He has risen to the position of Vice President of a large corporation. Throughout his career he has looked for new opportunities whenever he felt his existing job had stagnated. He radiates a high level of energy, activity, and enthusiasm. Now in his early 40s, he enjoys challenging work, which he approaches with strategic, systems-like thinking. He is open to new ideas of work organization and leadership, particularly those that contribute to team-building and participation, which he values. He described himself to me as a Gamesman, and he is right.

While Dan has cooperative working attitudes and desires to do well, this has required repression of some negativistic attitudes. He has a tendency to be initially resistant to demands that he perceives are being placed on him. He shows a tendency toward anxious worry, and often appears fidgety and impatient. And sometimes, in a flash, he becomes emotionally cool and distant. He says that he wishes he could feel more deeply and passionately about life, but something stops him. He also told me that he secretly admires people who give up a successful career and do something entirely different, because it shows that "they can live without the trappings of success as we've all defined it."

Dan's Rorschach test shows that he sees himself, unconsciously, as somewhat of an underling. This is symbolized, for example, by an image he sees of being down on his back, looking up at authority. He seeks love and affection, and does not want to be too adversarial in his work relations, perhaps because this might open up some anxiety-laden, unresolved issues like autonomy versus guilt, or rebelling versus performing. On the plus side, Dan shows real but underdeveloped capacities for love of life and creative, intellectual, and spiritual development. But he keeps his distance, and does not allow himself to become too emotionally aroused. I think his busyness and devotion to work has supported the more productive side of himself, overall. As a person he remains underdeveloped, more than he need be. This is partly because of some unresolved emotional issues, though no major ones, but also because his devotion to career and work has never supported any further development.

Perhaps careerists like Dan have developed as much as they can, given the limitations of large, multi-layered organizations and of contemporary leadership in our society. If more stimulation were to occur, from more opportunity for participation and development on the job, this might lead to more contribution at work as well as to more fulfillment for the person. Some recent experiments to improve work and leadership show that it is possible for this to occur, at least in some organizations.

Another example of an underdeveloped careerist who suffers is Ernest. In his late 30s, he originally studied for the ministry, but left when offered a position with a small manufacturing company run by his uncle. He liked the business, he said, but was squeezed out in a power maneuver by a cousin, the uncle's son. He eventually began doing human resources management for another, larger corporation. At the time I interviewed him he was second in command of the division, and was about to be given the top slot. He is viewed as hard-working and productive, who is particularly competent with detailed kinds of work, and who enjoys facilitating the career development of younger subordinates. He told me that he knows he is good at his work, and enjoys its perks, but that he feels, overall, bored with his life. He can't get interested in much of anything, anymore. Divorced for several years, he sees his two teen-age sons regularly, and they have a good relationship. But when he's by himself, he told me, he becomes "pretty lazy. I enjoy my comforts." Still, it troubles him that, for example, he used to enjoy reading Greek history, but now spends most of his spare time watching movies on the VCR.

Ernest described himself as a man of contrasts: hard working, but secretly lazy; outgoing, but also a loner; a pragmatic compromiser, yet a man of principle, with strong ethical-religious concern. These consciously felt contrasts reflect a deeper sense of being two people: an outer Ernest, hardened to organizational and career realities—an adaptive achiever within the system—and the inner Ernest, who is soft, compassionate, somewhat dependent, and seeks a bit too much of the all-accepting love of mother. His Rorschach shows that he unconsciously symbolizes himself as a crustacean: hard on the outside, but soft and vulnerable on the inside; and in another image, as a body in search of a backbone. He experiences some conflict, though not major, between outward aggressiveness and inward subservience and dependency.

Ernest is a man with real abilities. He has always been active and productive in his work and career. But he has come close to giving up on meaning. His desire for comfort and for minimizing risks is gradually overtaking his capacities for deep conviction, service to others, and spontaneity. His career advancement and adaptation has required, for him, a gradual hardening of his exterior and a softening of his heart.

WHEN VALUES CONFLICT

Some of the Working Wounded suffer from conflict between their internal judgments about what is important in life, including their sense of truth and ideals (or inner desire for such), and the values and attitudes one gradually comes to adapt to and acquire as the ticket to greater success and higher position. These conflicts over values are often unconscious, though not necessarily so. In a sense, values conflict is the more acute psychiatric version of the compromises, trade-offs, and anger we saw in Chapter 2, which all careerists experience to some degree today. The Working Wounded whose problems are rooted in values conflict have often embraced such values as money, fame, deception, or using people to such a degree that their value base gradually makes them disturbed, closer to the edge of sickness in their behavior and life-styles. This process was recognized as far back as the seventeenth century by the philosopher Spinoza, who in many respects was the first modern psychologist. He pointed out that passions for fame, power, and money, when they come to take over the person's reason for being and become ends in themselves, constitute forms of insanity.[4]

The Self-Betrayers. The most common emotional consequence of values conflict is the widely-found feeling of self-betrayal among troubled careerists who have absorbed, to too great an extent, the values of careerism. They have molded themselves too much for getting ahead in today's large organizations, and accepted their perks and payoffs as equivalent to a life of meaning and integrity. Diane is an example. She and others who experience self-betrayal have been affected by the situations that generate compromises, trade-offs, and anger, but in more extreme or severe ways, which lead to more acute problems. They may have crossed the border into values conflict because of the paths and opportunities that became open in their career development, the particular work and management environment they have experienced, or because of their particular talents, and overall personal orientation.

These elements typically converge into acute conflict when the path is easy, the person is talented and well-educated, and the behavior and attitudes which create conflict are reinforced by the culture and milieu of work. Or the person may have been seeking escape from gnawing questions or criticisms about the value or meaning of his or her work which had been filtering into his consciousness. Lacking understanding of the meaning of such conflicts, the person may worry that something must be screwed up inside for feeling any conflict at all over devoting too much of life to career, position, and money. The problem is compounded by the fact that the new careerist is willing to work hard, and has traits of flexibility and tolerance, but has to deal with constraints which require giving up something of oneself. Or operate in environments which require progressive and constant sacrifice, not so much in terms of hours, but in terms of personal beliefs, values, and expression of one's inner perceptions and judgments. The new-breed careerist suffers emotionally when he or she makes decisions and choices which are bad, in the sense of limiting or distorting personal development and inner sense of meaning, although they seem attractive at the time because they are good for the career. Some poisons can taste good, but will still make you sick or kill you.

John, a businessman who consulted me because of anxiety, illustrates the kinds of problems rooted in values conflict. A man of medium height with thick, reddish-blond hair and a mustache to match, John had risen to success with a large real estate development firm. Though well educated, he had flunked in and out of several prep schools, and had trouble in his initial years at college as well, because of his love of partying. Through family connections he got his start in the real estate development business, and, while a hard worker at times, his success was due, in great part, to his personal charm and likeable personality. His wife didn't work, but busied herself with various charity activities, the kind that put you in touch with socially prominent and wealthy patrons.

In his early 30s when he consulted me, he began to realize that he didn't think much of the life he was leading. He felt he (and his wife) were shallow. He had had numerous affairs, was drinking more and more heavily, and had reached the point at which he wanted help to understand and deal with what was happening to him. He had made a tentative decision to give up his career at the time he began therapy, and had begun volunteer work with his church. He joked that it helped "balance out my satanic proclivities."

John was a person with a great deal of unconscious creative energy. He was hampered by a questioning of who he really was, inside, and was plagued by feelings of anger and betrayal against himself. His Rorschach revealed a sense of always performing and displaying himself for applause, symbolized by images of show dogs and dancing bears. He also had unused capacity for human relatedness, and undeveloped spiritual longings, and desire to respond to life positively, with hope and greater aliveness. He was caught in a struggle between the limited person he had become and a person who was struggling to be born.

The development of values conflict and its manifestation in self-betrayal, which give rise to anxiety, depression, malaise, and unexplained physical ailments can be an insidious and circular process. The symptoms often intensify desire for the very behavior and values assumed to be "normal" and therefore unrelated to one's conflicts. An example would be equating more and more of one's self-worth with salary level and position, as a way of coping with the progressive loss of identity and individuality that often accompanies the successful pursuit of upward movement. Or assuming that good work will be automatically recognized and appreciated if one works more and harder, even though reality may contradict that belief.

Jill illustrated the latter. An editor with a large publishing conglomerate, she chafed against what she described as an atmosphere that "rewards negative behavior." She said that she found in her years there that the working environment brings out the worst in people. The reward system seemed to her to be highly arbitrary. And, she added, the environment was one in which you were expected to take on difficult projects to impress everyone around you, and never show signs that you couldn't handle it. When I asked her what her view was of how things should be, she said that she had expected a benevolent, egalitarian environment. But to get ahead you had to be aggressive and tough. She hated the atmosphere of "creative tension," in which people put down each other's ideas for new projects as a test of how hard you can push an idea forward.

The main problem Jill had found herself struggling with in that environment was that she had kept expecting that if she did good work and kept quiet, and did not participate in the culture of her workplace, she would be rewarded. She became increasingly depressed and troubled when she found out that it didn't work. My evaluation of her found that, while she had some negativistic tendencies, which were certainly being strengthened by her work environment, overall she was oriented to cooperation with others and had a positive interest in life. But she also had a great deal of anger, which was being strengthened by the conflict she experienced at work.

In a sense, the psychological problem of self-betrayal is a healthy sign, because it reflects inner rebellion against the Faustian trade-offs of money and position for careers which are thin and empty, isolated and fragmented, and make the person feel devoid of spirit and purpose. Feelings of self-betrayal mean the person hasn't fully given up yet. And it reveals some degree of inner recognition of the need for more fulfilling. meaningful work that is usefully connected with the outside world, and which provides for cooperative interaction and interdependency with others as part of the enterprise.

Symptoms of self-betrayal can be confused with the psychological residue of old values and attitudes about career development which are less characteristic of the younger careerists. For example, a 25-year study of 5,000 business careers found that the decade of the 40s is the most dangerous and turbulent on the job.[5] That people within this decade begin to find themselves increasingly isolated, fearing obsolescence, worrying about long-term security, and trying to hide unproductivity. The study found that they start to show symptoms of less productivity and boredom, as well as nervousness about mastering new technology. Because of the plateauing and leveling out that occurs during this period in career development, the study concluded that the careerist has to look inward more for satisfaction, and work at becoming more of a self-starter.

But the experiences of people in their 40s today are a very mixed bag. That decade contains the transition point from the attitudes of the new careerist, striving to combine success and fulfillment, and seeking more participation, decentralization of authority, teamwork, and quick recognition of competence, to the older values of careerists from about 47 on up, characterized by more passive acceptance of the trade-offs and dissatisfactions, appreciation of having gotten as far as they have, and acceptance of the traditional hierarchy. So some of the symptoms found in this study reflect the frustrations of the Working Wounded, rooted in the shift of values and motivations of the younger careerists, while other symptoms reflect the consequences of an older value system within the context of a rapidly changing career environment. Prescriptions for one group won't work for the other.

For self-betrayers, traditional success raises concerns which they may not discuss publicly with pollsters. But their anxiety and depression often spring from the feeling that what they have gotten isn't as good as they thought it would be. And they can no longer stuff their feelings about it as they used to. Success without fulfillment, without a value base that makes sense over the long run, feels too hollow to comfortably tolerate.

The theme of values conflict and self-betrayal is not unique to our era, except for its current link to career success within large organizations. The problem is that it is not perceived as a form of emotional disturbance by the mental health mainstream because it concerns issues of the spirit, values, morals, and the quality of life. Such issues are conveniently dismissed by today's practitioners as outside the realm of psychiatric problems. Ironically, novelists and playwrights have portrayed the effect of these conflicts upon a person's emotions and character with greater understanding and accuracy than most of today's analysts and therapists demonstrate. For example, many of Balzac's novels, as well as Ibsen's plays, such as *Pillars of Society* or *An Enemy of the People* portray the emotional effects of conflicts aroused by actions and choices which are good for one's career but destructive to one's character and spirit.

Throughout our organizations are examples of people who have become caught up with chasing career gratifications that are inconsistent with the ideals or values that originally attracted them to the career. An example of this is seen in the practice of law, one area which tends to breed values conflict and self-betrayal. In many ways, the experience of lawyers is a prototype of the value conflicts experienced throughout our organizations. Law attracts many bright, ambitious people who become captivated by the money, prestige, and other perks, while at the same time having to stifle their dislike of the work itself, much of which is boring, unfulfilling, and void of social purpose.

Harvard President Derek Bok has charged that law school has become the refuge of able, ambitious college seniors who cannot think of anything else they want to do, but are attracted by top money and the glamour of high-stake litigation. Bok criticizes what he sees as a massive diversion of exceptional talent into pursuits that often add little to the growth of the economy, the pursuit of culture, or the enhancement of the human spirit. Law students themselves commonly complain that law school is boring, repetitious, and that they feel malaise. These complaints are similar to what lawyers report years later, after becoming a partner in the firm. Reflecting the changing values of the new careerists, some law school students now balk at taking on the value system of the law firms, no matter how prestigious. They say they don't want their careers in the big firms to interfere with their "personal life-style."[6] Some firms are responding to this by shifting to avoid too huge a caseload. Some firms are having to admit that excess work, and the value system of the firm, can cause emotional breakdowns. One lawyer quit her firm to teach because she said she had no time left for a life of her own. On the other hand, another lawyer who often bills 65 hours weekly said that sure, he has a life outside of work: he goes home to sleep.[7]

One lawyer who struggled with these issues was Pat, a man of 40 who had skyrocketed to success in his law firm. By his own admission, he had always silently assessed people he met in terms of whether they could be of use to him in some way. If not, he wanted nothing to do with them. His relationships were strictly functional: no time to waste fooling around with people or conversation that had no bottom line. This attitude also applied to his wife and children. Though his wife was struggling to develop her own career, Pat had no interest or feelings of support for it. *His* work was much more important. After all, look at how much money he was bringing in.

One day he stopped home on a way to a meeting to pick up some papers that he had left in his den. He thought he heard some sounds coming from his bedroom. Feeling like he was watching himself in a made-for-TV movie, he entered the bedroom and found his wife with another man. Pat was devastated. He was both enraged and wanted to kill; as well as remorseful, feeling that he was to blame. His wife acknowledged responsibility for the affair, which had been going on for six months. But she added that if he had been more aware of her existence and needs she might have not been tempted.

This experience drove him to seek help to explore what he was doing with his life. It seemed to open the floodgates to an outpouring of conflicts about career, money, position, and the worth of it all that he never knew existed within him. He became anxious and depressed, and had trouble sleeping. During therapy he became aware that he never really enjoyed his legal work or found it very stimulating. But he was so talented at it, and so highly rewarded for it, that he stuffed those conflicts for years, and had come to identify with the values of success within his profession. He realized that he had no life outside of his career. Yet within him all the time were yearnings for more meaning and fulfillment. His Rorschach showed this, too, as well as tremendous intellectual and creative energy that was untapped. Like many careerists who suffer from values conflict, Pat saw images of people performing, dancing, seeking applause. He also showed capacity for critical penetration that he turns away from and doesn't use, as well as capacity to try to integrate diverse elements of things. While Pat's conscious struggle had just begun, it was clearly a battle over values, the way of life he had chosen, and the toll it had taken on him, rather than over internal pathology.

The Money Lovers.   Greed and money-lust also play a major role in the values conflict of some troubled careerists. This leads to the person's framework of values being thrown out of kilter. Just as power-lust is the Achilles' heel of people who develop surface sanity, money-lust is the equivalent for those Working Wounded suffering from values conflict. The desperate pursuit of money, fueled by socially-sanctioned greed within some organizations, serves as a compensatory trade-off for work that lacks meaning, challenge, and fun. Becoming a money lover has a seductive allure because, to the ambitious careerist, money is tangible, available, and valued by the social milieu and organizational culture. This can bring the person dangerously close to insanity, or lead to corrupt behavior, cases of which can be found in the newspaper most any day.

The effects of money-lust are seen, for example, among highly successful Silicon Valley careerists who find that success has its price. Studies of their life-styles and problems have found an atmosphere of enormous money-lust, wealth, and selfishness. The rate of giving to charity is one of the lowest in the nation, relative to the income level of careerists. Big money is the main force among fast-track careerists who see people around them generating large fortunes overnight. Young people just out of college are often offered equity in the company. In this environment, many decide that becoming a money lover is worth the personal sacrifice. An example of the latter is described by one yuppie-type who said that the experience of life there is boring: there is nothing to do besides buy things.[8] Money-measured success then becomes the main attraction, and the careerist gets farther removed from the technical and creative interests and needs that he or she originally brought to the situation. As this theme of conflict has become more widespread, some companies have begun offering sabbaticals, to help the careerist "recharge." But the problems are deeper than that. The success-oriented new careerist wants more in the way of fulfillment, not time off to lie on the beach.

People are starting to see this more clearly, because there are more and more examples of what happens to career professionals who abandon their values and principles in the pursuit of money and greed. A former General Dynamics executive who raised charges of fraudulent activity and corruption involving the defense industry acknowledged that he had taken the company line, and blamed personal ambition, defense industry norms, and being "maybe a little crazy." He maintains such attitudes are common throughout the defense industry. Underscoring this are the comments of a securities lawyer, who said that "If you take away or threaten something that is the source of one's power, prestige, or economic welfare, even the most rational person is likely to strike out and behave in a rather untoward manner."[9] And many organizations make sure that no "untoward" behavior is likely to occur, at least from those at the top, because there is a trend toward paying enormous salaries and bonuses to top executives. In 1984, 46 executives received salary and bonuses exceeding 1 million. These and other compensation incentives—stock options, golden handcuffs, and golden parachutes—set a tone of greed and support actions that are more in the interest of the managers than the stockholders. This affects the value system of the organization as a whole, and in turn, of the careerist.

Clark was someone who suffered from money-lust. A highly successful careerist in a lucrative field, he was a strikingly tall man who talked with a monotone that sounded both deadening and controlling. He spoke of feeling somewhat empty and dissatisfied inside, but didn't know why. He, like other money-lovers, had tried to buy his way out of his dilemma, but with no success. New cars, more clothing, the latest high-tech yuppie appliances, all to no avail. He began to think he had a biochemical problem, and sought out a psychiatrist who prescribed antidepressant medication. But I found Clark's mild depression to be not the product of an inability to feel pleasure, but the product of feeling too much of the wrong kind of pleasure. Inside, he was confused about who he wanted to be. He saw himself both as a predator—a self-image of a wolf who takes whatever he wants—but also as a victim. His capacity to respond positively to life and beauty was limited by his obsessive concerns with irrelevant details. Much like his focus on buying new things. which kept him unable to face and decide what would be more pleasurable and fulfilling in life.

Values Out of Kilter.   There are other forms of values conflict; other roots to the conflicts and troubles that careerists struggle with, in addition to self-betrayal and money-lust. A person's value system may be thrown out of kilter by adaptation to situations which support corrupt or deceitful attitudes and behavior. Of course, we must be careful to distinguish cases of neurotic self-sabotage, or of acting-out of unconscious attitudes, from behavior and values which become adaptive, yet generate disturbance within. An example of the latter would be a scientist who is not really neurotic, but who fakes data to ensure continued research money or to generate publications, in order to enhance his career reputation. One scientist who altered data to help out a company that was financing his research, but suffering economically from an inferior product, said, "It's so important to get a patent before someone else does. I had to earn the money for research or die."[10] An environment of intense competition for research positions and the shrinking research dollar can make these actions more likely to occur, as researchers become more frightened and desperate.

In other careers, the psychic or extra-monetary career highs can also skew one's values. The career may require subordinating so much of oneself to the job that one feels guilty or inadequate if he or she doesn't want to make that degree of sacrifice. For example, many physicians regularly place their career over their family; something they share in common with many corporate executives. They feel caught in a bind between what the career demands and the needs of their spouse and children, not to mention their own needs for a fuller emotional life. Moreover, medical training tends to enhance emotional detachment and a desire to be in control of everything. It may also enhance whatever difficulties they have regarding intimate relationships in the first place. Physicians I interviewed who told me that their work is more important than a love relationship with their children or spouses say that they are evaluated by how successful their practices are. That's the real bottom line, not how great a father or husband they are. But this also plagues them inside, and can underlie such symptoms as anxiety, depression, and alcoholism. But many feel more openly conflicted when faced with adapting to this kind of value system, which generates conscious conflict in its own right. In general, the younger physicians, like their counterparts in other careers, suffer more acutely when they violate their sense of integrity, or ignore their desire for love and meaning beyond the image, beyond the material.

Seeds of values conflict in its different forms are being sown earlier in life. For example, colleges across the nation report that record numbers of students are seeking counseling and psychotherapy for problems.[11] Most of their troubles seem rooted in worries that they will become emotionally trapped in careers. Of course, the high costs of college today plus the declining job market for college graduates understandably contributes to feelings of pressure. They are worried about future career opportunities. But there are also cases of depression, anxiety, and other psychiatric problems among successful students that reflect conflict over the values embedded in the career path lying before them. Conflict over the values of intense competition to beat out the next guy, and pursuing fields of study that may be lucrative but in which they have little interest. They start feeling conflicted, trapped, and hopeless about a future in which they see a lifetime of self-betrayals.

OVERADAPTATION

Problems of the Working Wounded can also be symptoms of adapting so much to the roles, attitudes, or behavior required for success that the person suffers emotionally. For others who overadapt, the more negative side of their orientation, and whatever latent irrational tendencies exist within them, become strengthened because they are so congruent with the work they perform.

Some people find themselves doing work which fits their character orientation, but in a negative way: it supports and strengthens whatever negative traits or irrational attitudes existed within them, but had been dormant. An example would be a lawyer whose obsessive–compulsive tendencies are strengthened by work which requires and rewards those character traits. There is congruency between the person's character and her work. But she does not develop as long as her situation supports and makes adaptive her negative side. She may perform well, as long as the environment remains the same. But overall, she suffers as a person. And if the work changes in a way which requires more creative, spontaneous, or flexible thinking, she may be in deep trouble.

The Heavy Copers. Kathy was an example. A successful economist, she told me that her devotion to her career had destroyed her marriage. She said she feels passionately about work, yet feels that it has made her into a "classic neurotic." By that she meant that she felt she uses work and her success to derive a sense of worth and adequacy that she otherwise lacked. In her work environment, she is rewarded for obsessive detail, performing analyses and research which, she says, would drive her crazy if she let herself realize how boring it really is. Her boss is a dominating man, on whom she has become dependent for praise and attention. "He's a daddy figure for me," she joked. She said that her life is all right, though it could be better if she tried to free herself from the way "work has locked me into my problems." She has been in therapy for eleven years. "Also a daddy figure," she laughed.

Similarly, Jean was a slender woman in her late 20s, and had undergraduate and graduate degrees from Ivy League schools in an engineering area, a field usually dominated by men. She had become troubled while working for a large energy corporation. She complained that the harder she worked, the more criticisms she received from upper management. In fact, Jean saw herself as a little girl inside, living in a grown-up's world. She rebelled against authority when faced with demands and expectations. While these were issues that she might have to deal with in any situation, the corporation she worked for had an atmosphere, at least in her division, of heavy-handed control. This was not a place receptive to participation by subordinates, particularly by bright women who talked back to the men. Jean dealt with this by trying to work harder, assuming that a benign father-manager would appear and rescue her. When it didn't happen she became increasingly troubled and unproductive. She finally sought professional help.

Some careerists, a bit farther along on the symptom-spectrum, find themselves faced with a work situation which is unhealthy, or which requires behavior and values that generate significant feelings of compromise and trade-offs. They deal with it by even more adaptation. It s simply business as usual, only more so. Their solution is to go along even more, adapt even more to the organization, and assume that their increased adaptation is the solution.

An example is Joe, a successful attorney for a prominent law firm. He said he had been bothered by "troublesome feelings" like anger and depression which seemed to "float around" inside him and were inexplicable in terms of his otherwise successful life. His response? More work. Longer hours. And an attempt to ignore those messages from within. But it didn't wash. It only made him more unhappy, and he began having nightmares about being a prisoner in a penal colony. What eventually came out was that he never wanted to be a lawyer. He admitted to me that he had gone to law school mostly to please his father, an ex-politician and prominent attorney himself. Joe had always feared yet craved the affection of his father. He had repressed awareness of this conflict because of the consequences of facing it. Now, at 39, he felt trapped by the prestige and perks of his career.

Joe became more open during our interviews and soon told me that about the only thing he enjoyed in life these days was the volunteer work he did teaching illiterates how to read. He kept it secret from his partners in the firm for fear that they would laugh at him. He said, "There's something fulfilling about helping these people, so different from the rest of my life." Although Joe created an outside source of fulfillment,

he still believed very strongly in seeking meaning from his career, though
he could not find it. Though his situation was complicated by his early
relationship with his father, he, like other careerists who try to cope more
heavily, had tried to involve himself even more with his work, even while
experiencing tremendous conflict over it. Up to the time of our interviews, he was only semiconscious of this conflict and had tried to conceal
it by working harder and burying his feelings.

Many of the overadapted Working Wounded try to deal with their
conflicts in this way. And it has wide emotional repercussions. Jack, in
his early 40s, had a successful, forward-moving career, but felt troubled,
with a variety of symptoms. He revealed to me a cynical attitude about
his experiences throughout his career. He told me that his career ambitions were partly responsible for the breakup of his marriage, because
he felt that everything should be subordinated to aiding his career. His
Rorschach contained many perceptions of Disney-like cartoon characters,
and silly-looking monkeys swinging around everywhere. Symbolically, this
represents his view of himself and how he sees the world: he trivializes
it, denigrates others, but sees himself as, in effect, engaging in too much
monkey business. (As a skillful user and manipulator, he had moved up
in his career through conniving and deceiving people.) On one card he
symbolized himself as a raccoon, suggesting a self-image as a clever thief.
He is emotionally hard and intellectually smart. More deeply, he views
himself as somewhat powerless, having to steal affection, and caught
between being terrified like a rabbit or hardened and powerful like a jet
airplane. Though not deeply disturbed, Jack's negative tendencies and
latent conflicts have been strengthened by his turning to work, almost
totally, for validation of his worth and power. It has caused further
confusion within him, as his manipulations have become rewarded, and
have resulted in an impovershed emotional life, which he can't quite
succeed in rationalizing away.

The nature of some people's work brings them even closer to the
edge of sickness, because the career environment and management can
arouse latent issues from childhood that might have otherwise remained
dormant. Ken illustrates some of this. He looks like a person with a clear-
cut neurotic problem: he has a vivid, overt symptom, he knows it is
irrational, but he can't stop himself from doing it over and over again.
Let's look at the role of his career situation over the years versus his
irrational passions in order to understand how his problems developed
and what they mean.

When I met him he was 50, and had had a moderately successful
career in journalism until he joined a media organization in a public
relations capacity when he was around 40. He told me he made that
decision because of what he thought would be the "extra security," which
had become increasingly important to him. After a series of steady promotions, Ken was passed over for the position of head of his unit, and

talk began circulating that a proposed retrenching of his organization would wipe out several positions, possibly including his own.

During this same period of time Ken divorced his wife of nearly 30 years and began having a series of affairs, including one with a woman whom he later married. Not long after Ken's remarriage his superiors discovered that he had been writing pornographic poems to several women outside his company, with whom he had conducted business as part of his job. When confronted about this, Ken acknowledged his "indiscretions and bad judgment," as he put it, and said that it would not recur.

But it did. Over the next several months he did the same thing with two more women. They both reported it to upper-level managers of Ken's organization. This time Ken received an official reprimand. Again Ken affirmed his intention to control himself. Upper management later learned, however, that at the same time he was making these assurances he was also making suggestive invitations to a secretary in another department. This came to light when the secretary's boyfriend threatened to come in to Ken's office with a gun. Ken admitted that he needed professional help, and asked for a referral to a psychotherapist. (This had never been suggested by management.) Ken said that he was scared his career—and his new marriage—might be ruined if he could not stop himself. He said flatly that he knew what he was doing was irrational, wrong, and a sign of troubles within him, yet he didn't know why he kept doing it.

My study of Ken revealed a picture of a man who has real capacities of the heart: a love of life, cooperativeness, attraction to beauty. But this side of himself has pretty much remained dormant. It had never been stimulated or developed within his work, either in journalism or in public relations work. In fact his description of his past working environments suggested sado-masochistic overtones, which might have been the features of the environments he found himself in. Or he might have sought them out; we just don't know.

But we see from his Rorschach that he feels increasingly weak and dependent, and tends to look for security through position and power. His attraction to power and potency has probably led him into masochistically-tinged relationships in the hopes of receiving it. One sees some of this, for example, in his relationship with his father, a stern and distant man who was not very affectionate. And also, to an extent, with Ken's first wife, with whom he felt deadened and henpecked during most of their marriage. Yet, Ken said that he felt too guilty to leave her until the children, one of whom was retarded, were more independent. Now, after his remarriage, he continued to give 75% of his salary to his first wife, even though she told him that she was willing to accept considerably less. From all this one could say that Ken has a tendency toward masochistic submission.

Throughout his career Ken has tried to be loyal and cooperative,

but has begun feeling increasingly angry and impotent over his circumstances. The loss of opportunity for increased recognition, his "plateauing out," and threats to his job security combined to trigger his symptoms
at work. His capacity for being a good institutional loyalist was undermined by the work environment, which drew out the more negative,
unproductive side of his character. His symptom reflects an unconscious
rebellion, through which he is trying to affirm love for life—through
sexuality—though in a very unproductive way.

Ken is a person who, despite his conflicts and overt symptom, is still
within the normal range of character, though of course he is close to the
edge of pathology. But his irrational passions are not that significant,
and he has shown outwardly normal, relatively successful adjustment all
his life, until now. Presently he finds himself seeking a kind of magical
refuge as a solution to his inner sense of increasing disintegration. Ken's
symptoms are not the product of serious, underlying irrational passions.
Rather, they can be best understood as the response of a relatively normal
person to feelings of insecurity and impotency about his future, which
has brought out negative and unproductive tendencies within his
character.

Would a better work environment have stimulated the more positive
and productive side of Ken? We can only speculate, but it is interesting
to consider what might have been possible in a work environment which
brings out the best in people.

Some respond differently than others to the same situation because
of the particular orientation—the emotional, intellectual, and social attitudes—that they bring to the situation. Normalcy, remember, is a range,
not a steady state. Careerists who become the Working Wounded show
a range of responses to situations, and differences in their attitudes about
them, without being neurotic.

But they do share the development of the less productive sides of
themselves. Their work and career experiences have aroused and supported their more negative sides, the negative traits of their personal
orientation. For example, traits which most of us would describe as positive, like loyalty, fairness, authoritativeness, and assertiveness have negative counterparts, such as submission, indecisiveness, dominance and
destructiveness, respectively. These negative traits often develop among
some of the Working Wounded who overadapt with more serious emotional consequences. For example, some tend to be less active and productive than others at work. Some are somewhat witholding, nit-picking
types of people, who wait passively for affection, recognition, and reward.
They have turned into the stereotype of the bureaucrat or complacent
careerist.

Joel illustrates this. He works in a financial area of the federal government, and complains bitterly about having been passed over for promotion several times. Most recently, he told me, the new head of his

division is a woman who "hates men. So naturally, I'm going nowhere as long as she's around." Joel doesn't do much work. But then he isn't given much responsibility, either. Upper management no longer has confidence in him, partly because they see him as too much of a vocal complainer. So he has a kind of stalemate situation: they don't give him much to do, and he's no longer too vocal about it.

He sits in his office much of the day reading, from the small arsenal of books he has on his shelves, unusual for a government bureaucrat. He proudly rattled off the titles of several books on management he has read. A few years ago, in exchange for a promotion which he was not going to get, he was sent for several weeks to a training course for government executives at Harvard. Joel is very proud of this, and keeps several Harvard mugs lying around on his desk and shelves for people to see. He was always resentful that he did not complete his graduate degree, at an undistinguished Midwestern university, because he ran into trouble with his dissertation and gave it up when offered the security of a government job.

Joel experiences conflicts with authority, particularly centering around sibling-type competition, which does stem from unresolved childhood issues. But he also has a systems-like mind and a value orientation of an expert and helper. He really does believe in serving the public. Would another environment, which did not foster diminished self-esteem and empty rewards, have helped him develop his more positive side?

Many of us experience career frustration, inadequate recognition, demotion, or worse during our careers, yet try to make the best of the situation. So do the Working Wounded. But those who overadapt through harder coping tend to deal with situations like these by becoming more passive, negativistic, and unproductive. At work they show a sometimes gradual, sometimes sudden development or sharpening of whatever un-resolved conflicts exist within them. But they don't show evidence of significant pathology. What we find are people with a somewhat unpro-ductive orientation, but still within the normal range of adaptation.

The kinds of work and management situations that limit more pos-itive and productive development, and feed ersatz neurotic problems include work that is isolating and often meaningless, with little relation-ship to anything, and too few opportunities for participation. All of which are of strong concern to the new careerists. The absence of career and work situations in which these issues are dealt with by management results in an increase in distrust, suspiciousness, and fostering of a police-like environment which makes people want to cover up and protect them-selves, and get what they can. This, in turn, causes management to tighten up and control more, which leads to overall deterioration of cooperation and communication. In short, a vicious circle.

So we can describe the overadapted heavy copers as people who are troubled, but not really sick, because their troubles arise from their work situations. Their work experience has aroused in them such symptoms as rebelliousness toward authority, holding out for love and affection from management, paranoid attitudes, and hostile and noncooperative attitudes. Some of these tendencies get strengthened over others, depending on the particular organization. For example, there are organizations in which people do "top out" at a high salary and position at a relatively early age. They can't go farther up the ladder in the forseeable future. The environment fosters an attitude of near-paranoid competitiveness for the "good" assignments among people who really need to be cooperative, given the nature of the tasks. The careerists then often develop destructive, suspicious, cynical, or undermining attitudes, alcoholism, or passive laziness, all to the dismay of upper management who don't understand what's going on.

As one person said, "It's not so much the work per se, but the situation, in which we are forced to claw like animals to get the goodies, the choice assignments, instead of working together, as we should be doing. It's either that, or you become burned-out, collect your fat paycheck, and drink a lot at lunch. So either way this situation makes us all act a little nuts."

Mel shows this kind of ineffectiveness and loss, both for the organization and the employee. A lot of people think he has emotional problems. He doesn't get along with many people, and he doesn't produce much, even though he puts in long hours and is a chronic complainer about how nobody believes in the work ethic anymore except himself. He also is always spouting off about how management "upstairs" doesn't look out for anyone except themselves. His subordinates dislike him because he spends much of his day recording in a little book how many minutes they spend away from their desks or making personal telephone calls. Mel spends much of his time trying to catch them at these things, and keeping tabs on how much time they appear to spend going to the bathroom.

Upper management dislikes him because they find that he can't work independently, for, despite his relatively high position, they have to constantly look over his shoulder. They are planning to get rid of him through early retirement. Mel told me that he grew up in a melting-pot ethnic neighborhood of a large Midwestern city. As a boy, he worked at whatever odd jobs he could find to help with the needs of his large family. After high school he decided to try his luck in New York, where he landed a job as a clerk-typist with a large company. Over the years he was regularly promoted, despite his limited education, and despite management's ignoring his requests for more training. It is possible that he was promoted beyond his capabilities, and then left to flap in the wind.

When Mel was younger he was more energetic, active, and ambitious. He even sounded more alive and spirited when he talked about his young adulthood. But his need for security and stability were gradually fed and strengthened by his work, and especially by his promotions which occurred without much achievement, risk-taking, or effort. Inside, he feels he is walking on thin ice, and may lose everything. And he knows that upper management considers him a thorn in their side. He has gradually given up hope for more stimulating work, which might, for example, require taking risks in return for greater development of his skills. Emotionally, he is somewhat blocked-off, and feels anxious around higher authority.

While upper management has been, in fact, unresponsive to the contributions and training needs of people in Mel's division, he has magnified his experience into total bitterness about all top management. This, in turn, has stimulated his most negative and unproductive attitudes at work. He has turned into a nitpicker. He is viewed by upper management as unproductive, probably hopelessly so. They have decided to tolerate him until they retire him. To complete the circle, management's view of Mel simply reinforces his worst fears and attitudes. So he does what he can do, with his limited resources: he measures people, and enters his measurements in his little book.

What people like this really need is not necessarily psychotherapy, but a better work environment, designed to develop the best of the human resources of the organization.

NEGATIVE COPING

People who have overadapted can come close to falling apart when conditions suddenly change. This can occur when circumstances change in what is required at work, or when the person has become so rigidly fixed upon career values or perks as a source of identity and meaning that the person loses flexibility and perspective. The result can be tragic and explosive. This can be seen, for example, in the case of a man who fell apart when his company did. He said his business always came first. He became extremely depressed when he was fired in disgrace as chairman and chief executive of a medical products company which had overextended itself financially. It later ended up in bankruptcy. He said that for the first time in his life he experienced failure, and it shattered him. His relationship with his family deteriorated and he attempted suicide.

Often those who have the hardest time facing failure are those who have become the most attached to their careers as a source of fulfillment. The fall from the top can be devastating. They have always experienced success climbing up the corporate ladder. They have worked long hours, loving it, thriving on the excitement of million-dollar decisions. Their jobs have become their lives.

One businessman who fell off the ladder said that inside he kept telling himself he wasn't good enough, that he had to do more. The man helped start the firm, and became a celebrity in the business circles where he lived. To meet overly optimistic sales goals his company started extending easy credit to customers. Sales were overstated and there wasn't enough money coming in to pay bills. He became extremely depressed. His firing was widely publicized in the newspapers. He wondered why he didn't see the problems coming on. He became secluded, dropped his friends, lost interest in everything. He decided his life was over and he would never be able to do anything. He began taking antidepressant medication, but became withdrawn and hostile. His family said what hurt them most was his saying that his career meant more to him than they did. His therapist asked him how he would feel if his family were killed in a plane crash. He said bad, but that losing his company was worse.[12]

He slowly began to accept failure as a part of life and admitted that he could not do everything, that he could not always be the best. He slowly made a business comeback, and says that it's amazing to discover that you can be happy without Brooks Brothers suits or Cadillacs. Obviously, this man had some internal problems. But we should not ignore the role his values and adaptation played in making it more difficult for him to deal with business reversal. He had adapted so much that he could not handle the reality of a setback without serious emotional consequences.

The Casualties.   This third form of the negative side of normalcy, negative coping, develops in situations in which a person struggles to adapt to a work environment, its conditions, management, or values which are unhealthy or destructive to such a degree that no normal person can handle them and remain unscathed. Careerists who try to adapt to a work or management environment that is alienating, boring, or unhealthy in some way will develop emotional problems, as in the case of Donna. For a time Donna was known as a disturbed person at work because she began acting pretty bizarre after being given a temporary assignment involving higher management responsibilities in her office. Bright and friendly, she had originally thought of becoming a teacher. Instead, she entered a management path in a corporation after graduating from a large Midwestern university, because the greater opportunities for career advancement and better pay she anticipated there appealed to her more.

Donna advanced steadily over the next several years. Then, a management position opened up temporarily because of a sudden death. Upper management recognized that the job was beyond her level of training and experience. But they saw her as having good potential. They recognized her intellectual and technical competencies, which they thought would allow her to perform adequately in the role. So they decided to try her out. Donna saw the assignment as a big challenge, and recognized that it would be a feather in her cap if she could handle it well.

But almost immediately there were problems. The biggest one was the person Donna now reported to, who was known around the office as "Jack the Ripper." He was a woman-hater who enjoyed slashing them to shreds if given half an opportunity. He was generally unsupportive of all his subordinates, male or female, as well as very hostile and demanding. In short order he began to severely criticize Donna's work. And he ignored her requests for help in organizing the work in her office.

Soon, people began to notice that Donna was becoming more and more irritable and suspicious in her daily relations with co-workers and subordinates. She began to accuse them of conspiring to ruin her career, and of stealing important papers from her desk. Around the same time she began writing long memos and letters to the company Vice President and to the head of personnel, charging that management was only looking out for itself, was trying to get rid of her, and was illegally persecuting her. On several occasions co-workers heard her singing loudly to herself in the bathroom, and shouting at people who entered her office. Her appearance began to look disheveled. Finally, Donna's boss told her that he was going to relieve her of her management duties and maybe fire her as well, unless she "controlled" herself. Within a short time her symptoms began to disappear, and she requested a transfer to another part of the organization.

Looking back on this episode when I interviewed her several months later, Donna told me that she had felt tremendous pressure because of the hostility of her boss and the lack of support she needed in her new role. "I realized that it was actually making me crazy," she said. And, she added, she had been shocked by the lack of help available to organize the work in her office, which had been in disarray from the illness and death of the previous supervisor. "It was a very different atmosphere from my earlier positions, where people seemed so much more helpful and friendly."

After a time, she continued, she was able to snap out of it. She saw the "handwriting on the wall" when she realized that it was all getting to her and that the reality was that she might get fired and her career might be ruined. So she began to force herself to "settle down" and do exactly what was expected of her, no more, no less. And with no complaints. Meanwhile, she started looking for another position where, she hoped, the atmosphere would be friendlier.

Had Donna been truly disturbed, it is unlikely that she would have been able to curb her symptoms. Without help, she probably would have gotten worse. Despite her symptoms, which were clear and dramatic, she is a person within the normal range. She has considerable intellectual capacity and an ability to work cooperatively with others. And she believes in the ideals of help and service. Her Rorschach does not show any particularly strong, irrational tendencies. It does, however, contain a theme of helplessness and a tendency to become angry, a bit frightened and rebellious when helplessness is aroused, or when she feels pressured to perform without adequate support. And this is exactly what happened when faced with having to adapt to a negative work situation and hostile boss. Donna experienced a very destructive environment to which she responded by coping harder, as she thought a competent professional should. Perhaps if she had consulted a therapist during her period of conflict, a therapist who understood something about how work can affect normal people, Donna might have been able to explore herself in terms of both the possibilities and strategies for developing her talents and capacities. And she might have been able to look at the real possibility that management made her situation more difficult for her because she was a woman.

Six months later she called to tell me that she had gotten married and had decided to take time off to think about her career plans, since she had become pregnant.

Another form of negative coping found in some Working Wounded occurs when the working conditions are demoralizing, unsafe, or destructive in some way. For example, accidents in railroad lines involving death and destruction have been attributed to the work force being significantly impaired by drugs and alcohol. In one study 20% of the workers were found to be regularly drunk when they arrived at work or got drunk once they were there. (This compares with about 1.5% of adult males in the work force nationwide.[13])

There have been dozens of accidents, some fatal, in recent years, in which the engineer, brakeman, and others were drunk and asleep. One survey found 25% of the employees to be problem drinkers, and one third said they had been drunk, drinking on duty, or had taken drugs at least once. The drinking and drug usage responsible for most of the accidents, as well as the damage to property and injuries, is a direct, though destructive and unproductive, response to the intense boredom and isolation of the work. Many of the alcoholics and drug abusers working for railroads say that education and counseling won't do the trick. What is needed, they report, is change in the nature of the work: eliminating long layovers far from home, irregular work hours, and lack of supervision. Many report stories of working while totally drunk, or blacking out and missing their destination by a hundred miles. One worker cited the mental stress of having to accumulate twenty years of seniority to get a weekend off, and that there is chronic loneliness when stopping over at isolated towns.

Workaholism can be a form of negative coping, as well. But the question is whether the person is driven by internal needs based in childhood. For example, a need to please parents which is being expressed through constant work, because inside he feels he can never please enough, or is compensating for deep rage over which he feels guilty. Or if work-aholism reflects overadaptation, with minimal, if any, underlying conflict. Sometimes the person realizes the latter when they do get away from work and discover they have difficulty not working. All they know about is how to work. Many new careerists are examples of this kind of non-neurotic negative coping.

Some believe that workaholics are normal, but in a different sense: that because they love work and say they thrive on it, they are therefore healthy. This is similar to the view of analysts who equate power-lust with emotional health, as we saw in Chapter 3. Similarly, without analyzing the meaning of devotion to work, and the values it serves, one cannot distinguish the cases in which the person is highly productive from those in which the person is acting out an internal conflict, or from those which reflect a form of negative coping to which the person has adapted.

Another group of casualties who deal with negative coping in a different form are the nonworking wives of senior executives. Their husbands typically work 60–70 hours per week, and are out of town on business about one week every month. The amount of time the executive spends with the family is severely limited. The products of the wives' negative coping are seen, for example, in the findings that, although two-thirds of them say they accept the sacrifices as a requirement for success, they also suffer greatly. While they say they enjoy the material advantage, wealth, prestige, and sharing of excitement and power, they also report feelings of tremendous burden, sacrifice, and physical and emotional strains. In addition, the wives suffer from damaged self-esteem and an inadequate sense of personal identity. Family relations and their children's development suffer as well.

One woman said that she feels sharing her husband with his career is probably worse than sharing him with a mistress because "there is no end to it and there is nothing that I can do about it." Another said her husband presumes that his time, his schedule, and his wishes are the most important in the family. That the good hours of his day are used up by the time he gets home, and he puts off the children. One wife has been seeing a therapist for years, because of difficultly "adjusting" to her husband's long hours, frequent travelling, and insensitivity when he is home. The implication, of course, is that there is something wrong with her for being dissatisfied with an insensitive husband. One said, "My husband always arrives home exhausted and detached. He's hundreds of miles away and preoccupied."

The most unhappy of the women say that in every respect their husbands take much more than they give. The most frequent complaints are that business dominates the husband's life too much, there is a lack of time with the husband, and the wife's role is very confining. Sixty per-cent of the wives describe their husbands as intense, impatient, insensitive, and poor listeners, who need constant ego gratification from those around them at work. Sex is unimportant and last. "He demands that I understand his problems, but he doesn't feel mine are problems at all," said one. Another said she watches her husband move through stages of depression because of circumstances over which he has no control. Twenty percent of the wives said that, aside from the toll on themselves, their husbands have suffered tremendous physical and emotional damage from their careers.[14]

There is a question of what is a cause and what is a symptom when spouses and family members suffer from the enormous time and energy devoted to work. Maybe the demands from the organization are tremendous, but the executive may also desire to escape the family through devotion to career. The latter can also be an unconscious escape from personal conflicts. And it is compounded when the organization supports attitudes that are pathological or when the career environment creates so many compromises, trade-offs, and so much anger that it, itself, generates severe emotional conflict.

TRAUMAS OF THE NEW AGE

5

Now here, you see, it takes all the running you can do to keep in the same place. If you want to get somewhere else, you must run at least twice as fast as that!
— *Lewis Carroll*

We have seen that the new-breed careerists' race for success has an emotional downside. That the career culture of large organizations, the work we perform, the way we are managed, and how we are rewarded all affect our emotional state. We began with the observation that career-oriented people describe the emotional affects of their careers in terms of compromises, trade-offs, and anger, which careerists deal with in different ways, and with a range of consequences. And we have seen that the meaning of this theme and its consequences depends upon the person's overall life orientation: how he or she adapts to the organizational environment.

We found that how we adapt to the requirements of success in large organizations, within our current economic, market, and political environment, determines whether or not we become overtly troubled and conflicted. Whether we become power-lovers—the surface sanity of disturbed people well-adapted to disturbed work and management—or the Working Wounded—normal people overtly troubled by disturbance and limitations within work and management, and by conflicting values.

This chapter deals with the second source of problems for careerists within the normal range, problems which are different from the value conflicts, overadaptation, and negative coping of the Working Wounded, but which can be equally as troubling for the new careerist struggling to navigate his or her way to both success and fulfillment. They are traumas of the New Age of work, which is rapidly transforming the landscape of organizational life and careers.

It was only after I removed the blinders of the clinician whose sights begin and end with the individual that I was able to recognize that major changes in the world of work link together to form the underpinnings of our potential for either fulfillment or conflict. And that they will continue to do so through the rest of the 1980s and into the final decade of our century. This New Age of work underlies, in particular, the traumas that career professionals call burnout, stress, and related problems that differ from the conflicts described in the last chapter.

That we have entered a New Age of work is, aside from its emotional affects, well-recognized by most careerists today. In broadest terms, the familiar landscape of work has been bulldozed by a steady evolution from an industrial–production to a service–information oriented economy. But what is not so widely recognized or understood is that this transformation, like others that have occurred before in our history, doesn't mean just that there are more careers within banking, financial, insurance, publishing, computer, and other information–service types of organizations. That is part of the story but not the whole story. This evolution has also changed the kinds of work, work organization, management, and reward systems that make for the most productive fit with the new-breed careerists populating these organizations. On a personal level, this transformation has a profound impact on our emotional attitudes and orientation to life: what we find satisfying or dissatisfying, ennervating or stimulating, inspiring or depressing. In short, this transformation is changing not only the rules of the game for career success and organizational productivity, but the game itself.

All of these changes, which form the emotional underpinnings of the modern career experience, underlie the range of potential emotional and emotionally-related physical problems found among non-neurotic, adaptive careerists. Knowledge of these changes and their effects provides us with a context and better understanding of phenomena like stress and burnout, which affects increasing numbers of non-neurotic, successful career professionals today. While problems like stress, burnout, and situational anxiety have been widely discussed by psychologists, psychiatrists, and others, the sources of these symptoms in the changing realm of work is inadequately understood. This, in turn, has implications for what helps or doesn't help the person.

Some of these conflicts are rooted in pure bombardment: the accumulation of too much work relative to the time we have, too many demands from our work and personal lives, and too many decisions facing us and not enough time to deliberate about them. In short, too much to deal with in a world which is too busy and too rapidly changing, in which we all feel tremendous pressure to make the right decision right now. This is experienced by most everyone today to some degree, and results in the typical symptoms of stress, situational anxiety, and burnout. But there are other, more complex sources of New Age trauma as well, which are easily overlooked or misunderstood. For example, some conflicts result not from the buildup of too much pressure per se, but from changing conditions of work or new situations over which we have no control.

There are four of these that have the most emotional impact as we try to navigate a successful career course. Spearheaded by the appearance of new technology at the workplace, these changes also include significant socioeconomic and political change in the larger society or within the organization that has specific emotional consequences for managers, executives, and professionals moving through or toward the middle and upper levels of organizations. Within the larger society, there is the impact of computerization and the new technology upon our work, and of economic, social, and political upheaval. All of this is potentially damaging and undermining to our self-esteem and security, our sense of stability and predictability. And the result is a range of emotional conflict that develops as we attempt to deal with it all. There is also the unrelenting growth of bigness and complexity—bureaucracy—in organizations that employ a majority of the work force, and the increasing and irreversible entry of women, and, to a lesser degree, racial–ethnic minorities, into management positions and the professions. All are potential sources of emotional trauma to the new careerist.

A RESHAPED LANDSCAPE

For the past several years, futurists—people who analyze trends occurring within society and what they mean—have been predicting and describing the impact of these changes upon our lives. Despite the danger of describing trends that are unsubstantiated by empirical evidence, recent books like John Naisbitt's *Megatrends*[1] and Alvin Toffler's *The Third Wave*[2] have been very widely read by the general public because, whatever their ultimate accuracy, they address a real desire: we all want to understand what is going to happen to us, why it is going to happen, and what we can do to prepare for it. No one wants to be left by the roadside, watching, as the rapidly changing world sweeps on by. We all want to know how to make sense of a world which seems to increase in both complexity and madness each day. And come out a survivor.

Most of the changes predicted by futurists concern the impact of new technology. Where it affects work and our lives in general, new technology may make the 1990s differ from the '70s as much as the nineteenth century differed from the eighteenth. The society is on the edge of a transformation comparable to that caused by the auto, the telephone, and the airplane. And all because of the silicon chip and the robot. For example, new technology may soon create intelligent machines which can serve many different needs. There is already growing use of robots in industry for work that is dangerous, extremely simple, or repetitive. Factory, construction, farming, scientific, and other kinds of work benefit from the ability of robots to perform repetitive or delicate tasks. Computerized technology is also being used to improve medical care.[3]

Benefits and Risks.   What can we say about the effects new technology will have upon our lives and society? One possibility is the increasing development of a high-tech and high-service economy. Futurists like Toffler see this development as part of a much deeper revolution in American life: societies created by the industrial revolution were based on mass production, mass consumerism, mass education, communication, entertainment, and political movements, but now there is movement to higher-level differentiation. For example, high tech de-massifies production. It allows greater market segmentation, mini-markets, home shopping through computers, directed communication to special interest audiences via cable TV, and precision guided weapons in place of mass destruction weapons. If "de-massification" continues to penetrate into all aspects of life, we will need dramatically altered economic and political institutions, as well as a changed mentality, to adapt successfully.

Stress and conflict develop in normal people whenever a society undergoes major transition. One doesn't have to be a futurist to recognize that we have already entered the transition from a production-based mass economy to an information–service economy. This new economy will increasingly deal with products and services that favor durability, design, and craftsmanship, as well as mass-oriented products. Information-based technology is already affecting growing sectors of the economy which integrate high-tech with high-craft, producing individualized, personalized products, often with an upscale flavor that appeals to career professionals on the rise.

This evolution has emotional impact not only upon American society, but in foreign countries as well, in which the introduction of new, high-tech industries affects the entire social fabric. This is particularly found in tradition-bound or third-world cultures which are suddenly catapulted into the New Age.[4] In a broader vein, Michel Poniatowski, French Minister of the Interior under President Giscard d'Estaing, and subsequently a member of the European Parliament, has observed that all the certainties of industrial society are disintegrating as we enter the New Age of work. That an erosion of ideologies, economic theories, and traditional cultures is occurring because they all come from the nineteenth century. He argues that 200 years ago society moved from the agricultural to the industrial era, which involved maximizing human and animal power through the use of machines driven by fossil fuels. But today we are moving towards a society marked by computerized information, telecommunications, and advanced technology. The question, here, is to what degree the human community can continue to assimilate these shocks without some form of damage.[5] How do people need to adapt, and what kind of help is necessary, for human beings to live productively in a semi-artificial world? It is possible that 20% of the adult population will be left out of the mainstream because they will be unable to adapt.

And what happens to them? For that matter, what happens to the 80% of the rest of us (and we all hope we are part of that 80%) who do adapt, by and large, to the New Age? What is the long-run cost of that adaptation? And are some forms of adaptation better for us than others?

Some clues can be found by looking at areas of work that are information-based and already use the new computerized technology. For example, we now have companies that don't produce anything. What they do instead is gather, process, disseminate, and manipulate information. They range from scientific information dissemination to money procurement, in which the company channels investment money to high-tech entrepreneurs. All together, companies whose business is information now account for 60% of the nation's workforce. Nationwide, 52% of all workers have white-collar jobs which increasingly deal with information in some form. Washington has the highest concentration, with 72%, followed by San Francisco with 65%.[6]

The impact of new technology on jobs and careers is also seen in the prediction that the greatest career opportunities by the year 2000 will be in high-tech and service jobs. Because of the unrelenting transition from a manufacturing economy to a high-technology, service-oriented base, we will find that by the year 2000 jobs in manufacturing will decrease by 50%, and only 11% of all workers will be employed by "smokestack" industries. But service-sector jobs will increase from 68% at present to 86%, with about 44% related to information processing.[7] The rate of increase of jobs will be higher for such industries as retail, finance, insurance, and health services. And the fastest growing will be in high-tech areas. In fact, of all the fastest growing careers, five out of six are technology-related.

The office itself is undergoing rapid change as a result of the mushrooming of new technology at work. Managers increasingly use computers, which lower the demand for secretaries. Fast retrieval of documents by anyone is made possible by the computer. For example, computers can pluck copies of documents from microfilm and display them on a screen. This sector of the information retrieval industry is predicted to grow about 9% annually. The new technology is supplanting not only typewriters, but also file cabinets, rolodexes, and mail memos. One result will be that routine office tasks will be made faster and easier. So on the one hand, new technology makes office work more efficient and office workers more productive. But it also makes obsolete the jobs of those who currently perform the tasks without the aid of computer technology. In fact, looming behind all these technological changes is the specter of job obsolescence for people at all levels, not just for secretarial and clerical workers, as is commonly believed. This reality makes increasing numbers of career-oriented professionals worried and insecure, something which all the "stress management" techniques in the world will not relieve, because it is a reality to be lived with.

One phenomenon, already here, that is related to this anxiety is more frequent job and career changes. People are more prone to drop out for retraining. And by 1990 more than 75% of all family units will have both spouses working. Testimony before a House committee session on technology and employment in 1982 predicted that we are headed toward a shorter workweek, job sharing, and several career changes within a person's lifetime. The work force will increase as more women and elderly look for jobs. And because technology is changing the work force and the work environment so rapidly the federal government is faced with developing policy to help promote a smooth adjustment.

New Age technology generates stress and conflict in a range of ways that are directly and indirectly related to work, and which affect people on the job as well as at home. For example, computers can be a source of problems in marriages, creating a "megabyte mistress." In fact there is an increase in cases of divorce and family stress which is directly related to home computers taking up more and more of a spouse's time and attention. Spouses often complain that their partners spend overly long hours at the terminal, and become withdrawn, unresponsive, and un-communicative. Sometimes the person begins giving commands to family members as one would to a computer. Also the rise of the "electronic bulletin boards" allows for easy, consequence-free communication with others through the computer. One can avoid faces, voices, or names. All this has the potential for breeding emotional detachment and alienated relationships. It fosters an illusion of possessing a computer-centered control of the world, without having to deal with the "messy" passions aroused in the ordinary give-and-take with people.

In Silicon Valley, the computer revolution is having a serious impact on family life. Because the computer uses logic, contains or has access to almost unlimited knowledge, doesn't criticize, and is at one's command, it can feed an exaggerated sense of control and mastery and have a negative rub-off on a person's intimate relations. Among students, com-puters can create an illusory self-confidence or insensitivity to social in-teraction. For example, one professor reports that students sometimes appear in his office without saying hello and begin issuing mechanical-type statements like "I have the following three requests to make, a, b, c," and so on, as though they are keying in an entry to the computer.[8]

The most significant emotional consequences of new technology, however, is seen in the dual impact on operators and consumers. That is, one set of problems exist for the operator of the technology—the computers, word processors, robotized equipment, etc. And another, for the beneficiary or user, including managers and professionals who make use of the analyses and operations it performs. For the first group, the mental health danger is the severe stress and boredom that often accompanies the operation of the new technology. For the second, it is the fear of being passed by in the career race by ever-younger careerists who are already comfortable with computers and who can adapt more easily. And the fear of higher-level managers accessing information directly rather than needing the mid-level manager to supply it, which can either make a person look like a fool in staff meetings or threaten to make one's position unnecessary. The general fear of job obsolescence and the fear of being unable to learn how to use the new technology combine to set the stage for anxiety, depression, psychosomatic complaints, and other problems for the careerist.

For those workers who must operate the technology, emotional conflict can arise because of the stress of having to adapt to and keep up with the dramatic growth of computers, automation, and robotization at the workplace. For example, many jobs become boring when computers take over and change the nature of work, without a corresponding change in management and work organization.[9]

The most controversial forms of automation occur in high-volume data-processing centers. There one finds highly sophisticated technology but also the most noticeable mental health effects on the workers. For example, one study of workers who use VDTs in such a setting found tremendous physical and mental stress, which was related to the observation that workers follow rigid work procedures and don't have any control over their work.[10] Some reported feeling that the machine was controlling them, particularly when they were aware that the machines are programmed to monitor workers' performance: a kind of surreptitious Big Brother.

The latter practice is becoming more widely used. Now, some phone companies program equipment to track the time operators spend on calls. Adverse action is taken against the operator if he or she spends too long with a call. A spokesperson for the Communications Workers of America union said the conflict between being monitored by the computer and the desire to help the customer is "very hard on your soul."[11]

This relates to another source of stress for operators: evidence that working in front of the VDT can take a physical and mental toll. Seven million workers in the U.S. spend a large chunk of their work day in front of VDTs. Some studies have found VDTs to be related to angina pain among operators whose times are monitored by computers, and who have little control over the process. They were found to have three times the angina rate as people in high-control jobs. And surveys have found that between 40 and 80% of users complain of eyestrain and other symptoms of stress.[12] It is increasingly evident that a work environment in which the computer is a central part can create conditions ripe for conflict and employee distress.

There is the possibility that VDT users lose so much time from work because of physical and mental health problems that it may have a growing impact on the economy. And it is likely that these and other problems are not only here to stay, they will be increasing, because computerized technology, by its very nature, has both a positive and negative effect upon the user. Computers can ease the boredom of routine task, but, as we have seen, they can also damage the health of workers who operate them, as well as threaten their jobs with obsolescence. This affects women, in particular. The typical American lower-level worker is no longer a man in a hard hat, but a woman at a computer keyboard. Women hold 80% of all clerical jobs, 99% of all secretarial jobs, 95% of all typing jobs, and 93% of bank teller positions. And all of these jobs are now using computerized technology in some form. Although the technology clearly has the potential for reducing tedium and enlarging worker responsibility, computers have transformed many jobs into deadly rote work. The issue may be not the use of the VDT per se, but rather the job design and management that accompany it, which limits opportunity for autonomy and participation, and can contribute to feeling that the work is unbearably stressful.

In a related vein, a study of the effects on workers of the introduction of robots in a manufacturing plant doing forging and machining of metal alloys found that worker attitudes became pessimistic, creating resistance that reduced productivity. The extent to which they were involved in the design of the technological and organizational change affected their acceptance and commitment to the change. They said that workers should have more say in deciding where the robot should be placed in the production process and who should operate it. They found that the robot changed the operator's job from a manual one to a cognitive one. Operators became busier and felt they had more responsibility, but also felt more stress, became bored, and had social interaction curtailed. This points to the need for increased job rotation and more job variety.[13]

A second consequence for mental health of computer technology is found among the consumers of its fruits. First, though, we must recognize the positive benefits of computerization that exist for career professionals. Overall, computers are reshaping the role of the modern careerist as well as the organizational structure of companies. The percentage of all professional, technical, managerial and administrative workers regularly using computers will leap to 65% before the end of the 1980s.[14] The reasons are straightforward: the computer provides immediate access to crucial areas of information. It can combine information outside the company with that inside, turn masses of numbers into easily understandable graphs, and provide speedy electronic mail services.

The computer also enables the manager to quickly analyze pricing, competitive product lines, and provide current information for decision making and forecasting. A manager can obtain detailed information about a subsidiary of his or her company in order to discover some unusual pattern of inventory or sales that might otherwise go unnoticed until it is too late. For both the company and the manager a flattening of the managerial pyramid is likely. Managers will have to know how to use the new technology to aid business strategy and decisions. As much as 25% of managers' time is now spent doing unproductive tasks, like waiting for meetings or for information. Such wastes of time could be completely eliminated by the use of computers.

Also, executives and managers can improve companies' revenues in many ways by using computer technology. One example is forming models that aid in decision-making related to investment, cash management, or the purchase and sale of goods and services. It is an indispensable tool wherever choice is possible and transactions are frequent, such as in product development, marketing, or sales, in which one can cross-reference and keep track of a multitude of data.

But now the downside: Managers' attempts to adapt to computer technology, whether out of interest or necessity, frequently create a climate of fear and threat, particularly for people at the middle levels. Roughly ten million executive and professional managers in this country are still computer illiterates, though they are under increasing pressure to adapt. Fear and anxiety account for most of this, and they take several forms. For example, a chemical company had to delay its installation of a financial planning system when many of its executives balked at mastering the computer. Some men said that they felt foolish and unprofessional, that working with a computer looked too much like typing, and everyone knows that's women's work. In other companies managers are worried that they will do something wrong and look foolish. One corporate Vice President refused to use his company computer, but secretly used his personal computer at home. He said he didn't want to look like a dope in front of his staff.[15] The managers who are most afraid of learning to use the computer and of looking like incompetent fools tend to be the older careerists, past the cusp of the burgeoning group of New Age careerists. Those who are frightened run the risk of being passed by in the career race by the younger careerists at lower levels who have grown up with the new technology, and are much more at home with it.

Another source of anxiety, particularly for mid-level careerists, is that senior executives are able to use computers to monitor information and, in effect, check up on what the mid-level managers are doing. Top executives can bypass their lower-level managers and get detailed information for themselves. Therefore, many at the middle levels fear a loss of influence, a loss of autonomy. Upper level executives have the advantage of cutting across several sources of information to test theories, compare budgets, and prepare forecasts. They say they are not trying to "check up" on the performance of their subordinates, but many middle managers don't believe it. They cite cases of managers whose careers were damaged when their boss acquired information that they, themselves, had not obtained. One said, "The boss knows more than I do and I'm in trouble."[16]

In addition, in the years that remain before our rendezvous with the next century we can expect to find that white-collar workers will continue to grow as a percentage of the work force, but with proportionally fewer managers. There will be some growth of demand for managers in service industries, but overall we will witness a general decline in growth of opportunities for managers. And despite entrepreneurialism being in vogue, the above trend will mean that the hardest hit will be the self-employed and the small companies. Big business will get bigger, and small independent companies will be squeezed out.

Therefore, one source of anxiety the New Age of work generates for careerists is the specter of job loss, although there are different views about what the final picture will be. And no one can say whether a fully automated service economy will absorb everyone. It may be that, in contrast to the 1800s, when the growth of factories took care of agricultural workers, the new technological revolution will not be as benign. Joblessness could become a permanent fixture, and society could be faced with a cadre of the permanently jobless, which includes white-collar careerists.

There is no question that all of this creates a climate of career anxiety: being left out, left behind, and losing one's self-esteem. Many express fears that they won't fit into the rapid technological change occurring all around them, and won't be able to control their lives. Most have some degree of fear of the new technology, though the older they are the worse it is. Many fear they will never be able to keep abreast of the new skills required. Automation and computerization create conditions ripe for damage to self-esteem, and danger to one's career identity. It is possible that the industrialized world is changing much too fast for the modern careerist to sufficiently comprehend or absorb, without some kind of emotional toll. Whatever the long-term impact will be, the transition is generating traumas for many careerists.

CHANGING TIMES

New technology is the most dramatic, but by no means the only change beyond our personal control which affects us at work. There are also changes in social, economic, and political circumstances which create mental health issues for well-adjusted careerists to deal with. A significant and recent example is the effect of the breakup of the nationwide Bell system upon the mental health of many workers. Some employees entered therapy because of stress related to the breakup's effect on their career future. Some even attempted suicide because of job uncertainties. And still others became deeply depressed when they were faced with a transfer to one of the regional spin-off companies.[17] Behind it all were tremendous anxieties about new job requirements, possible relocation, and the future of the eight spin-off companies. A Bell survey of 75,000 employees revealed that 30% believed the breakup would adversely affect their careers. At one of the spin-off companies, a nearly 10% increase of cases of job anxiety occurred during the period following the divestiture announcement in January 1982.

One person attempted suicide because, she later said, she didn't know what was going on and she felt unappreciated. Another interpreted a promotion as a rejection and became depressed. One could always say that such people have an underlying pathological condition that was revealed by their inability to "handle" the changes, and that a healthy individual could deal with whatever occurs in the workplace without developing symptoms. But such an interpretation reflects naïveté about the effect of adult realities upon normal people. That is, many employees experienced widespread feelings of anxiety and other symptoms because the new market orientation disrupted the previous norms of security and predictability. For example, a newly-unregulated unit for equipment and business systems no longer had a leisurely pace and straight salaries. Now the workers had to work harder with only 50–70% of their old salary guaranteed. The rest became contingent on meeting sales quotas. Physical relocations, new bosses, new co-workers, and new procedures all added to the stressful conditions.

Economic changes, gradual or sudden, can affect any kind of work, with mental health reverberations. For example, economic changes in recent years have created sources of stress and tension for farmers. Many farmers had assumed hard work would guarantee success. Now there are feelings of panic among people who are deeply in debt and who don't know if they'll make it. The conditions are compounded by, for example, the fact that farm machinery ties up a great deal of money, and repairs can run into the thousands.

Many farm families have become emotionally devastated as a result. The mental health effects of these changes are seen not only in anxiety, but also increased depression, violence, alcoholism, wife abuse, overeating, and suicide. In fact, the suicide rate in some rural Iowa counties is twice the national figure. And in Missouri, the occupation with the most suicides is farming. Financial problems coupled with the stagnant farm economy cause the farmers to feel that their whole way of life, identity, and sense of meaning are threatened.

A large group of careerists adversely affected by economic and political changes are employees of the federal government, not only in Washington, but in several regional centers around the country. During the first Reagan administration major cutbacks and demotions generated tremendous and debilitating stress for career civil servants who had come to assume stability and job security; perhaps too much so, in many cases.

But when security has been a norm and is then undermined severely, and coupled with a sense of betrayal, the stress that results can overwhelm even the most stable of careerists and erupt in uncontrollable emotions and behavior. One person in the Department of Housing and Urban Development suddenly attacked a co-worker with a metal coat tree, screaming "I'll knock your head off." In both my organizational consultations and private practice I found an escalation of eruptions of anger, threats, and anxiety throughout government offices during the early Reagan years. Many departments found a noticeable increase of employees taking valium. Stress-related behavior and illness in the government reached almost epidemic proportions. One Department found itself treating triple the number of people for symptoms like dizziness, stomach cramps, and diarrhea.[18]

In addition to cases of anger and stress, I also observed an upsurge of acute psychiatric symptoms among federal career professionals during this period. Cases of anxiety, depression, and bizarre behavior were flying, not crawling, out of the woodwork. All of which had a counterproductive effect in terms of the Reagan administration's objective of making the government run more efficiently.

An atmosphere of uncertainty will always create stress and anxiety for a normal person. If you are in a chaotic and unstable environment, with an objective threat to your situation, it is normal to feel disturbed. Federal employees began fearing loss of their jobs, feeling threatened by cutbacks, and seeing the ends of programs to which they had devoted years of service. Tremendous anxiety was stirred up, productivity suffered, and morale dropped. One manager said, "There's no work being done over here, at the cost of hundreds of thousands of dollars to government. Whole offices are grinding to a halt."

As a result of Reagan's "RIFs" (reduction in force: the government's euphemism for firing) and subsequent "bumping" of lower-level employees in order to retain a job—any job—high-level professional administrators sometimes ended up in the typing pool. One secretary had been directing a staff of ten and administered a twenty-seven million dollar budget. He ended up being paid $50,000-a-year to type. Another person who made $47,000-a-year found herself doing xeroxing all day long. A legislative analyst became a filing clerk. One person said, "When they offered me a clerk-typist position it devastated me. I had to take my sick leave to pull my head back together." One formerly high-level division director consulted me for acute depression and boiling rage because he had to take a position sorting mail in the mailroom, while earning his old salary of about $50,000. He had been directing a social-service-type program for several years, which was highly respected but had been completely gutted. He wasn't at all neurotic, but the previous therapist he had consulted interpreted his depression and anger as symptoms of underlying narcissism, which had been revealed by his "failure to successfully cope with the loss of gratification of narcissistic supplies."

The morale of federal workers has always been low, actually, in part because of the constant, politically popular attacks on bureaucrats. Federal career professionals, as well as those in state and local government, are frequently portrayed as incompetent and lazy, contributing to fraud and abuse, and with dampened motivation which inhibits performance. As a result of this public stereotype, fed by politicians looking for political fodder, many end up feeling as one federal official, who said, "In good conscience I cannot recommend to young professionals that they join the government."[19]

Surveys support this picture. For example, a survey of over 500 federal employees from 6 agencies found that 75% said that morale in their agency was low.[20] Nearly half said that, compared with the years prior to the Reagan cutbacks, federal work was much less satisfying. 62% worried about losing their jobs or being downgraded. One engineer said, "I don't like working in an environment where people could be cut anytime." In another agency a statistician said that he thinks the federal bureaucracy is totally demoralized and that "they're getting rid of people, but not the unproductive ones." Related to this is the particular stress suffered by the "whistle-blowers," who risk their career by calling public attention to graft, corruption, and fraud. As a group, they have been found to suffer from a variety of emotional and physical problems, such as depression, paranoia, and other situational stress-related disorders.

The normal individual will feel anxious in an uncertain environment, demoralized in a humiliating situation. Some are able to develop ways of dealing with this without the help of high-priced stress consultants by organizing self-help groups. Several groups were formed during the early period of the Reagan administration to counter the public image of bureaucrats as drones. One spokesman pointed out that because they are public servants and often have to perform an unpleasant job, they get a lot of heat from the public, aided by politicians who want some free mileage at their expense.

The Disturbed Middle.   Both business and government organizations are recognizing the need to tighten up, to become leaner and meaner in order to make it in our increasingly competitive economic times. For many previously successful, upward-moving career professionals this means a new source of trauma because of the haunting fear of unemployment and job obsolescence which is like a constant backdrop to their lives. There are frequent reports in the press of fear, shame, shock, and anger. One executive, who witnessed 20% of his colleagues laid off, said that although he was still putting in nine or ten hours a day, "more and more, I'm asking myself why. It's depressing. You end up feeling that what you do doesn't matter, that it won't make a difference."[21]

The worst can and does happen. In the last few years white-collar unemployment has been at a higher rate than at any point since the 1973–75 recession.[22] Middle managers who are in their 40s and 50s are being forced out, hit by the economic slump. The most severely jolted are those who had been comfortable in their positions and lives, and now experience anxiety and depression. There are cases of people who become immobilized for periods of time. An engineer let go after fifteen years said, "We get comfortable with the status quo and look at the big company as the security blanket. Well it isn't the security blanket you think it is." Another said he had played by the rules of the corporate game. He had given loyalty to get security. "I was a dedicated company man but they just didn't give a damn about the people."

The ranks of people in their 40s and 50s who are being fired are swelling to record levels, in the tens of thousands. And this is not likely to change. Companies can no longer afford the paternalism of previous times. An increasingly competitive world, industry shakeouts, and worries about productivity have all contributed to this. With companies trying to become leaner and more productive, people will get tossed out through no fault of their own.

Feelings of betrayal are common among people who believe they have given their lives for the company and then are rejected by it. Because the older careerists are often more committed to the organization than the new breed, they often don't know how to go about looking for jobs. They become depressed, feel they are stuck on the bottom and can't get out. Some become guilty about being unemployed. Many are told that they are overeducated, overqualified, and overpaid. A recurring theme among many is that the experience made them feel like failures, particularly difficult for people who had never gone anywhere but up.

Some displaced executives try to change careers, become consultants in their fields, or accept early retirement. None of these solutions are easy or that satisfying. One survey found that more than 40% of members of a self-help club who found new jobs settled for ones with salaries and perks substantially lower than those they left.[23] People in their 40s and 50s who have been with a company for 20 to 30 years and high-level executives often have more difficulty adjusting than middle managers. Having been accustomed to handling big decisions, they suddenly find themselves questioning even simple matters.

Loss of position typically affects self-esteem, which can make the person less effective in finding another job. This adds to their demoralization, and they enter a vicious cycle. Within the values system to which they had adapted, people are supposed to work hard, move up, and make more money. So if they get fired, they tend to think something is wrong with them.[24] A professor who lost his job said he has come to accept that he took a job as salesman for a subscription TV company and then lost that job. He says his self-esteem comes mainly from cooking for friends and he's thinking of becoming a bartender. Depressed and strapped for money, he said he often drinks six or eight beers a night to sleep. He said, "If it weren't for my friends I would have blown my brains out long ago."

Career Plateaus.   More common than firing, and likely to increase, are cases of people who find themselves on permanent career plateaus. This, too, can lead to depression, and marital and drinking problems. The plateau arrives when further career advancement is unlikely or impossible. With the baby-boom generation reaching their 30s and 40s during a time of widespread unemployment, and with record numbers of business school graduates entering organizations, career plateaus can develop in any profession and at any age.

At each step up the corporate ladder there are 30% fewer jobs than on the rung below. Bottlenecks develop. One person commented that you hardly notice it until you wake up one morning and you've had the same job for five years and it isn't anywhere near where you planned to be by that time. The plateau can become a crisis that contributes not only to personal problems, but also to heart attacks and high blood pressure. Some will accept a lower-paying job or one with less status just to start moving up in a new situation. Others leave to start their own business. But in most cases, the manager is reluctant to leave a company with the benefits that have accumulated.

Interestingly, in a reflection of changing values, some welcome it as relief from a culture of constant competition and pressure to keep moving ahead. For example, an AT&T survey found that after twenty years, one-third of the managers say advancement is not as important.[25] Only 36% say they would give up more personal time for career success. And two-thirds of *Fortune 500* executives in line for the presidencies say they have risen up as far as they care to. For today's younger careerist, however, the picture can look bleak from the junior manager perspective.

New technology can combine with changing social and economic circumstances at work to play a significant role in the development of such stress and other traumatic reactions among career professionals who had achieved stability, success, and status in their careers. For example, I pointed out earlier in this chapter that computerization allows senior executives to obtain information faster and more accurately, bypassing the middle managers. The consequence is not only that middle managers fear looking foolish when confronted with data and analyses their superiors have obtained on their own: There is also the stress of wondering why they are needed at all. Upper managers increasingly question whether middle management is becoming redundant. Coupled with the slow economic growth likely to continue for the next several years, this concern is showing itself in the one-third of the 100 largest U.S. companies that are already pruning management.

Not a comfortable situation for younger careerists on the rise. In companies that have started reducing their staff, many find it hard to block it all out and continue functioning, business-as-usual style. Some report having to deal with anxieties and feelings which they have never experienced before in their working lives. One manager said, "It's as if there has been a loss or death of someone very close." Another said that people have piles of work on their desks but don't care about doing it.[26] Often overlooked, here, is that the top executive who must make the decision about whom to let go also experiences a kind of anxiety the likes of which he or she has never had to deal with before, either. Like the dilemma of whether to fire an average employee with many years of service and a family to support, or a very bright younger person with no dependents.

The main source of trauma among career professionals in the middle levels is the fear that the new technology, in consort with the changing economy, will render their careers, training, and experience unnecessary. Related to this is the inability of many mid-level managers to make proper use of new technology. For example, managers in companies that join the high-tech bandwagon often don't know how to manage their technology efforts effectively. They fail to mesh their desire for technological expertise with business objectives. A survey of twelve of the largest American corporations found that most executives agreed that new technology is essential to productivity, growth, and new market development, but that many of them could not manage the technology in a productive way.[27] In contrast, the more successful companies took risks, didn't punish failure, and accepted lower earnings in order to finance big investments in technology for a longer-range payoff.

Situations in which fears and anxieties have materialized show us what we can expect to see more of in times ahead. They also show us how these problems can be misinterpreted by mental health experts who lack the understanding that there are adult traumas caused by a rapidly changing world that have little, if anything, to do with childhood. For example, executives in the American automobile industry have been particularly hard hit in recent years because of declining sales. Anxiety and depression have become almost commonplace among many auto executives—people who tended to assume that they were pretty much untouchable because of seniority and achievement. Psychiatrists who treated some of these troubled executives found that they were gradually forced to accept the fact that things will probably never go back to the way they were for many of them. These executives affected were people drawing six-figure salaries—part of a larger group of 20,000 career professionals laid off in Detroit. That figure, in turn, is part of a growing increase in executive and professional unemployment nationwide. For example, it increased 17% in just one year, from 1980 to 1981.

The mainstream psychiatric interpretation of such problems is to perceive them as Childhood Revisited. For example, they say the traumatized executives had always felt in control of things because they experienced the corporation to be a big family that would always protect them. Now, cast out from "family" security, or from fantasized favored-son status, they feel alone and unconfident. They therefore develop emotional and physical illnesses as a result. This conventional psychiatric view holds that since one's ego is attached to achievement, and achievement is directly related to happiness, if you cannot achieve you cannot be happy. And if the man at the top (i.e., the father-symbol) is himself in danger of being ousted, the person feels hopeless. The problem with such an interpretation is that normal people are not necessarily acting out a childhood experience when they are troubled. They can feel acutely traumatized when the values and norms to which they have adapted and adjusted are suddenly pulled out from under them. That can be a normal reaction. While those who experience severe or prolonged disturbance following a crisis may, in fact, have an internal problem that was triggered by the crisis, the mainstream mental health view doesn't distinguish this minority from the normal reaction to a threatened or disrupted way of life which had been socially and culturally sanctioned and reinforced.

Such threats and disruptions are likely to continue. Only the leanest, fittest companies are likely to survive through the remainder of the century. The executive ladder will become harder to climb, and some managers will find it difficult to maintain his or her standard of living. The days of rapid promotion are ending. Particularly for the younger, new-breed careerist, there will be fewer chances for promotion, partly because there will be fewer management layers. In general, middle management positions are becoming tougher, more competitive, and less secure. Those climbing up the ladder will find that the rungs get narrower and fewer as they move toward the top.

And even the winners will have to get used to living with little security. They will have to work at developing and learning more relevant skills and, in effect, periodically justify their existence. Increasingly, the people who can make sound decisions, not just recommendations, will be the only middle managers in demand. Winners in the newly emerging game will be those who are able to deal competently with complex financial transactions and the impact of technology on their products.

With layers of management being pruned by many companies, and organization charts being simplified, even in government bureaucracies, decision-making is being pushed down towards those who are closest to the marketplace. So there is also a trend towards more fluid organizations in which teams of managers are brought together to solve specific problems. Compensation will increasingly depend on performance. The overall picture will be mixed in the years ahead for middle managers, the group which earns between roughly $35,000 and $100,000, depending on the size of the company and the city in which it is located. While many companies plan to operate with leaner staffs or double up the work of middle managers, there are others which will increase their middle manager and professional staff. The savvy careerist is going to have to be increasingly tuned in to seeking out opportunities wherever they occur. But once past that career bottleneck, the person can expect the highway to be a few lanes wider, because an upsurge in demand for high-level executives is expected.

Like most middle-class Americans, the broad range of mid-level managers have always assumed that they would move in only one direction: up. The trauma of hitting the brick wall or tumbling off the ladder has created a range of emotional problems such as depression, anger, bewilderment, a sense of failure, alcoholism, and even an inability to function. The older managers are feeling that their skills are increasingly obsolete in the New Age, and that they are becoming the odd man out in a career world increasingly populated by baby-boomers and yuppies. The reality of a bottleneck ahead is starting to sink in for the latter group, too. For example, an AT&T study shows a big drop in expectations for career advancement among younger managers within AT&T.[28]

The size of one's staff has always been equated with power and money. But now the ball game is changing. Since information can be gathered more quickly and efficiently by computers than by middle management, the latter can actually undermine the ability of companies to adapt to changing markets. Lower-level managers are being expected to devise their own strategic and marketing plans. The function of management positions in general is being carefully rethought, as those who design, make, and sell products are being pulled out of staff bureaucracies in some companies, so as to liberate their activity within entrepreneurial enclaves.

To the manager, such changes are understandably frightening and undermining of security. Many feel the rules of the game have changed unfairly, and that they have been betrayed by top executives who, having failed to provide incentives for productivity or cost savings over the years, are now making them into scapegoats. Many middle-level managers worry that they are getting all the blame for all the problems and none of the credit for improvements. Many executives see themselves as quite isolated and not communicating with top management. And morale is lowest among executives whose companies have been hit by middle management layoff. Thirty-two percent report a decline of morale, more than twice the proportion of companies where no cuts have been made.[29]

Phil is someone who suddenly found himself in the middle of a different ball game, and on the losing side. In his early 50s, lean and ruddy, with flowing silver hair, he had been promoted regularly and consistently over the years of his employment for an energy corporation. He had also received numerous awards and citations for his performance, which he proudly displayed on the wall of his paneled den at home. Most people would think of him as a basically healthy individual. His orientation to work is that of a company man, an institutional loyalist who values service and helping his organization function smoothly. Though Phil never reached the top levels, he told me during our first interview that until the "incident" happened, he had been quite satisfied with his career and the recognition he had received.

Phil generally enjoyed his work, and personified the ideal of the good company man: a mixture of loyalty and dependency, with a desire to serve the organization well and efficiently, which one finds in many of the best, if not the most innovative, careerists in corporations and government service. People like him can be counted on to carry out the work of the organization at the middle levels with loyalty to whoever might be "calling the shots" at the top. He was considered a good careerist with particular competence in a technical area in which he had published papers in professional journals. And outside of work Phil enjoyed his life as a family man, and was involved in numerous charity and civic projects.

The "incident" he referred to happened when he was away on assignment to another part of the organization for a few weeks. The new administrator of Phil's division decided to reorganize and streamline it. When he returned, he walked into work one morning to find that his position was being abolished. He was offered a transfer to lower-level work in another office, at reduced pay.

Phil was stunned. "It's nothing personal," he was told, just part of a total reorganization plan. He could either accept reassignment to different work at the lower salary, or go look for another job. Being a loyalist, he tried to convince himself of the logic of the decision and that it was not a reflection on him personally.

But it didn't wash. He felt rejected, demoralized, and humiliated. Soon he was feeling severely depressed, and even had some thoughts of suicide. The money, he explained, was not that important. What really bothered him, he told me, was the blow to his prestige and status. Phil said that he didn't think he could survive such a "crushing blow" to his life—to all he had worked for. He said that his entire life and self-worth were synonymous with his career and position level. Without it, he was nothing.

Phil became immobilized by what happened to him, and could not bring himself to do anything on his own behalf. Friends and co-workers urged him to fight the decision. To look elsewhere, inside or outside his company, to do something, anything, but not just passively accept it like he was doing. But Phil felt listless and asked over and over how this could have happened to him after so many years of loyal service. He could not concentrate on his work at all, and began spending periods of time wandering down the hallways, and staring off into space. Upper management began assigning more and more of his work to others. His personnel office referred him to a psychiatrist to help him "adjust." He told him he was probably suffering from a chemical imbalance in the brain, and prescribed antidepressant medication. Phil tried it for a while, but complained that it made him feel too "drugged." Plus, he was still depressed. He consulted another therapist, who recommended that he come in three times per week for intensive treatment.

My evaluation of Phil found him to have a clear capacity for cooperation and service, as well as solid technical competencies. But there is an underlying theme of dependency and passivity within him. He has always required some direction, support, and recognition to fuel his loyalty and mobilize his performance. But still, these tendencies were not major. He was not exceptionally dependent. What had really happened with him had not so much to do with mother and father or his brain chemistry. It was mainly the values orientation and attitudes he had developed over the course of his adult career in a large organization. Not exceptionally ambitious or highly talented, he had made his entire life and self-worth synonymous with his position and career. Like so many careerists who are insufficiently challenged because of the lack of meaningful or substantive work, his identity had become his position and its security. Stripped of it, he felt he was nothing. Sadly, little effort had been made by his organization to recognize or develop the more active and productive side of Phil. So he, like many other middle management careerists, suffered.

What the Future Holds. A U.N. report from the International Labor Organization found that 500 million people—more than one-fourth of the global work force—are especially vulnerable to the effects of technological and economic changes because they are past their mid-40s.[30] These are the people just beyond the boundary of the shift of attitudes and orientation of the younger, new-breed careerists, and perceived by many to be too old to retrain yet too young to retire. The number of people over 45 will increase by another 200 million by the year 2000. Only a few industrialized nations have done anything to help this group. Japan, for example, has created special job categories for older workers, and requires that at least 6% be employed in full-time jobs. And some European countries have also developed programs to aid the middle-aged employee.

The threats of job displacement and new conditions to which older careerists must adapt or lose out are part of the New Age work and are likely to remain with us for some time to come. These new conditions generate a range of stress and emotional conflict for the most normal and previously well-adapted people. For example, there are basic changes in jobs and in the character of the labor force that even an eventual economic recovery will not alter. The question is whether a bigger proportion of the work force than ever before will be unable to fit into the new conditions because it lacks the skills or attitudinal orientation to work with the new technology. It is possible that both companies and people will adapt with time, but the picture is not yet clear. Take, for example, what is happening in some of the basic industries which have been damaged by shrinking markets. Some companies are trying to use advanced computer technology to manufacture various products with more efficiency and higher quality. Others have shifted to other kinds of products such as from machine tools to robots, or from mills to data processing. One example is a large, old General Electric locomotive factory in Erie, Pennsylvania, which was converted to a computer-controlled factory in which robots turn out diesel and electric motor frames.

But the fear is that, given the sweeping robotization and reorganization that will occur in the workplace in the next decade, the new technology will take the place of humans. To put this fear in proper context, we must remember that such fears have always existed. The Luddites in nineteenth century England, for example, smashed the machines that they feared were destroying their jobs. Some of this kind of fear can be irrational—a fear and hatred of science and technology—which is how the Luddites are usually characterized. But their actual target was not the new technology itself. The stocking-frame had been around since the late 1500s. They were reacting to the fact that the machines had become the property of men who did not operate them themselves, but hired and fired those who did. Similarly, there are fears today that the new technology renders the worker even more helpless in the face of massive changes beyond his or her control.

So if the new technologies are creating a shift in the workplace as fundamental as the transition from an agricultural to a manufacturing economy 100 years ago, and no form of work will remain unchanged, will there be dire consequences for the careerist? Historically, when old industries died out new ones took their place, like the new electronics companies in New England that replaced the textile industries. But the fear of upwardly ambitious careerists is that computer technology will eventually eliminate or negatively alter their jobs and roles. This particularly frightens people for whom career virtually defines their lives and provides much of their sense of meaning and purpose in life.

Economist Robert Samuelson, who has studied this issue, maintains that the anxiety over high-tech remaking the job market, with those who don't adjust being left behind, is sensationalized and exaggerated.[31] He argues that we have come to believe that everything must relate to a high-tech and service economy or be relegated to the trash heap of history. For example, 66% of the respondents to a poll said the economy is in the midst of a profound transition, and that middle-class society is doomed by the disappearance of well-paying middle-level jobs. But Samuelson points out that the job market has always been changing. There has always been new technology. And, in fact, industrial jobs as a percentage of total employment has been declining since 1950.

Also, while the new service-oriented economy is generating the largest number of openings in lower-level jobs, such as janitors, salesclerks, and secretaries, this increase simply reflects that these categories are keeping pace with overall economic expansion. The actual rearrangements are more modest, if one looks at Labor Department data which show no actual drift toward low-skilled or high-skilled jobs.

While it is unlikely that middle-class society will collapse, there will certainly be changes in the nature and emphasis of work for people pursuing successful careers. For example, professionals and managers will have to contribute more to the bottom line. They will have to understand competitive international markets and complex financial issues. And in many professions other kinds of rearrangements are occurring. For example, many law firms find their client base shrinking, with nothing to take its place. This forces them to become a more marketing-oriented, competitive business, more similar to the advertising or insurance business.[32] Lawyers as individuals find they have to learn more business management techniques and public relations skills: Lawyerly skills are not enough to ensure career success. One mental health consequence is that some lawyers simply can't adjust to the changes. They can't deal with pressures to improve their billing procedures or justify their expense accounts. It is a conflict between how they were trained, the personal orientations they have developed as they adapted to their work, versus what they now have to do to be adaptive and productive in the new ball game. Many say there is less time to develop excellence or quality of work, that the new atmosphere lacks grace and collegiality.

The bottom line regarding the emotional consequences of situations beyond the person's control in the New Age of work is that unless the labor market is able to generate opportunities for satisfying jobs and careers for the highly educated, ambitious, new-breed careerist, within the context of new technology and major changes in the structure and focus of organizations, a range of stress, anxiety, and other emotional problems will grow. As will escapist solutions into haute consumerism and compulsive pursuit of hedonistic pleasures as compensation.

CONSOLIDATED AMALGAMATED, INC.

So far, we have seen that careers in today's world are bombarded by large-scale changes beyond our control, including new technology and changes in socioeconomic and political conditions that affect the workplace. Another major change which affects us emotionally as we adapt and navigate our way to success is the increasing size and complexity of organizations—bureaucracy—whether they are private or public. "Bureaucracy," here, refers to multiple layers of organization, largeness, and slowness to respond to changing external circumstances, an impersonal quality to working life within it, and a tendency to move along and preserve itself at all cost.

Our work and career experiences occur today within a world of ever-larger organizations. Bureaucracy is increasing in all organizations, public and private. In contrast to the early 1800s, when 80% of the work force was self-employed, today only 8% is. And, despite the surge of interest in entrepreneurialism over the last several years, despite all the hoopla about its being the salvation of our economic system, and despite that it can provide a viable alternative to many bored and underutilized workers, there is actually greater dependence than ever on large organization as the prime shaper of personal identity and definer of adult values. For every person who becomes self-employed today there are twelve others who prefer a career within an organization.

Roughly half the American work force is employed by organizations of over 500 employees. And that figure is growing. Whether privately or publicly owned, the large organization sets much of the standard for normal adjustment, success, and their counterpoint: maladjustment and emotional disturbance.

One consequence of the reality of bureaucratic growth is that the conservative–entrepreneurial vision embraced by neo-conservative writers like George Gilder and by the Reagan administration—that of risk-taking adventurers and a free and competitive marketplace providing a renewed and re-energized capitalism—is not matched by reality. Large corporations and bureaucracies are dominated by people who minimize risk, and want protection from government. Large organizations do not want to adopt or advocate policies which rock the existing social and political structure. They want the population at large and unions to be content, and with a reasonable degree of security and justice for citizens. Comfortable maintenance of what exists is the value, not frontier, risk-taking adventurism. Even in Silicon Valley, synonymous in the public mind with creative entrepreneurialism, formerly tiny companies have sprouted into billion-dollar operations and grow ever-larger in the process. They often encounter tremendous difficulty trying to protect the innovative, youthful spirit which characterized their origins. And those who developed the companies with that spirit, like Apple Computer's co-founder Stephen Jobs, often find themselves, as he did in the fall of 1985, odd man out, no longer fitting into a large organization run by cadres of professional managerial types.

In today's world of large bureaucracy, technology poses challenges that existing institutions and social attitudes have trouble dealing with. Liberals who advocate a world which would be a throwback to small-scale business don't know how to contain and control high-technology, which is even more destabilizing today than when big business arose to make manageable the then-new technology of an era ago. At the same time, conservatives who advocate dismantling the welfare state don't ask who will provide the personal security or collective underpinning on which we all depend, including our corporations.

The trend toward bigness and less distinction between the private and public sector frightens many. Some see its worst consequences already upon us. For example, British historian and journalist Paul Johnson has argued that a decline of individual responsibility throughout this century has coincided with the rise of statism, that the state has proved its capacity to do evil when moral restraints are removed by largeness of structure.[33] But this is only a partial picture. The rise of the big organization, whether business or government, once served a useful purpose. If we go back to the creation of large organizations, Weber, the German sociologist who first described the workings and rationale of the organizational hierarchy around the turn of the century, spoke of a positive goal: creating an alternative to the instability and arbitrariness of charismatic leaders, and providing a consistent structure through which tasks could be performed with efficiency. But with time, the negative side of bureaucracy has emerged and strengthened. The historian Arnold Toynbee saw this as a process of institutionalization that is a price of durability, whether in religion, social institutions, or political ideals; that this is the paradox of durability of ideals or ideas over history.

Whatever the reasons, a central part of the changing landscape of work that confronts us as we head toward the twenty-first century is the specter of more bureaucracy. For many of us, of course, the bureaucracy of government symbolizes the worst of big organizations: the feared juggernaut of the future. Large bureaucracy and its workers have been described so often as mindless, passive, rigid, and robotized that it has become a stereotype. We commonly think of the bureaucrat as forever hiding behind rules and regulations which are inflicted with sadistic glee upon the helpless public.

And this image is not groundless, either. Most of us have a personal horror story about an encounter with a government bureaucrat which left us feeling helpless and infuriated. Erich Fromm described the sadistic pleasure some bureaucrats feel, through his example of the man behind the post office window: ". . . watch his hardly noticeable thin little smile as he shuts his window at 5:30 P.M. sharp, while the last two people who have already been waiting for half an hour have to leave and come back the next day. The point is not that he stops selling stamps at 5:30 P.M. sharp: the important aspect of his behavior is the fact that he enjoys frustrating people, showing them that he controls them, a satisfaction that is expressed in his facial expression."[34]

Both the political right and left have contributed to our fears by warning about the growth of government organizations. Ironically, both argue, but for different ideological reasons, that bureaucracy is bad for people and society. The reactionary right seems more concerned with the stifling of initiative and the ability to make a profit. Hence, the romanticized picture of the Horatio Alger entrepreneur, unencumbered by the "shackles" of modern organizational complexity. The left, on the other hand, worries more about the totalitarian potential of ever larger organizations in business and government.

The theme that our lives are increasingly dominated by large organizations, and that this is bad and destructive for people, so permeates our literature, social criticism, and popular culture ("Orwellian" and "Kafkaesque" are terms that have become almost household words) that it is hard to rationally evaluate its accuracy.[35] Erich Fromm made one of the earliest and most penetrating criticisms of the modern bureaucratic society and its effects upon people. Writing from a standpoint of both psychoanalytic theory and the humanistic–religious ideal, he argued in many widely-read books spanning more than 40 years, such as his 1941 classic *Escape From Freedom*, and such others as *The Sane Society, The Art of Loving*, and *The Anatomy of Human Destructiveness*,[36] that the "normal" character in modern society seeks escape from being fully alive, independent, and responsible. Escape through creating new objects of dependency which can be the State, as in Nazi or Communist ideology, sado-masochistic relationships, blind conformity to an ideology, or through material consumption, in an attempt to cover up feelings of inner emptiness and deadness. For Fromm, the modern "pathology of normalcy" meant the potential for becoming increasingly like the alienated, dead-ended, and robotized bureaucrats. The very people the literati have warned us about.

But the picture is not so one-sided. There are people, for example, who seem to develop themselves more fully, who come alive, emotionally and intellectually, working for large organizations, because their character orientation and talents fit what is needed in a productive, not pathological way. The trend toward more bureaucracy will not necessarily culminate in an Orwellian nightmare, though this expectation has become so embedded in our collective consciousness that it is hard to alter.[37]

Today, especially, fears of bureaucratic domination of our lives has been heightened by its potential for joining forces with computer technology. In this era of new technology and computerization, there is fear of its use by governments to increase repression.[38] This potential is no longer limited to the realm of novels or science fiction. For example, computerized bureaucracy can make it possible for governments and organizations to consolidate and perpetuate their power. Public and private agencies now collect and collate by computer pieces of information, including things that are false. Every so often one reads in the newspaper about somebody who was falsely arrested because of traffic violations or criminal charges that were pending against someone else with the same name. Other examples include the capacity of cable TV to store data about the watcher, or the capacity of telephone computers to store information about the calls we make.

To some extent, there is a tendency to feel powerless against the onslaught of such computerized intrusions into privacy. The push to centralize, collate, match, and compare data is a clear force within our governments and institutions. And while the computer has vastly increased the efficiency of institutions in dealing with large numbers of people or complex technical problems, the core fear is that the police-state mentality is fast closing in upon us. For example, a 1983 Harris survey on the impact of technology on society found widespread fears that the computer age and technological innovations will diminish human contact and make it more likely that nuclear, chemical, or biological weapons will end up destroying the human race. A large majority feared threats to their privacy.

The growth of bureaucracy affects our experience of work and social attitudes in three ways, which we must all absorb and deal with in some way while working in the New Age:

A Negative Spirit.   Surveys and studies of social attitudes within the U.S., Western Europe, and in the Soviet bloc all reveal a similar theme: growing deterioration of morale and increased depression over the weight of large institutions in society, whether government or private. Polls show a sharp plunge of public confidence in leaders and institutions, including business, labor, and government. In a 1983 book, *The Confidence Gap*,[39] Seymour Martin Lipset and William Schneider examined three decades of public opinion polls which show a persistent decline of public faith in virtually all major institutions and leaders. In their interpretation of these data, increased distrust of large organizations is the root. A related interpretation would be that the overriding assumption in post-World War II America has been that major institutions should serve broad public interests regardless of private purpose. The old notion of business as a good thing in itself is long gone. But while the public favors government regulation of business, it also distrusts government too much to permit much more. In analyzing this issue, economist Robert Samuelson has pointed out that institutions are still judged by their service to individuals, and this is the area in which people have become cynical and distrustful.[40] We are and will remain a society of large institutions. Small farmers, independent businesses, and day laborers no longer dominate the economy. The bind is that the modern worker wants and expects a career in a big organization, yet simultaneously feels the oppressive weight of bureaucracy.

Across the Atlantic we find a similar picture. A survey of 2200 people from England, Belgium, France, Holland, Italy, and West Germany found the respondents saying in overwhelming numbers that, in effect, they believed most people are no good and the world is a lousy place to live in. It also found rampant cynicism and alienation. All the people surveyed were between 21 and 45 years old, the European counterparts of our yuppies and new careerists. The survey reinforces the view that institutions are seen as powerless and meaningless to one's life by the European careerist class, too.[41]

Deterioration of Functioning. If the growth of bureaucracies has cast a pall upon attitudes about life and what the future holds, it has also contributed to a picture of deterioration in the actual functioning of our organizations, including the stifling of creative spirit and deterioration of work standards. Examples abound internationally, some bordering on the inane: In the U.S., the state of Maryland discovered in 1983 that one of its agencies had become defunct during the Carter administration. But no one in the government bureaucracy had gotten the word. The agency, the Criminal Justice Coordinating Council, had been maintaining a salaried staff of 19 with a budget of $446,000 of taxpayer money. In New York State, the Department of Environmental Conservation ran out of paper one day—pretty serious for a bureaucracy. As one might expect, the work of the Department came to a crashing halt. The Department was thus unable to submit briefs on time for an application of a utility company to convert a plant to coal. The company itself came to the rescue, trucking in 5000 sheets of paper to the agency's offices. A spokesperson for the council, which employs 2000 people, said he didn't know why it took so long to get paper, what goes into the decision, or even whom they buy it from.

This picture is found on the federal level, too, of course. One federal office has become known as the "Bermuda Triangle," because it is said that when something goes in, it never comes out. One administrator brought in during the Reagan administration was reported to have created a tremendous bottleneck because he insisted that a lot of routine decisions required his personal approval. In the private sector, also, are examples of the hindering of growth and productivity by multiple layers of management, something which is likely to increase rather than diminish in the years ahead. While it is true that many companies are increasingly pruning middle management, some—particularly the newer service industries—have been increasing their management layers. And these are the companies towards which the new breed careerists gravitate.

The most extreme examples of deterioration of functioning within massive bureaucracies are found in Soviet society. Soviet officials and management experts have become increasingly open about their criticism of the cumbersome, inflexible system of management, planning, and production. Reports have been published both in the Soviet press and in magazines for top managers about this, including examples which raise cause for concern regarding the long-range effects of increasing bureaucratization within our own society.[42]

Consolidation of Power. A third effect on people of increasing bureaucratization in the workplace is found in the effects of consolidated power.

One example is the tremendous power of the new megacorporations, huge bureaucracies which concentrate political power in the hands of a few top managers. The specter of megacorporation proliferation, with the potential of its managers influencing the political arena through lobbying, poses a considerable danger for the society. For example, campaign contributions through various PACs create significant potential power. The danger, in part, is that the corporate agenda for profit is not necessarily congruent with the public welfare and interest. More directly affecting the worker is the fact that "merger mania" can be destructive. Often small but profitable businesses that are taken over by large bureaucracies become ruined or are hurt economically. The problem is that the large companies are bureaucratic, and do not mix so well with smaller, more entrepreneurial enterprises. The latter usually suffer. And when the merger is between two large bureaucracies, the result is—surprise!—more bureaucracy. The extra layers of bureaucracy are likely to hasten deterioration and stagnation.

More than half of the diversification of the top 200 manufacturing firms from 1970–75 reflected mergers. What often motivates executives in such bids is a desire to aggrandize power through expansion and acquisition. Greed and ambition become socially reinforced perversions of the normal and adaptive desire for profit and responsible power. Existing corporations are strengthened and enlarged at the expense of newer or smaller businesses. In a similar vein, Yugoslavian social critic Milovan Djilias, author of *The New Class*,[43] which criticized the bureaucracy and earned him a prison term for his efforts, has observed that bureaucratic consolidation eventually stultifies the individual. In Yugoslav˙ , for example, he contends that consolidated power mixed with built-in sluggishness and ineptness combined with incompetence at the top has contributed to bureaucratic chaos.

WOMEN AND MINORITIES

The final transformation of our New Age of work is the steady entry of women, as well as blacks and other minorities into the ranks of management and administration of corporations, bureaucracies, and other large organizations, and into professions traditionally populated primarily by white males. While blacks and other racial–ethnic minorities are gradually filtering into the ranks of career professionals and organizations, women have been able to do so in greater numbers. Their entry presents issues to which the women themselves, as well as the men with whom they work as peers, subordinates, and superiors, must adapt. The issues raised, like outside circumstances beyond our control and the growth of bureaucracy, create new sources of stress and conflict for the new careerist.

Women on the Rise: Some Facts

- Percent of all women who work, married or single   52
- Percent of total work force who are women   44
- Percent of married women who work   67
  - Percent of married women working full-time   46
- Percent of mothers who work   71
  - Percent of mothers working full-time   65
  - Percent of married mothers who work   60
- Percent of women in managerial/administrative work   35
  - Percent of all executives who are women   1
- Percent of salary of male counterparts that women earn   60

What do these data mean in terms of their impact on both male and female careerists?[44] The opportunity for a successful career is as important to contemporary career women as it is to most men. Their career pursuits are occurring in the context of some historic changes. For example, for the first time, a majority of working women are now in the work force. Today it is 52%, and by 1995 it is predicted to be 65%. And over one-third of the 15 million women who joined the work force since 1970 have entered male-dominated fields. As of 1983, white male workers became a minority for the first time in history, and now make up 49% of the civilian work force. Women have grown to 44% of the total work force. By 1995 women are expected to make up two-thirds of all new workers.

Looking at married women and mothers, 67% of all married couples now have two incomes; and of them, 46% of the women work full-time. But the biggest spurt has occurred among working mothers. Today, 50% of married women with children one year old or younger work. And 60% of those with children 18 also work.

A theme emerging from these changes, when fleshed out with the experiences of real people, is that the woman is struggling to balance the demands and tensions between, on the one hand, the desire for career responsibility, competency, and success, and, on the other, the desire for children and a family life. The 60% of married mothers who work are faced with dealing with the conflicting demands of work and family. This reflects a jump from 42% of mothers who worked at the beginning of the 1970s. Many report feeling suspended between the ideals of family togetherness and personal independence. These dual demands are seen in several ways. For example, only 80% of full-time working women work at least 40 hours per week, compared with 95% of men. And they suffer in the job market when they try to return after having children. A study of women graduates of the Harvard Business School found widespread frustration over not being able to feel sufficiently rewarded by either job or family.[45] Yet most say they would not stop working, either.

Most men would probably agree that marriage consists of two people.

Yet women experience the dual pressures of career and family much more than men. For example, 60% of working fathers report that they feel they have enough time to themselves, but only 36% of working mothers do.[46] The career-oriented woman ends up sacrificing more in terms of a family and social life, also. For example, among senior women executives, about 50% are unmarried, but only 5% of the men are. Some men with career wives feel anger and resentment over the demands and pressures of balancing career with family. Some men speak of having to give up some of their own ambitions in order to be with their children more, or help with chores. Many also find they have to deal with feelings of anger and resentment over not being the center of things any more.

So most career women have difficulty balancing the competing demands of job and home. Those that are married tend to still do most of the household chores. On the other hand, single women careerists often worry about putting too much focus on work. All of them feel they make substantial sacrifices in order to advance their careers. Some women deal with this conflict by postponing having children. There has been a rise over the last 10 years in the percent of women without children in the 35- to 39-year-old category, from 11–15%. And 25 years ago, 24% of women in their early 20s had no children. Today, it is 43%. But the number giving birth in their 30s for the first time doubled between the beginning and the end of the 1970s. And from 1980 to 1983, the birthrate for women over 30 increased by a larger degree than any other age group: from 60 to 69 per 1000. Those who have children after 30 are part of the new breed of careerists: more affluent, better educated, and holding professional jobs, compared with younger mothers. Particularly in service companies like banks, retailers, computer companies, and law firms, pregnancies are increasing for those over 30 who also hold high-level jobs.

Increasingly, women want the satisfaction of having both a family and a successful career. Because of the conflicts, a growing number are choosing a slower track and shorter hours, when they can arrange it, so as to have more time at home. Others drop out until their children grow up. Women with children and a full-time career often have difficulty coping with the travel and long hours that may be required for career advancement. Some leave their positions for other companies where they can work a more normal workday. Others decide to forego getting to the top as fast, and give greater priority to their family. But emotionally, this can be difficult for an ambitious person to accept.

Adding to this dilemma for women is evidence that children whose mothers work and children from single-parent homes score lower on school achievement tests. According to a 1983 study by the U.S. Department of Education, the size of the gap was found to relate directly to how much the mother worked. A major conflict women talk about may relate to this gap: surrogate care for younger children, and "latch-key" children among the older. It has been found that some children from two-career families have feelings of joylessness and powerlessness, and often have diminished capacity to experience pleasure.

Dilemmas of the Woman Executive. The numbers of women in managerial and executive work is on the rise. The proportion of women in the traditionally male-dominated executive, managerial, and administrative jobs jumped from 18% to about 32% between 1970 and 1984. Even in professional areas traditionally closed to women, like judges, lawyers, architects, and engineers, the numbers of women have been steadily growing.

But the picture is far from rosy. Women who reach for the top find that they must deal with and adapt to long-embedded male attitudes that work against women's success. Women promoted to senior-level positions often have difficulty being taken seriously or treated with respect by male subordinates. The few women who have made it to the highest levels tend to be in their late 40s and 50s. Most women careerists plateau in the middle levels, and are often shunted into areas like personnel or public relations.

One problem for the men is that they are not used to seeing or treating women as peers or managers at work, and often don't know how to relate to them. As more women move into positions of power, men will be forced to better adapt to their presence. The women who have already reached the top tend to be more driven by power, and are angrier than their younger counterparts. Many feel quite willing to use deception, conniving, and other strategies of what Maccoby described as the jungle fighter orientation.[47] Younger careerists, more characteristic of the new breed of worker, are less driven and less angry than their older, pioneering counterparts. This, in turn, positively affects their interactions and relations with male peers.

The older pioneers rose up the ladder at a time when it was extremely hard for a woman to become a successful careerist. This contributed to the jungle fighter adaptation, though, of course, some may have had this orientation to begin with, which made them more willing to make their career their primary focus, and prove themselves to be as tough as—if not tougher than—the men around them. Those who couldn't or wouldn't do this, or who gave more emphasis to a home life probably got turned-off by the environment and what was required for success.

National surveys show that women, overall, are on the way up, but there are still few women at the top.[48] Sixty-three percent say barriers to women have not fallen at the senior management level. Seventy percent say women don't receive equal pay for equal work. They most frequently mention being a woman as the major career obstacle. They cite the old-boy network, insecure men, and the prevailing male attitude that they will leave their job and get married as factors which inhibit advancement.

They also see male bosses as unwilling to give them tough assignments, which would help develop their skills.

They are often restricted from the kinds of experiences in corporations that would prepare them for career movement into and beyond the middle ranks. For example, many American companies don't send women managers abroad for foreign experience. Yet, because foreign experience is so important, companies can't have people in its upper ranks who lack it. A neat Catch-22 for the woman executive. Also, some male supervisors undermine women by failing to give them difficult assignments or introduce them to as many senior officials. Consequently, women are often under much more career-related stress than men, based on the tension of working in male-dominated environments, with built-in limitations for women.

This, in turn, often creates problems for marriages. For example, the divorce rate is higher among women in male-dominated jobs than for those performing traditional work. The risk of divorce declines if the woman's occupation has a lower status than her husband's. Women in nontraditional jobs are substantially more likely to divorce, leave the labor force, or move to lower status than women in traditional positions.

So there are few women who get top positions in business, despite the progress that has been made. Among managers earning over $40,000 in the top 50 industrial companies, less than 5% are women. Some industries like banking, retailing, advertising, and computers are easier for women managers to crack, however, because those put more emphasis on managerial than on technical skills. And some companies actually seek women executives more than others. These include transportation, high-technology, aerospace, mining, and durable-goods manufacturing. These industries have taken the lead over retailing, financial services, consumer goods, and publishing, which in the past were most open to women executives.

Also, employment of women scientists and engineers jumped 200% between 1972 and 1982. Women now comprise 13% of all such workers. While women have been rising in high-tech firms, they are still less than 10% of the total high-tech management. In Silicon Valley, the heart of high-tech companies, women find it to be both the best and the worst place for women. The environment of intense competition and demand for innovation forces recognition of competence, regardless of sex. But the field has been long dominated by men. Women complain of a pervasive chauvinistic engineering mentality and culture, which forces them to be tough, aggressive, and to take on a male personality to survive.

In the field of law, women are making steady inroads into the profession. Women now constitute 40% of law school enrollments. But they encounter obstacles in the law firms. Many partners believe that they don't have the career commitment that men do, and that they will have children, which will affect their loyalties and priorities.

Overall, despite recent gains by women in moving up the corporate and professional ladder, they still don't advance as far or as rapidly as their male counterparts. Even when they are evenly matched, both having an MBA, the men still significantly outpace women in the race up the ladder. Nationally, women managers and administrators earn only 60% as much as their male counterparts. Those women who return to the work force at middle age, after raising children, often find themselves working for a boss 10 or more years their junior, which creates conflict for both of them, particularly if the boss is another woman. The older woman may resent the younger boss, thinking she had advantages that she, herself, didn't. All of these conditions have led some to develop criticisms of the values of the corporate world, maintaining that for the woman to compete with men at the highest level, they must imitate men, be cruel and conformist, and so on. For example, in a book about a woman's experience of Harvard Business School, Fran Henry has argued that the business world should change into one where there can be some compromise in values.[49] She concludes that business school training, in terms of its sink-or-swim atmosphere of constant pressure and the possibility for failure, should not be less like the real world, but that the real world should be less like itself.

Given the values and traditions within large organizations, women experience a range of conflict and stress over pursuing a successful career. They are faced with the emotional strain of struggling to reconcile the feelings and attitudes of motherhood with those attitudes they need to succeed in the corporation. Being both careerist and mother, and desiring balance between the two, they end up feeling torn, twisted, and unfulfilled.

Black careerists, as a group, often experience situations in their upward career movement that add an additional layer to the existing potential problems of working in the New Age. Their upward movement in organizations creates additional sources of conflict and stress for themselves, and for white colleagues who must adapt to their presence. Black career professionals' climb to the top is complicated by the extra dimension of racism—real or perceived, overt or hidden—and the strain of working in a white-dominated culture and environment. Culture shock, isolation, alienation, and loss of identity are frequently experienced. Black managers often resist learning the political game for fear of its conflicting with their cultural values. Stress is generated by racist attitudes and behavior, and by the withholding of information by white supervisors, which would aid the black executives' performance and upward prospects. Blacks often feel that they get shunted into dead-end jobs or that promotions are withheld. Their attempts to cope with this often lead to repressed anger. Psychiatrist Jeffrey Speller has found that, as a result, they may explode, like anyone under severe stress, or develop a variety of physical ailments and other signs of severe inner conflict and turmoil.[50]

An underlying issue is that many blacks feel torn between two worlds. Because there are certain rites of passage for newcomers in an organization, black or white, there are added dimensions for blacks to deal with. For example, the transition is often more alienating because they are surrounded mainly by whites, within a white culture. They often feel forced, as they climb higher, to make choices that aid their career at the expense of their blackness, such as becoming isolated from their black milieu, or having to choose between it and the white culture of work. Consequently, black career professionals often report physical complaints, migraine headaches, sleeping disorders, back pain, nausea, heart trouble, and high blood pressure. Speller believes many of these symptoms reflect underlying anger which almost inevitably builds up during the career adaptation and upward movement of the black executive and professional.

STRESS AND BURNOUT REVISITED

The features of the New Age of work which underlie many of the emotional problems of the Working Wounded and those who develop Surface Sanity give us a better framework with which to understand stress and burnout. The traumas of the New Age of work, which can be debilitating and destructive, have emotional and physical consequences for today's careerists which often take the form of the stress/burnout syndrome. For many, this syndrome serves as a warning signal: something like the way physical pain or a fever is a feedback mechanism that tells us something is wrong, so as to help us avoid permanent damage that might result if the signal were ignored or if the symptoms were stifled without diagnosing and treating the underlying problem producing the symptoms. Numbing the pain too much, or unnecessary suppression of a fever, will prevent both the necessary warning signals and the necessary restorative processes to occur.

Any of the three major changes in the world of work can trigger stress or burnout. Any of us may experience difficulties as a result of trying to cope with the mental health consequences of these changes, which can bombard us to such a degree that they diminish our capacity to respond effectively or efficiently. All careerists are vulnerable. Everyone has a burnout level. But what it means is not the same for all people. Not everyone responds to the same kind of stress in the same way. To help understand this, let's review, briefly, what happens inside us when we are under stress. The brain perceives danger and triggers the release of chemicals that heighten the sensitivity of our nervous system. For example, it raises our pulse and sharpens our reflexes. At work, this heightened sensitivity can be aroused by difficult decisions or multiple tasks that we have to perform. Or by the pressure from dealing with new changes to adapt to, the stultification of bureaucracy, and the juggling act between career success and family values. On the positive side, this arousal can provide clear thinking and extra energy, but if left "on" for long periods, the body and mind can be damaged. If instead of slowing down the system continues to race, we get the common symptoms of stress, like anxiety, headaches, sweaty palms, and irritability. The stress reaction can actually disable the person and prevent normal functioning. Most of us can probably think of someone who, previously hardworking, aggressive, and apparently well-balanced, suddenly became sullen, angry, or volatile. Often the person's productivity declines and a pattern of increased absenteeism may occur. Stress causes or worsens an estimated 70–90% of all illness, and costs industry about $75 billion yearly, by spawning hypertension, heart attacks, depression, anxiety, and other problems.

Burnout, as many career professionals have learned through direct experience, is a state of fatigue, cynicism, or apathy brought about primarily by work activity that either fails to produce reasonable satisfaction, or results in chronic frustration. The person often feels he or she is receiving diminishing returns and less enjoyment. Other common symptoms that appear are boredom, irritability, depression, loss of enthusiasm, and declining job performance. Frequently, the person turns to a "quick fix" to restore vitality and energy. For some, that may mean a vacation, drugs, alcohol, sexual escapades, or gambling.

Stress is a broader concept than burnout, and can be related to both personal and work situations. Burnout, on the other hand, is more closely related to work experiences, and often affects, in particular, the upward-moving career professional who hits the brick wall of debilitating circumstances in the organization. Many career professionals become vulnerable to burnout when they try to cope with the mental health consequences of the three transformations of work, particularly when they don't understand them, and feel increasingly beaten and worn down.

The people most vulnerable to burnout are mid-level managers and professionals, or owners of small businesses, rather than heads of large corporations. Owners of small businesses complain of stress twice as frequently as those who run giant corporations. Forty percent of top executives report that they experience stress. The larger the company, the less the top executives complain about the stress. Among the top 200 companies, only 8% of the chiefs said, when polled, that they consider stress or burnout to be a problem, compared with 24% of the chiefs whose companies rank between 500 and 1350 in size. One chairman of a medium-sized company said that the dangers of stress occurs in middle management. "People who get to my position have the stomach of a goat," he said. That may be true, but it is also the case that the top manager has the power and authority to take action which can help alleviate stress and circumvent burnout. Those in the middle, or those running smaller companies, do not. Without an outlet, the system is all revved up but can't go anywhere. It's like pressing the accelerator to the floor while keeping your foot firmly on the brake. Something's got to give. The highly successful new breed careerist is often a victim of burnout and stress because the combination of high ambition, willingness to work hard, and latent ideals make the person more vulnerable to impediments in the desire for success and fulfillment. Thus, we find that 50% of the chiefs of organizations under 45 find stress and burnout a problem, compared with 29% over 45.[51]

We have seen that there are traumas of the New Age of work which generate a variety of conflicts for the new careerist, and which underlie much of the stress and burnout so widely experienced by career professionals today. More broadly, the massive changes in the world of work are shaking the foundations of our norms of adjustment and adaptation. They are contributing to a gradual evolution in the range of attitudes, values, and motives which constitutes the life orientation of the new careerists. And they are also creating a new range of problems and conflicts which are becoming normal to experience in our times.

THE NEW NORMALCY

6

It is a law of life that one must grow or else pay more for remaining the same.

— Norman Mailer

What does it mean to be normal? Is it the same as being untroubled? Or successful? If so, successful at what? Questions like these scurry around hidden corners of the minds of new breed careerists today. And understandably so: The sea change underway in the world of organizations and careers is rocking the foundations of our lives. It is creating psychological earthquakes and a topsy-turvy world in which, as we have seen, it can be adaptive and rewarding at work to be emotionally sick. In which intelligent and hard-working career professionals feel trapped and emotionally conflicted over the bind between ambition and personal values. And in which nearly everyone is at risk from the danger of becoming stressed-out from the daily impact of the New Age of work.

All of the changes regarding work directly affect the values, motives, attitudes, behavior, and sanity of the new breed careerist. They force us to question, rather than take for granted, what it means to be normal or maladaptive in our times. And to ask whether there are any standards that make sense, or will we have to flounder until the debris of social change settles before we can figure it all out? These questions arise because the sea change underway at work has generated a new set of circumstances and conditions which people must deal with and adapt to in some way. A new, and much broader range of feelings, experiences, desires, and motives that constitute new norms for career-oriented men and women. This is the New Normalcy.

Its main psychological feature is that our self-definitions and self-evaluations regarding our achievements, success, and virtually all our worth as people is largely equated with our work and career position. Particularly for the career professional class, work increasingly defines and describes our lives. As one 32-year-old architect said, "All I do is work. I have no other life. My work defines me totally." Because of this merger of our careers with our identity and self-worth, work has, in effect, provided us a framework and definition for what we perceive to be normal or well-adjusted. These new norms are particularly seen in the changing attitudes and behavior regarding what people want from work, and in the desire for greater fulfillment, meaning, and development in life—in one's work, personal values, and intimate relationships.

The New Normalcy is also seen in the kinds of conflicts that the new careerist must deal with. These conflicts reflect a bind that has grown out of the merger of our self-definition and the work we do. In essence, careerists feel caught between wanting to become and thereafter remaining successful career winners, but also wanting more personal fulfillment. They want to perform work that is more meaningful, as well as to be able to enjoy work more fully, and with less conflict. The rise of the New Normalcy is pushing the careerist to rebel against the self-betrayal which has traditionally been the price for overadaptation to success at work.

The tight job market, shifting and changing career opportunities, and the specter of downward mobility for new entrants into the career professional class as well as those already in it, also contribute to the psychological and social mosaic that presents new areas of emotional conflict and trauma—some, not necessarily solvable—that are part of the New Normalcy. The careerist is faced with the task of adapting to and dealing with them in some way. That is, the traumas of the New Age of work, the conflicts of the Working Wounded, and the conditions that feed Surface Sanity are all part of a broadened realm of problems, binds, and disturbing emotions that exist for the careerist. This is why fear, anxiety, depression, and other psychiatric problems that usually reflect a neurotic personality can all be normal experiences and reactions of people who are adapting to a changing world.

To help understand the New Normalcy, and how we can identify the areas in which it has broadened the range of emotions, desires, attitudes, and conflicts that are normal to experience in these times, we need to clarify what motivates us to adapt in the first place, what the pressures are upon us that generate the range of normal adjustment.

WHY ADAPT?

The sea change underway in the world of work affects our standard of normalcy and, in turn, the kinds of emotional problems we develop, because nothing in our society occurs in a vacuum. Any changes that create or resolve economic, political, or social crises are part of a network that affects our attitudes and values, as well. Like shared attitudes about what we "should" value and do that enable us to fit in: to be successful and adaptive. The pressures to adapt to what others do to obtain success and fit in is something that affects everyone. In the most basic sense, we all have to be able to get along with people around us, at least to some minimal degree, in order to function in society. Also, most of us need to earn a living, to support ourselves through work. Although there are different ways in which we can do this, and with varying degrees of "success," depending on what we value, we all have to adapt for both social and economic reasons.

This results in an individual's life orientation, what the late psychoanalyst Erich Fromm identified as the "social character" of people: the pattern of traits, motives, attitudes, values, and behavior shared by members of a group, class, organization, society, or culture. It grows out of adaptation to the existing economic, technological, and social circumstances, and is transmitted to a person both through the family and through institutions of society like education, government, and religion. Shared attitudes, values, and behavior enable people to function effectively. So in this sense, it defines what is normal or well-adjusted.

Social character is often difficult to understand, partly because the current fashion is to divide things into either healthy (i.e., normal adjustment and adaptation) or unhealthy. But there is an in-between range of attitudes and behavior shared by people within a society or group which is neither sick nor fully healthy. It is simply adaptive. Although adaptation means giving up something of oneself in return for the benefits of fitting in, some people do it more than others, and some begin at an earlier age. For example, most of us can think of some two- or three-year-olds who show more willingness to conform than others of the same age. The mainstream of psychoanalytic thinking holds that adaptation is pretty much over by the age of about five, and that one's later adult character, including one's mental health, are determined by this age. But this view is being forced to change, because of increasing evidence that adaptation does not cease when childhood ceases. It can continue throughout adulthood, particularly in the arena of work.

Social character is not really a new concept. Aspects of it have been described since antiquity, in terms of how culture, work, or even geography shape how the masses of people think and act. In early American history, the most classic description of our own social character at that time was Alexis de Tocqueville's early 1800s study *Democracy in America* [1] What Fromm did was to combine the older tradition of interpretive observation of society and social history with psychoanalytic insights into unconscious motivation and human development.

A person's orientation is reinforced while growing up and throughout adulthood by the social attitudes, motivations, and values conveyed by institutions of society, such as schools, religious institutions, government, and, in particular, by the kinds of work people perform. In effect, a society (or organization) needs its members to *want* to act and think as they *have* to act and think in order for the society to function effectively. That is not necessarily good nor bad, in itself. But it has the potential for becoming good or bad, depending on what it is people adapt to.

Most people accept and adapt to the dominant values, ideology, or attitudes, and interpret them as "normal," even though they may change over time, for a variety of reasons. There have been different views of normal adjustment, success, and, correspondingly, of emotional problems, in every historical era. These views, or shared assumptions, have changed over history as the kinds of work people perform have changed. In fact, our views about normalcy have evolved not so much as a result of increased scientific knowledge about mental and emotional functioning, but as a by-product of new and different modes of work that come to predominate in society, and the paths that become open to success.

Changes in work, in turn, have been largely determined by changes in technology, which create new conditions and requirements for successful adaptation. That is, socioeconomic and technological changes are the usual causes of large-scale change in the shared orientation: in the emergence of a new life orientation which comes to predominate in the society. For example, the hoarding, thrifty, self-reliant person who was adaptive to the largely farming culture in early years of the United States underwent change with the growth of industrialization and entrepreneurialism following the Civil War. Different attitudes and traits became more adaptive during that period, such as risk-taking, adventurousness, and longer-range planning.[2]

The roots of our present evolution lie in the beginning of modern industry and in the development of mass-production technology during that period—roughly, from the mid-1800s onward. And, also, in the development of ever-larger government and business organizations that began about that same period. These changes shaped the predominant assumptions about what social adjustment, success, and normalcy were. From today's viewpoint, the "normal" person of the early 1800s would appear quaint, unnecessarily hoarding and tight, reserved, perhaps even neurotic. But from the standpoint of that person, today's adaptive careerist would probably appear wasteful, self-indulgent, shallow, and lacking moral fiber.

The content of "normal" attitudes can also change with the national need. Look, for example, at the change in American perceptions of the Japanese or Germans from World War II to the present. And, currently, investment opportunities and the political agenda are reshaping our shared attitudes about formerly "Red" China; aided, of course, by changes within China itself.

So what we call normal or well-adjusted is really the constellation of attitudes, values, and behavior of the dominant social character orientation, which we all share or are influenced by, to some degree. At this moment in our history what we call and define as normal or well-adjusted is undergoing another, but much more far-reaching transformation. Such change always brings with it some degree of upheaval; fallout from the evolution of shared perceptions about what is the most normal, adaptive, and successful kind of life. Changes in our work have sometimes abruptly, sometimes slowly, changed the rules regarding what makes for normal, successful adjustment, creating new standards of it. And, by contrast, of maladjustment.

Today's predominant orientation, shaped by contemporary work, is one in which people tend to view themselves as commodities or products to be sold to others, by presenting the most marketable appearance or image. It is adaptive to want to spend and consume material things, partly to fill up, psychologically, the emptiness that results from giving up parts of oneself in order to fit in and be approved of. Like all traits of a particular orientation, this one can be expressed in more or less rational ways. For example, a person can express the consumer trait through active, productive activity which results in pleasure; or in an indulgent, passive, or self-centered manner.

The current transformation which has given rise to the New Normalcy also brings with it a new range of conflicts and troubles that are normal to experience. Because normalcy refers to adaptation, and is not necessarily the same as emotional health, it provides a potential springboard into Modern Madness for the new careerist. This is because the unspoken definition of normalcy and successful adjustment in life now coalesces around that which best makes one into a successful careerist. If your attitudes and values conflict with this, you are in trouble. We have seen in previous chapters that some people's "normalcy" at work camouflages serious problems because the work "requires" sick and irrational attitudes. When people adapt to that kind of situation, they don't show any overt symptoms on the job. But they suffer deeply, inside. Their Surface Sanity is reinforced by career environments which make their disturbance functional and adaptive to success.

For others, a range of mild-to-severe emotional problems or value conflicts develop. Not because they are neurotic, but because their work environment is unhealthy or affects their emotional development in a negative way. The Working Wounded therefore suffer values conflict, overadaptation, and the work traumas of stress and anxiety. The conflicts that spring from this new set of norms are more a product of a clash of values, or overadaptation, than of unconscious, irrational passions. The conflicts are a part of the culture of our times, and do not reflect internal sickness. For people with these conflicts, like Yossarian in Joseph Heller's novel *Catch-22*,[3] their maladjustment is that they are sane.

Emotional conflict, then, can be a product of attempts to cope with the New Normalcy. Anxiety, depression, and other psychiatric symptoms can be a by-product of the experiences and situations facing the new breed careerists. For many, part of adjusting to the new realities means having to live with the conflict between achievement and fulfillment, which cannot necessarily be resolved satisfactorily, or at all. Part of the reason for unproductive or negative solutions to the more acutely troubling problems of the New Normalcy is the fact that the mental health mainstream doesn't understand the changes that are occurring, and are applying an obsolete view of normalcy to their treatment of the troubled careerist. But, more broadly, a central reason is the virtual absence of role-models and leadership—nationally, culturally, and in our institutions—that could help articulate the changes occurring and provide some examples, albeit imperfect ones, for navigating the uncharted waters that we are in. There has been no semblance of framework, no directions, no appeal to the positive elements of the New Normalcy that, as we will see, are present, but remain at low idle.

TWIN DESIRES

What are these positive elements, and why have they not emerged more forcefully? We have seen bits and pieces through the kinds of problems the careerist experiences and deals with while trying to become a winner in the career culture. In essence, this newly emerging standard of successful adjustment—a description of the new winners, in effect—is the desire for achievement plus fulfillment. To the new careerist, achievement means working hard and performing well, but with a sense of meaning and authenticity; and direct and undelayed recognition for excellence and quality, but with freedom from constraints on initiative and creativity. It is a hard-driving ambition to succeed, and to be well-rewarded for it. To be competent and creative, not solely in terms of one's personal batting average, without regard for how the team as a whole is doing—that's part of the old norm—but in terms of achievement which contributes to the group, and helps the team as a whole. It means working as part of a winning team but also having more pleasure, freedom, and opportunity to participate while doing it.

The other desire is for more pleasure, development, and fulfillment, not just from career, but from life in general. At work, this is seen in seeking and expecting opportunity and support for development of new competencies, new skills, in an atmosphere of trust, openness, and respect. And in expecting participation in decision-making, along with increased responsibility and authority.

But more broadly, the desire for fulfillment means combining success and achievement at work with more enjoyment, pleasure, meaning, and overall personal development. All within an atmosphere of tolerance, openness to working and living cooperatively with different kinds of people and lifestyles, and a sense of community. The positive side of the

New Normalcy also includes the desire to express and work towards
ideals, including concern for others, and living by values that are practical
and realistic, but which also have some depth of meaning.

In previous years, such strivings would have been perceived as unrealistic and naïve. And they still are, by older careerists past the transition
point of about 45–47. From these ages on up, I have found that careerists
share many of the same yearnings of the new breed, but are more resigned to limits and frustrations. They grew up to career maturity during
an era in which the person tended to accept trade-offs, frustrations, and
limitations as a given: a necessary part of a successful career. As one 54-
year-old executive said to me, "In my time, we felt lucky to get a good
position, or an opportunity in a good company. We accepted the hierarchy, the system, as is. We thought if we performed well and were loyal,
we would get our gradual promotions and rewards. The younger people
don't seem to feel any of that. They work hard, but they want to be
consulted about things that we never even questioned. And if they don't
get quick recognition, they leave." As a group, the older careerists don't
experience as much conscious conflict, because the New Normalcy doesn't
touch them as directly. As we will see later in this chapter, this blend of
success with fulfillment of the self has created new opportunities for
some but the potential for serious conflict for others.

The Yuppie Caricature.   Now what about all the selfishness and materialism which supposedly characterizes the new careerists—the yuppie
attitudes of self-indulgence, greed, and lack of concern for those who
aren't winners? The yuppie characterization is actually a caricature of
the negative side of the new-breed careerist. The negative traits of the
New Normalcy quickly grow when the opportunity for personal development, participation, and fulfillment is either absent, blunted, or insufficiently present in organizations and careers. Or, when the negative
potential is actually supported and encouraged by leaders within the
organization or in the political arena. It is not a coincidence that the
negative side of the new careerists that has been so visible has, in fact,
emerged in a period of encouragement of greed, concern for self at the
expense of anyone else, and of uncertainty and fear about the future.
All of these are part of the climate created by the Reagan administration's
illusion of supporting economic renewal by appealing to selfishness and
greed.

But the yuppies must be understood in the larger context of the
striving for success and fulfillment. In a sense, they are the direct de-
scendants of the hippies. They have absorbed the legacy of the '60s,
including the positive values of the counterculture; the anti-war, civil
rights, women's, and ecology movements; and sexual openness. They
take all of this for granted, and go on from there.

The yuppies have been misunderstood because they are a partial

picture of the new careerist, which reflects the negative traits that appear
when the positive are not supported. Many speak of hating their work,
because it is too dead-end, without sufficient substance or meaning, or
too bureaucratic. But they don't want to give up the benefits of a successful career. So it is understandable that some members of the generation of new-breed careerists develop attitudes of throwing concern
for others, for ethics, or morality, out the window. They have concluded
that these aren't relevant to getting ahead. After all, life is short, you
may lose out, the Bomb may drop. So what the hell. Go for what you
can get. Without support for their positive motives and ideals, the new
careerists opt for what they can get: using discretionary income to obtain
tangible, concrete things, hoping to eke out some pleasure and fun, even
if it is short-lasting or transitory, which it is. For some, the desire for
achievement and success has understandably become perverted into greed;
and the desire for fulfillment, into hedonism and escapism.

A New View of Achievement. In the attitudes and behavior of careerists
in our organizations and institutions, in both the public and private sector,
we see illustrations of the new view of success. The new careerist seeks,
overall, a deeper sense of meaning from work. And a more rooted life,
not so devoted to career as the sole purpose of existence. For example,
recent surveys find that people are much less willing today than in past
years to accept transfer and relocation in order to advance their careers.
Many report willingness to sacrifice, if necessary, career advancement,
or switch to a slower track in exchange for the greater rewards of an
enriched and more rooted personal life, including interests outside of
work. A common complaint from careerists is that they want to be able
to derive feelings of greater pride and satisfaction from their careers,
but that both are elusive. That the most desirable balance is to work
within an organization at something you enjoy, while having an active,
fulfilling life outside of work.

For a growing number of managers, this means working part-time.
Since 1976, the number of people working less than 35 hours a week
expanded by 63%.[4] For others, work provides opportunities to pursue
self-development. For example, some activists from the '60s are fusing
self-fulfillment goals with computer technology. They enjoy the appealing mixture of excitement and independence, the pleasure of working
in a field that rewards original and unconventional thinking, and being
on the leading edge of change. Creativity and flexibility are hallmarks
of these new career winners, and companies are beginning to realize the
benefit of nurturing these traits and attitudes. At a 1983 conference on
humanities and careers in business that drew heads of corporations from
all over the country,[5] several said that corporations should look more for
people who have a broader education in the humanities, which helps
them become more developed human beings, rather than those who are

trained only in engineering, finance, and marketing. This recognition has begun trickling down to the MBA level: at Stanford's Graduate School of Business, a course in business creativity involves study of Zen and Eastern relaxation techniques, to stimulate creativity necessary for business success. The underlying theory is that what makes some people more creative than others is their ability to overcome blocks to innovation.

Part of the desire for achievement and success at work involves wanting more from the work itself. This is seen in several ways. For example, the Opinion Research Corporation has found in attitude surveys that the new breed of managers and career professionals are increasingly dissatisfied with the companies they work for and the work they perform. Fewer like working in their companies and fewer said they would choose the company as a place to work again. The reason? They dislike traditional management systems. The younger careerists resist the traditional top-down decision making and the hierarchical structure of the typical organizations. Moreover, they perceive their companies as insufficiently responsive to their concerns. There is more than a communication gap between top management and the rest of the company. There is a values gap.

The increasing complexity of organizations, together with the multilayering which has come to characterize the bureaucratic hierarchy, turns off ambitious, action-oriented younger careerists. This relates to the shift in values among careerists. Older careerists developed more of an orientation to things like job security, pay, and benefits. The new generation of managers and professionals, from the mid-'20s to the mid-'40s, wants and expects much more involvement in decision making, greater meaning from work, and more opportunities for development. Having absorbed the legacy of the '60s, they do not hesitate to criticize people in leadership roles. One implication of this for the future of our organizations is that human resource executives will have to adjust to these changes by opening up lines of communication, delegating more authority, and insuring fair treatment of up-and-coming managers.

Where the younger careerist has found a more responsive environment is in high-tech companies. For example, the telecommunications industry, like cable TV and video games, and other service industries like publishing, appeal to them. As a group, careerists at the younger end of the spectrum—say, from the early 20s to the early 30s—show less corporate loyalty and more willingness to move to other careers or companies as opportunities open up. In particular, they believe that the paycheck is not the only reward. They want more time off and opportunities for personal development. They also want to know exactly where they stand in both their own job and in relation to competing peers. For them, this is an essential part of life on the fast track. In brief, they are talented, motivated people who are fighting hard to get it all, right now. The younger careerists grew up with prosperity and with new technology, with which they are quite comfortable, and not at all frightened. To them, concepts like corporate loyalty or job security seem like relics of the depression. One such careerist said, "I didn't grow up in bad times so I don't understand job security. I think I'm real good so I never worry about getting fired. All I worry about is winning."[6] These attitudes also include wanting to be viewed as an individual, but integrated with a winning team. For example, they often want performance ratings every six or eight months instead of every year.

The New Normalcy, revealed through changing worker attitudes, is steadily filtering into other industrialized cultures, too. An example is seen in Japan's fast changing high-tech fields, in which an increasing number of executives are experimenting with new management and organizational techniques, especially in areas demanding individual creativity which conventional management inhibits.[7]

The attitudes of the New Normalcy reflected in work also include the desire for work that is satisfying and allows for personal development on the job. Today's new breed simply doesn't have the lust to climb the corporate ladder that management recruits had twenty years ago. For example, a 25-year study of AT&T managers' careers found a significantly diminished desire for upward mobility.[8] In the 1950s, most of the managers were white males with homemaker wives. In the 1970s, half of the study participants were women, and one-third were minority members. They are more prone to question authority and pay less homage to higher-level positions. Some say that they came to realize that meaning and enjoyment were more important to them in a job than power and prestige. The new careerist wants to work to fulfill inner needs, as opposed to conforming to standards of the past.

As a result, a new definition of getting ahead has emerged, centered around meaning and enjoyment at work. The person is highly committed to the work he does, but less so to the company. Consistent with these new attitudes, several polls show that now both men and women rank attainment of a personal sense of accomplishment as the main reason for working, beyond supporting a family. The priorities of managers and professionals are shifting away from near-exclusive emphasis upon career to more emphasis upon one's private life and outside pleasures, as well.[9]

Related to this shift in the definition of getting ahead is the increased desire for rootedness. Census Bureau data show that for the past 25 years, 20% of the work force moved each year. But now, the number is dropping. Companies must deal with this new reality in their recruiting, training, motivating, and promoting activities. Managers and professionals want to remain in one spot. Many feel committed to dual-career marriages, enjoy community involvement, and are concerned about the quality of life. For example, a manager at Boeing in Seattle was offered a 30% raise by a Los Angeles company, but decided it wasn't worth it to leave the pleasant life and disrupt his wife's career. At the same time, some corporations are starting to believe that frequent moves for young managers are wasteful and disruptive. At IBM, where shifts have been common, the percentage of its 200,000 work force that moves each year has been cut to less than 3%, down from the 5% of the mid-'70s. And they plan further reductions.

Of course, two-career families are one source of the new rootedness: over 50% of all marriages involve dual careers. And when half of a dual-career couple gets transferred, the company often makes more trade-offs, helps them relocate, gives advice on housing, and assists with job prospects for spouses. Nevertheless, at a time when between one-third and one-half of employees are resisting transfer, there is more going on than just the reluctance of the dual-career family to move. This trend clearly reflects part of the evolution of a new orientation to life, based in part on the desire of career professionals to stay where they are, if they like it, and continue developing outside pleasures and interests. To them, it's worth more than a raise or a better-sounding title. The reduced mobility is greatest among those who in the past were most willing to move: the highly-educated professionals and managers. No longer are frequent transfers necessarily evidence of fast-track career success. Even when entire companies relocate, the new careerist may not.[10]

The Drive for Self-Fulfillment. The desire for achievement and success, redefined in the New Normalcy as a combination of competency with increased participation, more meaningful work, and opportunities for development on the job, is one-half of the twin desires of the new careerists, which represent the positive side of the New Normalcy. The other is the desire to reach beyond success, to a greater sense of personal fulfillment, and continued development of the self, in terms of one's values, spirit, and emotional experience. Not in the indulgent and ego-centric "self-actualizing" sense of the late '60s and early '70s, but rather, in more practical and concrete forms, which make room for relating to others with mutuality, respect, and cooperative, team-oriented attitudes. It includes a search for values and a way of life which have deeper personal meaning and stability in this fast-changing world; which reflects ideals that can be practiced and put to work in one's personal life.

In essence, the desire for more fulfillment is a quest for a more enriched inner life, with spiritual, though not necessarily explicitly religious, overtones. It also includes greater concern for health and exercise of the mind and body, and a search for greater freedom and creativity in life. For some, as we will see, this quest, like the desire for success, can become perverted into self-destructive channels, or lead to a dead-end street of escapism and hopelessness, a perversion which blurs self-indulgence with self-fulfillment.

The most striking part of the search for fulfillment is seen in the reaching out for new and positive values to live by. A search for a more active, honest, and pleasure-oriented way of life, in which both productive work and responsibility to others are embraced. It is akin to the kind of hedonism described by Aristotle: pleasure derived from the active use of one's powers and passions, as opposed to pleasure that results from passive consumption and taking in. A sure sign that there is a solid core to this quest is that even Madison Avenue has begun trying to tap this market. For example, some companies have begun altering their advertising message to yuppies, recognizing the inaccurate stereotype of materialism and selfishness. They see the positive elements of the new careerists that have been missed by the media caricature: untapped idealism, capacity for giving, and interest in involvement in issues outside of the next big purchase. An American Express executive commented that his company believes that the yuppies are "turned on by more than material possessions and will become the most public-spirited generation ever."[11]

One ad agency created a new coffee advertising campaign based on the theory that self-indulgent hedonism, which used to be the appeal of, for example, soda commercials, is out. The agency that produced the campaign found in a survey of young, career-oriented men and women that 80% wanted traditional lives, good jobs, close-knit families, and nice homes. In fact, 70% explicitly said that self-development is one of their long-term goals. Also, 85% said hard work paid off, and 86% expressed confidence in controlling their own destiny.[12]

Some elements of this shift were found in the early 1980s by pollster Daniel Yankelovich's public survey methodology. In *New Rules*[13] he reported evidence of the emergence of the desire for self-fulfillment. He found growing desire for deeper satisfactions, meaningful work, meaningful relationships, and having more concern for the quality of life than for piling up possessions. This theme has become more fully developed by the educated career professional class who are spearheading the New Normalcy: growing realization of the emotional cost of competitive status seeking, the desire to develop one's own goals and to seek greater creativity, leisure, autonomy, pleasure, and participation. This positive side of the New Normalcy has been largely overlooked by those who see only the self-absorption, hedonism, and narcissism of the yuppy caricature.

The emergence of self-fulfillment as a central part of the New Normalcy is sometimes hard to see because it can be masked by this negative side, which is also there. Or by unproductive, inadequate expressions of it, such as impulsive behavior, the appearance of breakdown of morality and standards of conduct, or illegal activity; all in a half-conscious attempt to experience greater aliveness and freedom in a world of topsy-turvy values and behavior.

We need to distinguish between unproductive behavior which is a symptom of the push for greater self-fulfillment, and degenerate behavior based on taking the easy path to self-indulgence and self-centered payoffs. The positive struggle toward self-fulfillment involves experimentation and struggle, but the values involved, such as greater meaning, responsibility, and active pleasure, are actually consistent with the positive tenets of the Judeo-Christian, the Islamic, and the Buddhist–Taoistic religious and philosophical traditions.[14]

This core of new values is not only found among male careerists, who have formed the bulk of the career work force, but also in the attitudes of contemporary career women, who are entering the ranks of management and the professions in increasing numbers. This value shift shows up in the struggle women report over the desire for both independence and self-fulfillment. This requires balancing the desire for freedom to compete in a male world, in which the woman has to prove herself, against the undermining, but understandable, tendency toward anger at men as a group. The career woman is often caught in a conflict between having to fight men to achieve position and success, and at the same time being tempted by a *Love Boat* fantasy of giving it all up for the ideal man.

Career opportunity is very central to the self-fulfillment desires of women. More then ever, American women think their place is on the job. Consistent with the New Normalcy, they regard work and independence as basic elements of life, as satisfying as husbands, homes, and children. In fact, men and women are growing closer in their attitudes about work. In 1970, 53% of women said motherhood was one of the best parts of being a woman. In 1983, only 26% did. Fifty-eight percent said they would want to work even if they didn't have to, and 59% think employed women are as good mothers as those who don't work outside the home. One said, "Being a wife doesn't say who or what you are." Eighty percent said to get ahead the woman must be better at what she does than a man. They rate independence and career choices as the best things about being a modern woman.[15] The growing numbers of women in the work force reflect not only the expansion of options available to women but also the possibility and the wish to fulfill more needs that are personally satisfying.

Another area in which we see the emergence of the desire for greater fulfillment in life concerns what both men and women want from a relationship. Part of the New Normalcy involves a shift of goals in relationships to more equality, respect, and mutuality: relationships which preserve individuality while deepening intimacy. There is a growing convergence of views around this desire by men and women. But at the same time, there is recognition that it is very hard or even impossible to achieve.

Single people show increasing commonality of views about love, sex, and expectations from a relationship. A major study of their attitudes found a marked decrease in casual or promiscuous sex over the last several

years. Many who were in the forefront of the sexual revolution of the
'60s question whether casual sex and its life-style are that great. Many
see it as a symptom of an empty life. And this trend began before the
herpes and AIDS scare. Also, singles at the upper end of the spectrum
of new careerists, in their 30s and 40s, value tradition, are fairly conservative in their social and sexual habits, and do not lead swinging,
permissive lives. What they want are monogamous relationships that
develop slowly.[16]

One consequence of this aspect of the New Normalcy is that new
issues are raised for people to deal with, for which there are no precedents
or rules. For example, many singles and formerly married men and
women feel unsure and insecure about dating. Single people who live
together show a desire for greater compromise, tolerance, flexibility, and
openness about problems, particularly around the issue of mutual desire
for successful careers.[17] And despite the shared attraction to monogamous relationships, people still commonly speak of anger, frustration,
desperation, and hard-heartedness. Men complain that women want them
to be both passive and strong. Men and women both complain about
self-centeredness that often affects the search for a high-powered career
along with a strong supportive relationship. Women say professional men
are too narcissistic and babyish, too influenced by power, and insufficiently capable of mutuality. Women also complain of the difficulty of
trying to develop caring and relating. That they find male careerists
arrogant, conceited, and leading empty lives in which career is placed
above all else. They don't want to go through the time and effort to
develop long-term relationships, so they go for the immediate and tangible thrill. They want to avoid the pain of failure. But most of these
same complaints are also made by men about women. Both dislike the
selfishness, overambition, extreme self-interest, and lack of satisfying
emotional life that limits intimacy and sharing.

Today, women commonly speak about men's lack of commitment—
that men come to the threshold of making a commitment but then back
off. Men are often perceived to be more frightened of permanent commitment than women because men confuse being independent with being
alone, and perceive relationships to be traps. But both men and women
share the fear of intimacy in an age in which strong emotions are feared
or numbed. They want to protect themselves from the pain of the eventual breakup which they perceive as inevitable. But the positive strivings
of the New Normalcy of relationships cause people to recognize
that the best ones are those in which individuality is supported and
encouraged.

One of the most prevalent fears among both men and women careerists is that they will be exploited, used for personal gain, and then
discarded; not unlike a strategy for career advancement. Part of the
negative side of the New Normalcy is a tendency to take and not give.
Highly educated and motivated to win, the new careerist often deals with

relationships in the same way he or she assesses and acts upon opportunities for career advancement. Some, of course, are disturbed inside, and may have been either deprived or overindulged in childhood, which has led them to unconsciously seek restitution for deprivation, or expect entitlement regarding their personal desires.

A symptom of this confusion is the growing trend of repeated remarriage, a kind of short-term bonding. There is often a flip-the-dial attitude which leads to a quick exit as soon as problems or boredom set in. Personal needs are put ahead of sharing and compromise. Though the person may rationalize that this attitude creates more chances to find the "right" partner, the ultimate result is diminished self-esteem, and feeling like a loser. It adds to the feeling that nothing lasts, and to a loss of faith in relationships.

Because of the desire for career success, it can be easy to ignore or postpone relationships. But this reflects a negative response to the lack of examples which illustrate greater fulfillment in relationships. There is frustration over how to combine freedom and independence with honesty and understanding. So given the absence of examples of happy couples, it is no surprise that the goals are often abandoned, though with bitterness, because male and female careerists all feel the push of the New Normalcy, to give concrete expression to the emerging consensus about equality and respect in relationships.

Finally, the desire for self-fulfillment also shows itself today in an explicit spiritual or religious quest which some careerists undertake. This is reflected in the resurgence of interest in religion and prayer in recent years, particularly among successful careerists, and shows a need for spiritual values that careers and fast-track, high-tech lives cannot supply. The renewed interest in prayer shows the growth of interest in an inner life that has greater depth and meaning. Many who undertake this quest speak of wanting to move beyond the superficiality they associate with a life limited to careerism, and to develop a sense of real meaning in their lives, beyond career success or acquisition.[18]

Radical career changes today, while rare, are usually a response to this search for greater self-fulfillment. People who have discussed their motives for such changes point to the growing awareness that there is more to life than money. They describe wanting more depth and meaning in their lives. One former accountant with a big corporation said, "I was frustrated. The more fulfillment I got out of making inspirational talks at civic groups the less fulfillment I got out of the job I was being paid for." And a former businessman said, "I chased success hard. But when I got to 40 I realized there is something more to life than what I had been chasing." A former millionaire stepped down from heading five corporations in search of a simpler and more fulfilling life. He and his wife moved into a boat in Key West and lived on money from odd jobs, scraping boat bottoms, carpentry, painting, and investment income. He said he, his wife, and family changed as they became more successful.

"We used to measure people by the money they had. People around us enjoyed drinking, big steaks, but they were phonies. I didn't want to be like them. I have a bigger life now."

Of course, the above examples sound more like the old-style "drop-out" of the '60s, in which the person moves away from productive activity. But the search for self-fulfillment which is part of the New Normalcy, when it leads to radical change, usually takes the form of maintaining productive work, but often in a different realm, in the form of something more meaningful to the person.

One example of an alternative which supports a life of more fulfillment and outside pleasures is found in an ex-Chicago lawyer who uses technology to combine city work with a life in the country. He moved to a town of 175, where he has an office linked to his Chicago office 200 miles away, by computer. He handles the same cases, and has the same phone number, so many clients don't even realize that he is not in Chicago. A nationally known food and drug law expert who has been with the firm for 26 years, he said in an interview that he doesn't miss the frills of city life and harbors no grandiose career ambitions. "I'm not as wedded to money as I am to the quality of life." His firm's only worry is that it may start a stampede.[19]

The blend of successful work with fulfillment and ideals takes a variety of forms. For example, an organization called the Creative Initiative Foundation in Palo Alto, California, has been attracting successful, intelligent, and wealthy people in their 30s and 40s who are willing to abandon lucrative careers in the Silicon Valley, site of the computer and electronics firms south of San Francisco. The Foundation deals with such problems as energy conservation, chemical contamination, and the nuclear arms race. It was founded and is directed by some affluent dropouts from high-tech firms, many of whom are on unpaid leave from high-salaried positions. One person said he and his wife got involved because they "realized we all follow a pattern, grow up, get married, get a career, have children, but somehow it doesn't all add up. The idea of meaning in life becomes important." The people working at the Foundation are encouraged to look beyond their daily concerns to the factors that threaten survival of the world, and to address mutual problems rather than just concentrating on personal gain. One person in his 50s said he had been so totally preoccupied with career that "I didn't even know I had been searching for something like this."

The desire for self-fulfillment is also found in the growing interest in assuming responsibility for one's own health and thinking of one's development in terms of the whole person, rather than isolating one area, like muscular fitness, meditation, or nutrition. There is a greater desire to move away from the passive, dependent attitude about health, and developing programs to maximize physical well-being. A physician who speaks of a link between disease and the way people live their lives, in terms of overeating, drinking, smoking, and inactivity said, "Normality is killing America." There is a growing consensus among medical researchers that much disease involves life-style choices.

The floundering and new conflicts that often accompany the search for fulfillment and greater meaning take several forms. Popular literature and the performing arts increasingly portray the tension between the desire for greater fulfillment and meaning, and the appeal of traditional values that contradict or inhibit that desire.[20] This dilemma, when experienced in the context of one's daily work, often leads to struggle and questioning. For example, work within the weapons industry increasingly bothers the conscience of some engineers. One man who used to design radar-jamming gear for B-52 and B-1 bombers, and parts for submarine-launched Trident missiles, decided to leave the field. The number of defense engineers agonizing over their work is growing because of concern over participation in weapons manufacture and the extent of the U.S. military buildup. One said, "Do I really add to peace and deterrence? Or is that just a sop to my conscience?"

The Wave of the Future.   The views of young people—those of college age and on the cusp of career entry—complement the theme of success and fulfillment found among 25- to 47-year-old careerists. The attitudes and goals of students are a mixture of strong determination to be traditionally successful combined with the desire for an opportunity to express ideals, though in a practical and result-oriented way. The image of materialism and self-preoccupation that seems so pronounced among youth are there, but they are really a response to fears of being closed off and excluded from lives as good as those of their parents. There is good reason for this: Data show that these young people's big brothers and sisters actually have less earning power than their counterparts did 30 years ago.[21]

Because of this fear and pressure, adolescents and college-age men and women share much of the same orientation to life as their parents. There is an absence of rebellion and hostility, coupled with a basically positive view of the family. No greater evidence of this can be found than in the preoccupations of Hollywood, which is always quick to pick up and capitalize on a social theme. The plethora of youth-oriented movies of recent years are light-years removed from the *Rebel Without a Cause* or *Easy Rider* genre of past times. With little to rebel against, today's youth are portrayed in movies as embracing—not rejecting—the materialistic, success-oriented life-styles of their parents. They want in, and fast. They don't want to waste their time or future on alternatives that may make them losers.

Of course, there is another side of this coin. For example, a study of children of senior-level executives of corporations with sales of $70 million or more shows that money and the perks of success buy them security and contentment, but at the expense of inner fulfillment, independence of thought, and a social conscience. These characteristics tend to be underdeveloped within them. These offspring feel weighed down and pressured by their fathers' ambition and success.

Typical college students demonstrate an acute blend of pressured ambition plus latent ideals. Surveys of college freshmen find them to be materialistic, though liberal on social issues like disarmament, women's rights, and integration. A total of 68% said a very important reason to attend college was to make a lot of money. This reason rose from ninth place in 1970 to number two. But ranked first was the desire to become authorities in their field of interest. Their conservatism is seen more in economic issues, like balancing the budget.[22]

Materialism and greed are there, all right; no question. Money is extremely important to today's college students. And they also have a tendency toward cynicism: They think everyone is on the make, and things are falling apart. Yet at the same time these students are filled with pragmatic idealism. They actually express more optimism about the future than older people. But fear of being left out, or losing out, is very strong. They are trying to cope with economic uncertainty, global instability, and fears about personal survival in an uncertain world, one in which a high level of education guarantees nothing.[23] One said, "In spirit, people agree with what the students were protesting in the '60s and early '70s, but they realize that mistakes were made in their approach. Now they're less absolutist. They want to be cooperative and work through the system." Another said, "If you want to change things, you have to work with those in power. There's a greater sense of realism, knowing that things are complex and that issues aren't so black and white."

So: Our college students today want tradition, stability, and security, combined with personal development and fairness in society. Thus, a 1983 survey by the American Council of Life Insurance and the Health Insurance Association found that young adults favor marriage over being single, frown on drugs, and would like to see more respect for authority. A large majority prefer a marriage in which both spouses share responsibilities for home and child rearing. A total of 56% said they approved of unmarried adults living together; 93% expressed the want for placing greater emphasis on traditional families.

Not surprisingly, worry about career opportunities leads college students to select more marketable, career-oriented courses, rather than the liberal arts. More are seeking professional training because they feel economic pressure to be highly marketable. This is seen most vividly at highly selective schools that offer both liberal arts and engineering. For example, both at large universities like Stanford on the West Coast and small colleges like Union on the East, the percentage of the student body seeking to study engineering and computer science has shot up several points over the last several years, compared with those seeking the liberal arts. Many traditional liberal arts departments like history have become, in effect, service departments to other majors. The downside of this development, of course, is abandonment of more genuine interests because of fear of being unmarketable. Yet another negative aspect of this trend is the premature narrowing of specialization—just at a time when corporations are beginning to realize the need for more broadly educated people among their ranks of managers.

Other examples of this pressure to get a head start on a career are seen in the trend of students who become entrepreneurs. They run a variety of businesses, providing goods and services, doing the marketing, making the financial decisions, and keeping the books. Some finance the business with their savings, while others use family money or get friends to invest. They believe they are helping insure a successful future for themselves. This reflects the view that large corporations will not provide the creativity, mobility, and enthusiasm they seek from work, a view that mirrors the one expressed by many already in the thick of their careers in large organizations, as I described earlier in this chapter.

Overall, both male and female young people are after the same goals regarding career and family life.[24] Only 3% of women students have aspirations similar to those of a decade ago—that is, traditional women's fields like teaching or social work. Male students now give a higher priority to child rearing and family life than their earlier counterparts. Over 90% of both males and females plan to get graduate degrees; over 90% of both also want to marry; and 88% want children. But 33% also say their career goals are not the ones they would like most to pursue. They end up compromising because of family pressure or of the difficulty of getting into graduate school.

Some of the emphasis on materialism and career among the young is a product of seeing the emotional effects of the broken marriages of their parents and the general economic and other uncertainties of our times. One young person, for example, wrote that people like him believe they have little to feel bad about. They want money and stability. Seeing former hippies having sold out, and having only vague memories of Vietnam, Watergate, and civil rights, they are looking for reasons to be proud of our country. But, he added, they don't lack compassion. They want, however, financial security, good jobs, and politicians who make them feel good as a kind of foundation for adult life. Beneath this mixture of self-oriented concerns and latent ideals, young people are frightened of a world that seems to them to be on the brink of careening out of control. So they want to make sure first that they are at the top, that they have taken care of themselves. Yet, at the same time, they want and hope for more.[25]

NORMALCY YESTERDAY AND TODAY

There have always been both positive and negative sides to our standards of adjustment in society, to what we accept as normal. Normalcy has changed and evolved along with our work and our standards of successful, well-adjusted lives. We must recognize that everyone who pursues a career in the United States must accept and be motivated by, to some degree, the values of profit, power, and position. These realities, including their good and bad consequences, are cornerstones of the American work experience. But it is difficult to analyze their role in our working lives, historically or in the present, because they raise very emotionally charged issues about ideology and values that are deeply ingrained in us. Therefore, these are difficult to see clearly, let alone critique. Moreover, it is difficult to examine power, profit, and position in a way that balances respect for making a fair profit within a free market economy with a fair distribution of wealth and social justice.

The dialectic between material pursuit, success, and accomplishment versus inner fulfillment and the development of ideals is a running theme through our history.[26] It plays a major, though overlooked, role in the development of our emotional attitudes and problems. The passions for profit, power, and position (and their more extreme forms: greed, domination, and selfishness) provide a potential springboard into social and emotional conflict, depending on how and to what ends they are expressed and channeled. This potential has been an implicit part of the ongoing debate about how the socioeconomic system of our and other societies affects human development. A rough distinction can be made between those who argue that selfishness and greed, when properly channeled through competition in a free market, create social wealth and benefits for everybody—the basic argument of neoconservative gurus like George Gilder and Michael Novak—and those who believe that greed and selfishness are undesirable human qualities, and lead to destructive competition, estrangement, alienation, injustice, and inequity.

Princeton economist Albert Hirschman shed some light on the relation between passions like these and our work in Western culture. He researched the prevailing ideas among the influential philosophers, moralists, and religious teachers of the seventeenth and eighteenth centuries, and their impact on the growth of capitalism.[27] He found that during those centuries a view evolved that the desire for money is more rational than, and can balance the desire for, passions like power and fame. It was believed that the latter passions were destructive to mankind, although a part of human nature. Furthermore, it was recognized that they were too powerful to be controlled by intellectual ideals or religious commands. Therefore, the only way to keep them in check was to balance them with another passion: the "self-interest" economic motive within a

market economy. Economic self-interest was anointed as, in effect, a new
passion that could balance the destructive passions of greed and glory.
And it did just that, because to pursue economic self-interest—money—
one is forced to be more rational. Binges of glory-seeking, blood-drink-
ing, and unbridled grandiosity tend to undermine that pursuit. According to Hirschman, the criticisms of capitalism—that it is alienating, creates
artificial values, and so on—are misplaced because these are exactly what
capitalism was intended to achieve.

The development of capitalism in relation to the experiences of
people regarding their work has also been studied by the eminent French
historian Fernand Braudel.[28] Emerging preindustrial capitalism, rooted
in overseas trade, became the great motivating and unifying force in the
development and spread of European civilization, and ultimately transformed the experience of life in Western civilization. Merchant capitalism
provided a civilizing function, and the acquisition of money established
the great merchant families who formed the social and political hierarchy
of the time. But that's not all capitalism established. It also created a kind
of consensus and standard as to what came to be perceived as "success"
in life. People whose talents, character, and attitudes were most adaptive
to the new merchant capitalism became the most successful in the emerging societies of Europe. The unspoken consensus regarding normalcy
and successful adjustment coalesced around the attitudes and behavior
of those who were most adaptive to the new system, to the changes that
were transforming society.

Standards of normalcy and success are a product of the kinds of
work that predominate within a society at any given time. Normalcy
reflects the standards for the most effective and efficient personal functioning that are generated by work and the existing economic framework.
This is seen more clearly by looking at how and why prevailing attitudes
about work, and what work means, have changed over the 300 years of
American history. Maccoby's analysis[29] found four different kinds of
work ethics that have prevailed in different eras of American history,
each of which represents the positive side (i.e., the ideals) of the dominant
social character orientation of the time. These four attitudes predominated because they were the most adaptive to the changing conditions
of technology and work in that era. The four attitudes, or work ethics,
were the Puritan (Protestant), the Craft, the Entrepreneurial, and the
Careerist.

The earliest work ethic, which developed in the initial colonization
period of America and lasted from about 1620 to 1700, was the Puritan,
or Protestant, ethic. It embodied the Calvinist and Quaker spirit of co-
lonial America, a time in which work was seen as a kind of religious
imperative, a vocation that combined a sense of productivity with purpose
and participation in "God's plan." Accordingly, it was marked by rigid
self-discipline and attitudes that were functional for success at the time.

The Craft ethic, which supplanted the Puritan, lasted until the early 1800s. It was, in effect, a secular version of the Puritan ethic. It was popularized by Benjamin Franklin, for the free-thinking craftsman. It represented the hoarding–productive attitudes necessary for success in the emerging craft and small business of the period. During this time, 80% of the work force was self-employed, either in farming or in some small business.

With the new dreams and opportunities created by the expansion of the frontier and the Industrial Revolution in the nineteenth century, a new work ethic emerged: enterprise, a race for fame and fortune. Individuals who were the most adaptive and successful in the post–Civil War era of expanding business were not those whose attitudes of caution and moderation led to success in the previous era, but those who had new attitudes of daring, speculation, and long-range vision. These attitudes made them successful entrepreneurs in the new era of mass production.

Our views about disturbance and successful adjustment follow a route that parallels the evolution of the work ethic. Medical and psychiatric textbooks from the 1700s and 1800s, particularly those written after approximately 1850 (a period which coincides with the growth of mass production and industrialization), defined and explained neurotic maladjustment in terms that reveal this link with changes in work and technology. Of course, early healers lacked modern knowledge about human development, irrational passions, and the effect of childhood difficulties. But they often expressed an intuitive, if primitive, recognition of how adaptation to work and to the way a society is organized to produce affect people's emotions and motivations.

A collection of descriptions of several thousand patients written by a British doctor in the early 1600s[30] reveals that only about 5% of his patients seemed to have psychological problems of the kind we see today. In contrast, current estimates indicate that about one-third of all patients who consult a physician for a physical problem have emotional problems. Of course, it is possible that cases of psychological problems were simply overlooked or wrongly diagnosed, given the state of psychological and medical knowledge of the time. But this picture also suggests that the kinds of emotional problems widespread today were relatively absent from preindustrial society. Not because it was any "healthier" back then; rather, the nature of work did not stimulate the kinds of conflicts and frustrations found today. Instead, it stimulated other kinds, related to the kinds of work and life situations found then. For example, most of the emotionally disturbed people, aside from those who were delusional, suffered from deep depression, much of which was probably a realistic reaction to the situation in which the masses lived.[31] The concept of disturbance gradually evolved and broadened to a view of emotional disturbance closer to how we think of it today. This occurred during the same period in which mass-production technology began to develop. Although cases of severe depression and psychotic delusion had been described since antiquity, the term "neurosis" was never even used until 1777, and then it only referred to what we now would call psychosomatic problems.[32] What we have come to describe as neurotic problems really began to be observed and described in the late 1800s, a period in which more and more people began to work for organizations that were increasing in size, and which culminated in the rise of the careerist work ethic around the turn of the century.

Up until the late nineteenth century, mental illness and "nervousness" were only dimly thought of as something within the mind.[33] Most practitioners lumped them in with physical illnesses. But one view—shared by some of the minority of practitioners who tried to understand neuroses in their own right—was that these "mind" illnesses related in some way to modern life. One practitioner argued that "city life" destroys mental stability, and several spoke of "railway neurosis," relating to both a fear of the new technology of the time and to the pressure to adapt to an increasingly business-oriented and organizationally-oriented work world.

The transition to a view of normalcy and maladjustment that was implicitly linked with work is found within psychiatric and medical texts written during the 1800s, as the Industrial Revolution built up steam. First, the impact of the environment, in general, began to be discussed in relation to people's problems. A British preacher who worked with disturbed people wrote in 1856 that insanity had to be a product of the dull, flat, and unvarying scenery around Cambridge;[34] and that a boring environment must be a cause of emotional problems. Daniel Tuke, the author of a widely accepted psychiatric textbook published in 1878, *Insanity in Ancient and Modern Life*,[35] attributed emotional problems to the haste of life in the railway age, an age in which people were busily pursuing commerce and personal gain. He added that in a "civilized community" of this type there always will be found, by far, the greatest number of insane persons.

Tuke and other authors of psychiatric textbooks from that period claimed that the increased incidence of emotional conflict was the result of the competitive spirit of modern civilization. According to these writers, defeat was inevitable for most competitors. Somewhat earlier, pioneering French psychiatrist J. E. Esquirol had written that emotional problems were the natural response of human nature to life's injuries,[36] which he defined as the stress of rapidly changing life in the Industrial Revolution.

Tuke's books on insanity in 1878 and 1885 stated that the largest number of insane persons will always be found in a civilized community. Was he on to something, without knowing what it was, exactly? Perhaps so: a theme emerging from Tuke's and others' books, and from case histories published during that period,[37] is that much of the emotional problems of the kind that today we call neurotic were related to the norms of successful work, and how well people adapted to them. One doctor stated that "over-study" and "business worry" produced more cases of emotional disturbance than any other source. Another attributed the depression of a young man to the "strain of preparing for the intense competition of business life." Also, an 1885 study of admissions to mental hospitals,[38] which listed the occupations of the patients, revealed that a majority worked for others in a small business or other organization. They were not self-employed craftsmen or farmers.

Case studies published in the late 1800s reveal that much of the emotional disturbance at that time reflected conflicts over adaptation to careers in growing organizations, and the feelings and conflicts they aroused. By 1894, Freud, in his early papers, was already starting to talk in terms of the core of neurosis being a defense against threatening inner feelings and fantasies—the hidden passions.[39] While Freud was concerned with wishes and impulses that are part of human development, such passions are also affected by circumstances and conditions outside the family that affect relations within it. For example, Fromm has shown how the two intertwine by describing how the Oedipal conflict was characteristic of the particular pattern of social relations in the late Victorian period. During this era, middle-class business activity provided the model of personal and social relations.[40] The male was the patriarch and the locus of power within the family, and the mother the nurturer and emotional provider.

ON THE DARK SIDE

The technology that was created and utilized by the individualist entrepreneur in the late 1800s made possible the development of complex managerial hierarchies of organizations, which became increasingly larger. And the result? The rise of the professional manager—the careerist—in the late nineteenth and early twentieth centuries, in both business and government. Beginning with this period the concept of the career ladder developed, and the hierarchy itself became the focus of a person's successful adaptation. This established the careerist work ethic, which has predominated throughout most of this century.[41] In this ethic, success is equated with adaptation to and upward movement within a hierarchical organization to positions of increasing responsibility and management authority. Such an ethic is intertwined with the kinds of emotional problems and conflicts today's careerists develop. These difficulties have arisen because the New Normalcy is ushering in a different work ethic, one centered more on personal development. In recent years, a combination of forces—the growing rejection of paternalistic authority, the demand for self-expression and rights growing out of the civil rights, the women's, and the antiwar movements, and the growing desire for a fuller emotional life—have nurtured this shift. This change in attitude is pushing against the constraints and limitations of the careerist work ethic that has dominated most of this century. The positive side of the twin themes of the New Normalcy—striving for success and self-fulfillment—are increasingly visible: tolerance for diversity of life-styles and racial—ethnic differences; a spirit of cooperation and flexibility; interest in personal growth; and willingness to experiment. But there is also a negative side, seen in unproductive attempts to achieve success and fulfillment, and also in such traits as self-indulgence, escapism, aimlessness, materialism, amorality, indifference to others, and lack of deep belief in anything. We see examples of this growing New Normalcy, its positive and negative sides, in all spheres of the lives of new careerists.

In this context, many psychiatric symptoms, such as anxiety and depression, feelings of guilt and self-betrayal, and lack of enjoyment of one's success, can be interpreted as a product of the struggle to deal with the New Normalcy and the problems it poses for the careerist. Part of the adjustment to the new realities means living with a degree of these conflicts, particularly those generated by the twin desires between achievement and fulfillment, which creates a tension which cannot necessarily be resolved satisfactorily under our present conditions in our organizations and society.

The values people acquire and develop as they learn to navigate through our large organizations can be destructive both to the economy and the individual, yet all the while being "normal," because they are functional, adaptive, and widely shared. An example in the realm of business is found in the orientation of most business schools to training people to focus on short-term profit. This creates more concern for the immediate benefit to one's own image and career than in developing competence for long-range growth and development of the organization. Today's managers tend to organize production and work under traditional systems that worked in the past, but are dinosaurs today.

Today, managers are more oriented to making money from fast-return investments, clever financial strategies, and speculation in commodities, all to the detriment of production competence. As one critic put it, "Managers are a frustrated breed in American industry. They don't know what they are doing and they know they don't know. They are caught up in a high-pressure swirl of events that prevents them from ever stopping the action long enough to get things sorted out so they can start doing them right."[42] Today, productivity depends on efficient coordination of people and information more than on equipment. Aloof senior corporate officers, too-large and too-layered organizations, and managers whose vision is narrowed to their own short-term interests, are all supported by business schools which teach specialized, overly narrow skills at a time when management requires the opposite. So here is an example of a standard for normal, successful functioning which also contains the seeds of disturbance, both for the manager, who knows better inside (yet is rewarded for doing what is good for his career in the short run), and for the organization, which suffers in the area of long-term stability and productivity.

On a more personal level, the emotional troubles of the new breed careerists are often a product of the negative side of normalcy, the downside of successful adjustment and adaptation to our career culture. But it can be difficult to understand that one can be troubled as a result of being normal. As we go through life, adapting to its demands and pressures, we tend to assume that our attitudes, priorities, and values in our work and lives are "normal" because they are widely shared by others. And that they are therefore unrelated to emotional troubles. But the new breed careerists inevitably experience conflict as they push against the limitations of the career ethic in the struggle to combine success and fulfillment.

Many people today, whether they have ever sought professional help or not, become troubled while struggling to deal with the link between their career success and their emotional lives. Some people develop emotional troubles and dissatisfactions with life because of the negative side of the New Normalcy which has developed within them.

In our current climate of economic crises, limits, and doomsday fears, the more negative side of the New Normalcy is strengthening. As I described earlier in this chapter, that is reflected in the yuppie stereotype: attitudes like wanting more for oneself, and to hell with everyone else; like cynicism; like the kind of pervasive semi-depression about life that infects more of us each day. This negative side of normalcy, and the attempts we make to escape from it are a product of the transformation now taking place within what makes up the most adaptive attitudes, desires, and behavior in our times. When the positive expression of this new orientation cannot find outlets or support from leadership, work organizations, and institutions, the negative side blossoms—attitudes of self-indulgence, self-marketing, aimlessness, shallowness in personal relations, interest in giving by not getting, escapism, and lack of deep convictions.

We have seen that the emerging New Normalcy is marked by a strong, though often thwarted, sense of ideals, of caring, of compassion for others, and desire for ethics and values which are based on something more meaningful than selfishness or greed. But as the new careerist waits for leadership, for examples and support in this direction, the negative side can develop. And the negative side is also strengthened by the standards of success which support over-concern for power, position, and profit, as well as appearance and self-inflation.

The new breed careerists who develop emotional troubles today are more likely to be suffering from problems which originate in this negative side of normalcy, rather than from a childhood-based neurosis. Many of the careerists within the normal range whom I studied spoke of feelings of inner emptiness, of no solid self, no values that mean anything anymore, no leaders that they felt inspired by, and no overall vision about life beyond the immediate moment. A kind of perverted existentialism, in which we become victims of ourselves—what Sartre called "bad faith."[43] Some have recurring dreams in which they look into a mirror and see nothing.

How do most of us attempt to deal with this part of the New Normalcy? Primarily, through the orientation of consumerism. Losing ourselves in seeking (then discarding) new possessions, new experiences, new people. The desire to acquire things or fill up on quick, disposable pleasures—like emotional junk food—is something we all engage in to some extent. We all seek quick relief from the inner emptiness that goes along with being normal in our times. Of course it is adaptive and normal to want to consume material things. But the negative potential of this develops when consumerism takes on a driven quality and serves as compensation for the emptiness that results from regularly giving up or betraying parts of oneself in order to be approved of, fit in, and acquire success. This is most visible in the consumer traits of the yuppie.

There are different ways in which we do this. Some describe their main diversion from inner emptiness as a search for new electronic or video gadgets to turn them on, or consuming new and constantly changing experiences in order to "get" more aliveness. Others indulge heavily in escapist drinking, cocaine, or endless TV watching to try to fill up their inner emptiness or numb their awareness that they have given up too much of themselves while grabbing hold of the American dream and hanging on for dear life while it whips them down the fast track. And others take hold with fervor a religious or political ideology from which to obtain some inner solidity, conviction, or spiritual excitement. One man, a heavy-drinking journalist whose real life came closest to the literary persona of Hunter Thompson of anyone I have ever met, told me, "My friends and I all lead 'diversionary lives.' And we know it. But you got to go for it while you can, you know? Tomorrow it may be all over."

Consuming things and transitory pleasures to the degree that they begin to dominate and take over one's life numbs the reality of feeling empty or deadened inside: the reality of semi-depression which increasingly plagues us all today. These attitudes and behavior all reflect the negative side of the shifting standard of normalcy. The people who become more openly troubled feel these conflicts more acutely, by virtue of either the makeup of their character orientation or their particular situation.

Thus we hear complaints like John's. He works for a congressman in Washington, and is caught up in the whirl of activity, glamour, and party-going that characterizes much of Washington's culture. Twenty-eight and already twice divorced, with children from both marriages whom he seldom sees: "I know there's something pretty empty about wanting to be turned on all the time, then getting bored. But I don't know what to substitute for it. I just want to consume things, take things in. It's pretty shallow to live this way, I know. But sometimes I feel I can't create anything or give much to anyone, that I'll never change."

In personal relationships, the downside of the New Normalcy is seen in dealing with people in the mercantile, selfish terms of profit and investment. While complaining about the lack of real intimacy or love in their lives, the troubled careerists also speak, in the same breath, of "investing" emotion in people and calculating the expected "return," like a human money market fund. Or, they find themselves appraising their potential partners not in terms of shared goals, values, or capacity for feeling, but in terms of a checklist of appearance-oriented traits, much like the accessories on a new car. And often the underlying concern is how much the prospective partner will aid or hinder their career ambitions.

This reflects an emotional attitude toward people that they are objects to be possessed and consumed for personal pleasure, then discarded when used up, like throwaway cans. Issues like trust or commitment raise too much discomfort, and so are avoided. At the same time, awareness of the shallowness and limitations of these attitudes is very close to the surface. The careerists, pushed on by the emerging New Normalcy, feel very self-critical and often guilty about the quality of their relationships and friendships. Not surprisingly, there is a price for these "normal" attitudes about relationships. It is found, for example, in the complaints of being unable to love anyone, of feeling guilty exploiting people, of a lack of real interest in everything and everyone, which they force themselves to mask over each day.

The negative side of the New Normalcy can also lead to escape as well as to unproductive or destructive solutions. Many people, unable to find the key that unlocks greater meaning, or, lacking the capacity, discipline, support, or opportunity, turn the corner onto the Boulevard of Blue Dreams: a realm of passivity, unhappiness, and disconnection. Many become one-dimensional computer-age casualties, scared of feelings and fixated on minute concerns of the present, to avoid a sense of guilt or anguish over unlived lives.

Some become near-caricatures—people who are severely unconnected, bland, alienated, passive, and uncommitted to anyone or anything. They no longer strive for meaning. Some casualties of the search for meaning have lost their dreams and abandoned their plans. They often become drawn to escapism or illusory meaning—perversions of the quest. Often highly intelligent and narcissistic, they are unable to be related to others in a mutual way. Theirs are vacant lives, drowning in their own emptiness, and often wasted by affluence and indulgence. These people, living on the dead-end streets of the 80s, have become the subject of some contemporary novels, which portray lives adrift and trapped, filled with doubt about everything and unable—or uninterested—in pursuing anything that has meaning beyond the immediate moment.[44]

The winds of the New Normalcy are sweeping across our landscape, affecting career attitudes, people's views about the quality of their lives, relationships between the sexes, and the goals of youth. Many people develop troubles rooted in this emerging new orientation to life, which is now pushing against the old career-based standard of normal adjustment. As this rumbling within people's hearts and minds becomes louder, pressing for clearer and more defined expression, and flinging psychological debris around like an emotional earthquake, it is understandable that we find some people feeling that they lack an inner core, that they have no solid self, no values or dreams that mean anything anymore.

These conflicts of the talented, motivated, new breed careerists are the by-product of mounting tension between what they have to do to be career winners, and the growing internal demands for fulfillment and self-development. There is a high probability that a person who decides to seek professional help because of conflicts generated by this sea change will encounter a practitioner who has an obsolete view of normalcy. One that is grounded in social and psychological realities that fit a rapidly disappearing age. But the practitioner does not realize or understand this, because of the isolation and narrowness—intellectually, emotionally, and culturally—of the mainstream of mental health practitioners. The practitioner is likely to fail to comprehend the meaning of problems that are linked to the emergence of a new form of normal adjustment, and fail to help the person deal with those problems, no matter how intensive the treatment; or, if he is medication-oriented, no matter how many tranquilizers or mood-stabilizers he prescribes.

In most people's lives, and in most organizations, the push towards the New Normalcy has not yet found sufficient positive expression and support. Without relevant help or available opportunities, many end up feeling incapable of changing or struggling with anything. So they opt, instead, for getting what they can, while they can. And for indulging themselves with disposable pleasures. But they feel frustrated and stuck, alienated and confused. They want to change, but don't know how.

SHRINKING THE SHRINKS

7

*I think of my psychoanalyst friends . . . they are working
with torsos and decapitated heads. In Aesculapian times
man was still a whole being. He could be reached through
the spirit. Today not even the greatest psychoanalyst can
restore to men what they have lost. Each year there ought
to be a congress of analysts meeting at Epidauros. I
would give them first a month of complete silence . . . I
would order them to stop thinking, stop talking, stop
theorizing. I would let the sun, the light, the heat, the
stillness work its havoc. I would order them to listen to
the birds, or the tinkle of goat bells, or the rustle of
leaves. I would make them meditate not on disease but on
health, which is every man's prerogative.*

– Henry Miller

*We must not forget that psychoanalysis is based on a love
of the truth—that is, recognition of reality—and that it
precludes any kind of sham or deceit.*

– Sigmund Freud

There is an irony attached to that Freud quote. Though legitimate criticisms can—and have—been made about some of Freud's theories and interpretations, his views about the kinds of people who should become psychoanalysts and what they should do with their patients to help them sounds refreshingly radical, almost like heresy, when contrasted with what you hear from practitioners today.

And there is an additional irony about contemporary psychoanalysis in general. At a time when public interest, at least among the career-professional class, has been swinging back to psychoanalysis as the most solid means of understanding and dealing with our problems, the mainstream of psychoanalysis is less able than ever to help with the kinds of problems people seek help for today. The major reason for this is found in the kinds of people who become analysts and other mental health practitioners today, how they differ from the pioneers of Freud's time, and how these differences affect what they do with troubled people who enter their offices.

The difference between practitioners of yesterday and today, in combination with the shift in the kinds of problems people suffer from related to work, and the consequences of the New Normalcy, result in the reality that patients today are often not helped at all. And sometimes their treatment makes them more disturbed than they were to begin with. Practitioners, whether originally trained as psychiatrists, psychologists, or psychiatric social workers, often just don't know what they are dealing with when people enter their offices. This is because their own character, values, ambitions, and life experiences have combined to render them ill-equipped both to understand the source of contemporary troubles and to know what would help people deal with them. Specifically, the mental health mainstream tends to be ignorant about what goes on in a person's life context, the daily world of careers and organizations, and how that affects the person emotionally. It has difficulty grasping the fact that our work and careers affect our emotional lives in ways that are far deeper and more complex than they think. It is not just a case of understanding that neurotic or psychotic problems interfere with performance of job duties, or that some people experience a mounting up of burnout and stress. One reason for this ignorance is that too many of the people who become practitioners today are, like some of their patients, careerists who fear examining their personal values, decisions, and assumptions too closely, because of the conflict it might stir up.

As a result, practitioners have lost that penetrating, truth-seeking spirit Freud spoke about. Some become, in the process, comfort-seeking and complacent people whose prime interest is using their trade to make a fairly lucrative and easy living. And others are compassionate people who are genuinely motivated to help, but are too soft-hearted to grasp and deal with the emotionally-charged realities and painful choices of patients' lives. They are sensitive to human suffering, but don't really understand what life is like for their patients in the outside world, mainly because of a lack of personal experience with it.

There are, of course, practitioners whose sensitivity, understanding, and skill have immeasurably helped many troubled and suffering people overcome their disturbances and develop happier, symptom-free, and more productive lives. But there are also those who are unable to understand or help their patients because of the kinds of people they are, how they are trained to think, and what they actually do with patients behind the closed door.

THE SPIRIT OF THE PAST

The psychoanalysts of Freud's time had a more radical spirit. A willingness to penetrate into the underlying truth about a person's motives and relationships, their unconscious wishes, attitudes, and passions, which reveal themselves through outward symptoms, dreams, slips of speech, and in our daily behavior. Freud thought in terms of a central truth operating within a troubled person, and that with help we can face and experience it, once we realize that it is human to weave illusions and rationalizations to hide it from ourselves, to project it upon others, or to distort it to avoid pain or the burden of responsibility for the way we are.

Some examples would be a deep desire to stay attached to mother, to remain a protected and secure baby. Or a desire to rebel against and destroy father; or a passion for greed, conquest, subjugation; or for cheating and using people.

As Freud described it, analysis involved a commitment to strip away the sham, deception, and illusion which can distort and pervert reality in any area of life, individually, socially, or politically. He attacked the illusions we create about our motives and intentions, and recognized that there is a core of irrational potential within us all: a "cauldron of passions," as he put it. With a directness and simplicity that would put today's detached and overintellectualized practitioners to shame, he said that neurotic symptoms conceal our hatreds, our disappointed ambitions, our guilt over evil intentions, as well as our reproaches against all these things. And that taking responsibility for the truth about ourselves would "require people to be honest, confess to the instincts that are at work in them, face the conflict, fight for what they want, or go without it."[1]

Much straighter talk than you would ever hear today from most analysts. The early analysts were pioneers by necessity: The field required people to be adventurous enough to explore the uncharted terrain of character development and unconscious motives. And courageous enough not only to withstand tremendous ridicule from the general public and fellow scientists, but also to risk ruining their careers by calling attention to the effects of repressed sexuality.

And what was the benefit of liberating the truth? Overcoming misery and suffering, and, ultimately achieving fuller human development. By the latter Freud meant growth of the "heart," like love, truth, reason, and the development of responsibility and independence. Development also includes the capacity to be more fully alive and awake: engaging life with spontaneity and passion. These, of course, are ideals. Few human beings are saints or models of perfection. But as ideals they represent a focus and direction for guiding one's development, emotionally, spiritually, and morally.

But something happened along the way. You don't hear much talk of passions, ideals, or values anymore from practitioners. It's considered irrelevant to analyzing childhood trauma so that the patient may "cope" or "function" better in our world; or irrelevant to satisfying the checklist of "needs" that the pop psychologists write so glibly about.

I recall a discussion several years ago with a well-known senior psychoanalyst in Washington who was supervising a group of us on our cases. One of us asked him about the motive of greed in the emotional problems of a case we were discussing. He suddenly became very agitated, started squirming around in his chair and shouted, "Greed? You mean G-R-E-E-D, GREED? You don't know the most elementary things about neurotic theory!" He then proceeded, flush-faced and sweating, to give us a condescending lecture, filled with sarcastic put-downs, about Oedipal conflict and orthodox psychoanalytic theory.

Many of today's practitioners are, themselves, well-adapted career-ists. But adaptive to the norms and ideology of the profession, not to an organizational culture, since they don't work for organizations. Thus they have become uncritical supporters of an ideology of social adjustment; adjustment to conventional values and norms of a world which is rapidly disappearing. Too often they collude with patients to make minor ad-justments here and there, exploring the relationship with father and mother ad infinitum—or, perhaps, ad nauseam—but without analyzing what might really be wrong with a patient's emotional life, especially if it would require analyzing their adult motives, their responsibility for the situations and values they have adapted to, and its emotional con-sequences for them.

So what has happened? The kinds of people who become psycho-therapists and psychoanalysts today are no longer interested in uncov-ering the kinds of truths which can really help people do something about their problems. Instead, they have a view of coping and adjusting, in which helping the person adjust to external circumstances is equated with health. So they spend years ferreting out tiny truths, minutiae about childhood, to help the person adjust better to adult reality, with less complaint. Often the patient learns a great deal about early experiences with father and mother, toilet training, and other issues while remaining as neurotic as ever.

Another important difference between the early years and today is that the earlier analysts were more well-read, and liberally educated in literature, history, and culture. More curious and respectful of life's miseries and ironies that people have always struggled with. They were able to help their patients more than their counterparts today because of their awareness and understanding of the human passions and con-flicts that have been expressed through the literature, art, music, my-thology, religion, and philosophy of the major civilizations.

Freud's writings were grounded in this. He quoted freely from Shakespeare, Goethe, the classics, and other works of literature, drama, and mythology. He used their themes, plots, and character portrayals to illustrate and illuminate the motivations, unconscious strivings, and moral dilemmas underlying his patients' neuroses. For example, he drew from his knowledge of Sophocles' version of the Greek tragedy *Oedipus* as the basis of what he interpreted to be a universal feature of the male child's relationship with his mother and father. Few, if any, practitioners today even know the story of the Oedipus drama, let alone have read Sophocles. Many would probably have trouble identifying who Sophocles was, or describing the themes symbolized in any of the Greek tragedies. Yet they present themselves to the public as experts in understanding people: the complexities of motives, passions, and workings of the heart.

Many practitioners today are basically technicians. They are ignorant of and disinterested in the actual conflicts and passions of people, like those portrayed by such writers as Shakespeare, Balzac, Ibsen, or Dostoyevsky. And they are ignorant, as well, of the themes expressed in major religious writings of the Old Testament, the Christian mystics, the Buddhist, Taoist, and Islamic traditions, all of which describe a core of human experience, including sources of emotional suffering. Overall they are ignorant of the philosophical, religious, and cultural traditions, as well as of the socioeconomic history of our civilizations. Yet all of this has profoundly influenced how and why we think and behave as we do, including, as we saw in the last chapter, our views of what is normal and what is disturbed—views which have changed over history.

The original concern of Freud and his followers was alleviating the misery of clear-cut neurotic symptoms like hysteria, phobias, obsessions, and compulsions, whose source was repressed childhood conflict. But after Freud, analysis became more ideological, abstract, and technical; and it was removed from the immediate emotional experience of its patients. And at the same time, the nature of people's problems was changing. Some analysts recognized this and attempted to keep their focus on understanding and helping the patient. But most did not.

From the end of World War II and into the 1950s, psychoanalysis was thought by the educated and increasingly affluent managerial and professional middle class to have the answer to personal unhappiness and the desire for increased social adjustment. The symptoms present in Freud's time had diminished. Patients now sought help to understand how their early childhood frustrations interfered with and limited their social adjustment: their desire to conform. They sought help in dealing with, for example, rage, guilt, inhibition, and need for approval. In resonance with the times, they didn't enjoy acting or feeling too different from others, but they felt conflict over their conformity, and often fantasized or dreamed about being free from what Hugh Hefner, founder of *Playboy,* has called "controlled environments." This was often depicted in popular literature and movies of the time, such as *The Man in the Gray Flannel Suit.*[2]

Then, from about the mid-'60s through the early '70s, in the context of an explosion of social and political ferment, many people sought help in "liberating" themselves from oppressive relationships, social conventions and institutions. Unfortunately, as many people later realized, this often led to exploitation, ruined lives, chic radicalism, and ultimate bitterness over the fruits of liberated attitudes.

Later in the '70s people's problems began to focus around their growing desire for personal success, especially at work and career. Interest grew in developing successful winning strategies, and learning how to adapt successfully with a minimum of conflict—at least consciously. How to mold behavior, appearance, and overall image into maximum personal and material success. One legacy of this period was a turning away by many people from the traditional, detached, passive, silent analyst. People now wanted quick action and results to help them become winners before they lost out. The rise in popularity of all the "how-to" books, focused on winning and looking out for "No. 1," reflected this.

Along with the evolution of people's problems, there has been a movement away from the radical penetrating and liberating spirit of early psychoanalysis, and toward stagnation and retreat into conformism and respectability. The latter tendency was always dormant within the psychoanalytic movement. After all, Freud himself was rooted in all the prejudices and ideology of his historical period and class. A Jew living in Victorian times in anti-Semitic Vienna who entered medicine because his first choice, law, was barred to Jews, Freud was a patriarch who accepted urban bourgeois culture as the most fully developed and rational possibility for civilized people. This led to the orthodox ideology that took root after Freud's death,[3] and which is espoused by analysts who have become compliant careerists sharing in, rather than critiquing, the social norms, values, and anxieties of our times.

So as analysis and the various psychotherapies it spawned (an NIMH study estimates that there are over 250 different psychotherapies on the marketplace) became more accepted, respected, and absorbed into the mainstream of culture, its practitioners became more technique-oriented and narrow people working at a job. The original spirit and focus on the workings of human passions got lost as the mental health practice evolved into a conservative, comfortable, career path.

Today the field no longer attracts the numbers it used to, nor the sharpest, most imaginative, creative minds from psychology, medicine, or social work. For example, only 4% of medical school graduates currently choose to enter psychiatry, which is an all-time low. The response of the profession has been to market itself better, promote a better public image of psychiatrists, improve recruitment techniques, etc., all of which look at the problem as one of advertising or packaging, rather than as something that needs some work on the inside. Non-psychiatric physicians and non-clinically trained psychologists tend to view psychoanalysis and psychotherapy as low in status, low in efficacy, and selected only by their more fuzzy-headed and neurotic colleagues. In some quarters there has been a recent trend to focus more on the biological and drug aspects of treatment, probably because the latter appeals to practitioners who feel they aren't doing anything of value, or who fear their own irrationality which might get aroused in the course of helping patients in a therapeutic relationship.

Today, those who do become analysts uncritically equate social adjustment—outward success, functioning without complaint, and acceptance of conventional values like power-seeking, with mental health. They assume that all conflicts a person has are based in childhood. They don't understand that there is a normal range of character adaptation which is different from childhood-based neurosis. And that adaptation has problems of its own for the contemporary careerist.

The spirit of early psychoanalysis applied to today's world would require a critical and penetrating attitude toward values, and toward any social situation which has the potential for warping or deforming a person's attitudes and emotional development. It would recognize that a person can repress not just the memory of early childhood conflicts, but also adult experiences such as self-betrayal, criticisms of self and of one's situation, impulses to be more free, more alive, or loving. We saw in Chapter 4 that emotional problems can be a product of values conflict, overadaptation, or negative coping. This is the price paid for too much adjustment to a bureaucratized and careerist, consumer society—to work which limits rather than stimulates more responsibility and fulfillment. All of this causes alienation, escapism, fears of feeling deeply, inner emptiness, anxiety, depression, and other symptoms of the New Age, which the analytic mainstream doesn't realize has arrived at our doorstep.

The Catch-22 is that therapists are, themselves, examples of all these traps. Many not only fail to see the forest because of the trees, but often can't see beyond the branches and twigs. Look, for example, at how the career of a therapist or analyst develops, and what it leads to. He or she usually goes directly from college to medical or graduate school, then to post-degree training, and then to treating patients. Often in a clinic or hospital at first, and then, gradually, into private practice. Around that time, he or she may also begin some advanced training and some teaching and supervision of younger colleagues.

Notice something: Throughout this process the person has had little, if any, experience with life in the outside world. Virtually no interactions with the diversity of people and their lives outside of the doctor–patient relationship. And what does this sequence of training prepare the person for? Mainly, personal career development: using acquired skills and "tools" to make a secure and comfortable living. They end up complacent, often more interested in understanding their investment portfolio than in understanding their patients' lives. I have heard some of the more cynical therapists make jokes about how this patient has paid for the new Mercedes, that patient, the beach house, another, the skiing trip to Zermatt.

Another dimension to the therapists' lack of experience with the outside world which creates a severe limitation upon their abilities to help people is their lack of exposure to the working world, particularly that of large organizations, in which most patients work. The typical practitioner seldom leaves his or her office and has never worked for organizations, particularly as a subordinate part of an administrative hierarchy. Practitioners confine their personal interactions to their treatment hours, in which they are the boss. People come to see them, and they set all the conditions and the rules. While there is a rationale for the latter related to conditions that enhance the bringing forth of the patient's inner experience, it also helps distort the practitioner's view of his power and role in relation to the outside world.

If the practitioner has worked for an organization at all, it was a hospital or clinic, and usually as a student or while building a private practice. So in addition to being high on the totem pole to begin with, as "The Doctor," working in a hospital or clinic is usually a stepping-stone to the boss-free work of private practice.

It wasn't until I began to leave this comfortable but limiting atmosphere of The Office—its green plants, subdued lighting, and Oriental rugs, that I discovered an interesting irony: Most practitioners have less knowledge and "street smarts" about the outside working world and how it affects people—its realities, pressures, politics, conflicts, and limitations—than do their patients.

The consequences are damaging to the practitioners' treatment of patients, and to their own sense of reality. For example, therapists often naïvely assume that a person who is a mid- or upper-level executive can simply alter his or her job duties at will, shift to another part of the organization, or to a different superior, if this is desirable to alleviate pressure or reduce stress which may be aggravating an emotional problem. I have heard therapists say their patients are "resisting" treatment when the patient explains that this cannot be done so easily, if at all.

In other cases, private practitioners treating patients who have suffered a breakdown requiring hospitalization have called the consulting psychiatrist or psychologist at the patients' place of employment to dictate what type of work situation the patient must be reassigned to in order to aid the therapy and expedite a return to work. They become incredulous and suspicious when they are told of the organizational obstacles and difficulties involved. But most patients, even if psychotic, could probably have explained that.

The upshot of all this is that therapists are very mixed up when it comes to understanding the difference between problems that originate in the person versus those caused by a situation that is bad for them. Having little, if any, personal experience with the working world, practitioners don't understand it. They are trained to interpret all conflicts and symptoms as being based in childhood. Within that view, any healthy person would be well-adjusted to his or her work and not experience conflicts about it to begin with. Another Catch-22. And one consequence is that both therapist and patient end up avoiding emotionally inflammatory issues or conflicts about the patient's ambitions, values, and motives in the here-and-now.

There are always different possibilities, many questions that can be explored. But this doesn't sit well with the patients (or practitioners) who want something quick, slick, and definitive. After all, if you have a sore throat you want the doctor to know what's causing it and give you something to make it go away. Therapists and analysts are trained to be able to always come up with a plausible diagnosis and formulation of a patient's conflicts. The problem is, these formulations are often so theoretical and abstract that they don't relate very well to the emotional reality of people. But they help us mask the vast amount we simply don't understand about the problems people experience. One can read an article which uses patient case material in most any psychoanalytic journal and come away without any notion of what the patient actually experienced, or what actually occurred during the treatment sessions.

The more orthodox analytic treatment methods help only a very small fraction of troubled people. The irony is that some practitioners themselves admit this. For example, in Janet Malcolm's book about the New York City psychoanalytic establishment, *Psychoanalysis: The Impossible Profession,*[4] a typical analyst is quoted as acknowledging this, and adding that he thought most patients changed only "a few degrees" this way or that, even after years of treatment. This was certainly true in his own case. After years and years of orthodox psychoanalysis he was still very neurotic: He had very babyish attitudes about his relationship with older colleagues in his professional organization, and was too nervous and inhibited to speak in front of groups.

With people like him as practitioners, no wonder there is a turning away from the traditional "talking cure" in some quarters. Because of therapists' poor knowledge of human, social, and political affairs, their interest in understanding what the patient actually experiences and struggles with is also limited, often to thinking of the patient in terms of a disease entity or a symptom cluster. I find that many are simply not very interested in understanding people, their experience of life, their aspirations, their conflicts—what it is like to be them.

A report by the National Council on Medical Education of the American Medical Association expressed a similar criticism about the training of physicians. It charged that medical schools stuff students with so much detailed, technical information that they end up churning out detached technocrats who can't understand the patient as a human individual, but rather as a collection of separate, unrelated parts. This seriously affects their ability to diagnose and treat illnesses.

Medicine today is focused more on disease entities, than on the patient. Young doctors who lack experience or a heart rely too much on technology to get by. But students themselves are starting to react against this. (Remember, they are part of the new breed of careerists, seeking greater self-fulfillment.) They find medical school, internship, and residency very dehumanizing. Many complain that they entered their training with compassion for the ill, and find that what they are taught is cold, inhumane, incomplete, and detached. They see harm to the patient resulting from an absence of personal caring. One can also say that medical education has failed to help the student deal with feelings of being responsible for casualties, and that this is one source of the alcoholism, drug addiction, and depression the students are often prey to. The training experience can push the student into a self-imposed isolation from experiences that help them develop the values and perspectives essential for them to become caring physicians, not to mention interesting, alive people.

All of this can affect the diagnosis, proper treatment, and recovery of the patient. For example, residents and interns at hospitals increasingly make serious errors in these areas, often because of inadequate physical examinations and too much reliance on equipment and machines to make diagnoses.[5]

Lewis Thomas, in his book *The Youngest Science: Notes of a Medicine Watcher*,[6] said that the healing arts have become a technology since about the time of the development of antibiotics in the 1930s. Technological achievement has fostered a diminished role for the doctor, who cares less and less about what it feels like to be a patient. Similarly, C. P. Snow, the British scientist, novelist, and government official, said in his discussion of the "two cultures" that it is important for the scientific, technological community and the literary, artistic one to have a degree of knowledge of each other. He was concerned about the possibilities for distortion and perversion of the individual who is warped by one area, particularly in the area of power. In one of his novels, *The Masters*,[7] he says, "I want a man who knows something about himself and is appalled and has to forgive himself to get along."

I have discussed at some length the issues affecting the kind of people who become physicians because they mirror the experiences of psychiatric, psychological, and psychoanalytic training as well. In fact, the same issues exist in other areas of professional career training. For example, in the business world we find increasing recognition of the consequences of failing to take the long-range view and consider longer-range possibilities, when making strategic decisions. Such failure has a direct negative impact on long-range economic productivity, though it may make the short-term earnings statement and the image of the manager look good— at least, for a while. The view that has prevailed is that all managers need is a degree from a top business school. But without the broader perspectives from exposure to history, literature, and the humanities, they cannot properly analyze events within their broader context, or put them into the kind of perspective that aids sound decision-making. MBAs, like mental health practitioners, have had no real work experience. They are geared to leap from one high position to the next without absorbing a sense of the organization's culture or developing loyalty to anything beyond their own career advancement.

The bottom line regarding such training-bred limitations where therapists are concerned is that their understanding of psychiatric problems suffers. They end up ignorant of how social conditions and historical change affect our deeply held attitudes, our desires, our ways of dealing with each other, and the kinds of conflicts we experience. They are unaware that what we define as normal is adaptive, but not necessarily sane from the standpoint of what is humanly fulfilling or rational.

The theories—really ideologies—we currently have about the mental and emotional effects of work are based on little real understanding of how different types of people—reflecting different value orientations they bring to their work—are affected by their work situations. When theories are not grounded in systematic, actual study of adults in the context of their career environments and experiences, the result is something like prescribing a medication for an ailment which has not been diagnosed. For example, what is stressful and negative to one person may be stimulating in the most positive sense to another. People respond very differently, physiologically and emotionally, to external stress. One person may thrive on it, while another may crack up. Some people can even become addicted to their own adrenaline, the hormone secreted when the body is under stress, which may then produce an addictive high, characteristic of some workaholics.

In short, contemporary practitioners have taken what was once a discipline with a humanistic. radical, cutting edge calling for a penetrating critique of values, motives, and needs, and made it into a technical, mechanical, tool of support for smooth adjustment to the status quo. Treatment, then, often amounts to verbal Rolaids: something to swallow that quells the inner distress and complaints of people who want to eliminate feelings of conflict and guilt without having to change anything about how they live. As careerists who are uncritical about and disinterested in analyzing their own values, and who can therefore easily rationalize self-indulgence, greed, or power-seeking, both in themselves and in their patients, they have become examples of the kinds of people they should be trying to help.

IN THE INNER SANCTUM

Because of the first two problems—the kinds of people who become therapists, and how they are trained to interpret emotional problems—there is a third problem: what actually goes on behind the office door is frequently off the mark regarding the person's core dilemma. This often results in a setting-in-concrete of the patient's problems. Treatment may drag on for years while the patient continues to be troubled and the therapist continues to collect the fee. The late Truman Capote humorously described this dilemma in *Music for Chameleons*:[8] "Anxiety, as any expensive psychiatrist will tell you, is caused by depression; but depression, as that same psychiatrist will inform you on a second visit and for an additional fee, is caused by anxiety." This sort of circular activity is an example of a "gentleman's agreement" between patient and analyst. Neither wants to be shaken up by new experience or awarenesses. Both are satisfied by small "improvements" and are grateful to each other for not bringing into the open their unconscious collusion to avoid emotionally inflammatory material.

Unhelpful treatment is made worse when the practitioner limits his interest in his work to maintaining a comfortable career, applies "techniques" which are really pat formulas, and fails to develop active interest in understanding people. To an extent, this is understandable. We are all members of the same society and historical era, and therefore want to share in the desires and values which are a part of being normal today, especially career success and the opportunities, pleasures, and comforts of an affluent society. But the therapist has a special responsibility to be aware of the two-sided face of this context; to create an atmosphere of truth-seeking and courage to confront the irrational and the painful, and of willingness to analyze the norms of social adjustment, which can have a negative as well as positive potential upon our personal development.

The Reductionists.   The tendency of the therapeutic mainstream is to reduce all conflict—in fact, nearly all adult experience—to early childhood fantasies and conflict. The values conflict, over-adaptation, and negative coping of the Working Wounded, as well as the traumas of our New Age of work are seen, through this reverse magnifying lens, as simply the manifestations of inner pathology. Lacking a view of a normal range of adaptation as distinguished from pathological development, conventional practitioners see primitive strivings and conflicts lurking beneath the surface of nearly every adult behavior or attitude.

Curiously, they maintain this reductionistic ideology in the face of the reality that no one has a perfect childhood. There are no ideal parents, no ideal circumstances in which to be raised. Yet this does not mean that everyone grows up psychologically diseased. Recent research, in fact, shows that many who have bad childhoods nevertheless come out all right, and that many children who suffer turn out, as they grow up, to be pretty resilient in the face of their pain and suffering. Subsequent life experiences heal them and they become adults who are more or less psychologically well. The research found that even the most profound childhood trauma can be overcome to a great degree. Most of the troubled children studied grew into stability with adulthood.[9] We can also question the assumption that early deprivations automatically create later psychological crises and developmental setbacks. For example, Harvard psychologist Jerome Kagan has cited evidence that the specifics of the parent–child interaction are not so crucial, and that what happens in one stage of development does not necessarily determine what occurs in those that follow.[10] In this view, development can be seen as an unfolding process through which the brain matures, and new cognitive abilities as well as various emotions emerge. All of this is constantly interacting with, and being affected by, ongoing experience.

Evidence like this requires that we broaden our understanding of the roots of emotional conflict beyond the reductionist ideology that they are nothing but the expression of primitive, infantile, and childhood material. But many mainstream analysts and therapists are unfazed by such evidence. They cling to old ways of interpreting reality and old methods of help that don't work. This is something like the old Sufi story of a man who sees someone searching around on the ground, and asks the person what he's looking for. "My key," he replies. "I've lost it." So the first man joins the search, looking intently all over the ground. Finally he asks, "Where exactly were you when you lost it?" "At the other end of the street," he replies. "Then why are you looking here?" the first man asks. "Because there's more light here," he answers.

This kind of frozen thinking is seen, for example, in the case of a mid-level career professional in a state government agency who experienced mounting anxiety over cutbacks which were eliminating positions in her division. There had been no communication from above about which positions were targeted, why, or how many would be affected. I presented a summary of this case to a sample of psychiatrists and psychologists, and asked them to comment on what they would want to learn about her work environment, what they thought the problem was, and what they thought would help her. The typical response was that there was little that they needed to know about her work, that she was obviously suffering from anxiety neurosis, revealed by her "inappropriate response" to the situation—that she was unable to cope effectively with it, possibly because of a narcissistic injury, and that the recommendation would be three times per week intensive treatment.

The reductionist view typically sees childhood-based issues underlying whatever difficulty a career professional experiences on the job, and fails to consider any other source. Career frustrations and conflicts among managers and executives are often interpreted in terms of the person's ego ideal. The ego ideal is similar to the superego, but concerns standards to which one feels compelled to conform based on early idealized love objects, usually parents, rather than on internalized fear of punishment. The interpretation would be that the person's conflicts regarding work represent frustrations of the ego ideal: The person is seeing himself as less strong and powerful than his internal, childhood-based idealization demands of him.

Another variation of this one-note samba is that the essence of every interaction between manager and subordinate is a reenactment of the parent–child interaction. Perceptions, evaluations, and criticisms of one's superior are interpreted in terms of reacting to the person above as though he or she is parent and oneself is the child. So the interaction is replete with parent–child-related fantasies, distortions, unrealistic desires, and irrational resentments, which determine the substance of the interaction.

Similarly, there is the view that disturbance in the career context reflects an unconscious childhood "crime," which people unconsciously punish themselves for by sabotaging themselves. The crime usually reflects some behavior or attitude toward a sibling or parent for which one feels unconsciously guilty. It is expressed through undermining one's own success, or through unconscious motivation to make restitution for bad desires and impulses, or to remake a relationship with a parent.

Of course, examples of these unconscious conflicts and motives can be found. But to interpret virtually every action, decision, and interaction in these terms is both naïve and way off the mark. Another area in which this is found is in the recent vogue for treating the narcissistic and "borderline" disorders. While there are somewhat different developmental roots to narcissism and borderline conditions, and they have been explained through different psychoanalytic interpretations (mainly through the work of Kohut and Kernberg)[11] both of these conditions represent more serious disturbance than the usual neurotic personality, but not so disturbed as the psychotic. As a result of the attention to these conditions, practitioners, particularly students in training, tend to indiscriminately apply the diagnostic criteria for these disturbances to a wide range of patients, and therefore misdiagnose and mistreat the problems. The most damaging results of this concerns the failure to discriminate the narcissistic and borderline patients—the actual percentage of which seems to be very small in most practices—from patients more within the normal range of adaptation, who may show narcissistic or borderline traits at times, because of the attitudes and values to which they have adapted.

In general, the reductionist argument is most accurate in cases of fairly visible behavior which forms a recurring pattern, particularly when it undermines the person. For example, careerists who manage to sabotage themselves or feel acute anxiety around promotions are often acting out an unconscious conflict between a desire to achieve success versus a strong fear of it, in which the latter wins out. Often such a person believes, unconsciously, that his or her success will lead to something terrible, such as punishment, rejection, or abandonment by parents. Promotion might arouse unconscious fear over provoking the anger of father if he competes with or outdoes him. A woman might fear abandonment or rejection by mother if she becomes too successful, and therefore becomes, unconsciously, too much like father. In addition to these Oedipal issues, other problems related to sibling rivalry, narcissistic attitudes, and poor self-image can all effectively interfere with successful career functioning and advancement.[12] For example, a person who has difficulty in a position of responsibility may be feeling the consequences of having lacked good role models, which are important for developing a sense of competence and capacity to work cooperatively.

While such cases exist, the error of the reductionist viewpoint is that it sees such unconscious, neurotic forces operating everywhere, and therefore ignores other parts of reality. As we have seen in examples of the Working Wounded and the traumas related to the New Age of work in Chapters 4 and 5, some types of conflict or maladaptive behavior are a product of negative coping with a bad situation, based on the person's values or the reaction to the realistic elements of a difficult situation. The person's attempted solution may be unproductive, but is that of a person in the normal, not necessarily pathological, range.

That is, a neurotic-appearing reaction to a career situation can be a human response to a real problem for which there is no easy, if any, solution. For example, a person may show what looks like fear of success for reasons that have nothing to do with neurotic conflict. Among the Working Wounded are people whose belief that there is a lack of substance inside is a realistic appraisal, because they have marketed and puffed themselves up so much that they have come to confuse their image with reality. Then, when moving into positions of greater responsibility and weight, the anxiety they experience is that born of the inner recognition that they do lack sufficient substance, and have not developed as much skill, competency, and mastery as their image indicates. In other cases, anxieties may develop because of a frightening reality. For example, having to deal with declining revenue in an unpredictable market, with no solution in sight, or a natural disaster that wipes out the supply of raw materials for your product. Assessment of one's competence, business strategy, and management practices all may be right on target, but one is still subject to tremendous stress as a result of situations beyond control.

There are also the effects of being on center stage, having to perform constantly, particularly in a volatile and highly competitive environment. The isolation that often characterizes executives at the top can take an emotional toll which illustrates this. In the realm of professional sports, former Yankee superstar Mickey Mantle has described, in interviews, anxiety-laden dreams which reflect some of the performance anxieties that many normal careerists experience, but which the therapeutic mainstream would have a field day with. In one, he is making a comeback. He is at the plate, the pitcher throws the ball, he sees it but can't swing. His bat is paralyzed. In another, he can swing the bat, and hits a line drive past the infield, but he's thrown out at first base. He hits another off the fence, and again is thrown out at first. No matter where he hits the ball it always beats him to first base and he's out.[13]

The reductionist interpretation would be Oedipal—that he lacks and fears sufficient strength, symbolized by the ineffective bat (penis) because of fear of retaliation by father. But it is also possible that his dreams reflect the kind of anxiety experienced by careerists whose conflicts and anxieties over their work relate to human failings and having fallen short of performing as well as their talents might have enabled them to, because of market or political forces beyond their control, or events that realistically limited performance. (Mantle was plagued by injuries during his career.)

The point is that we must be careful not to blur the distinction between an extreme or recurring reaction which reveals an underlying instability or irrational tendency—like the cases of self-sabotage discussed above, or those of executives who kill themselves or crack up when they are discovered to have taken bribes or engaged in corruption, or when they lose out in a power struggle—with a reaction that reflects value conflicts, realistic circumstances, or lack of training and experience, in which the person perceives no recourse. With sufficient difficulties in these areas, most anyone may be prone to anxiety, turn to alcohol or drugs, engage in corruption, or become physically sick. It is not surprising that middle managers have a higher rate of severe heart attacks than chief executive officers. The former may have less responsibility, but the nature of middle management involves fewer options and actions available to deal with the kinds of conflict that mount up in normal people in those roles.

Some executives, if not reductionistic analysts, recognize the environmental context which creates conflicts for normal people. For example, a former Senior Vice President at General Electric said in an interview that as a person climbs the pyramid it becomes colder and lonelier. Every quarter the executive gets a public flogging or a public celebration. When he goes out to play golf the other chief executives either look at him as if he had the plague or as if he walks on water. Commenting on missing the trappings of power, he said, "My limousines are yellow now and they used to be black. I don't care if there's a meter running in them, I still get to the airport in fifteen minutes."[14]

Hand-in-Hand Madness. Ironically, Freud anticipated and warned about most of the problems which now exist with therapists and analysts. He could see what was coming. For example, he always stressed that the character of the analyst is one of the most important influences on the outcome of psychoanalysis. He pointed out that in medicine, a doctor who happens to suffer from heart disease is not necessarily handicapped in diagnosing or treating a heart problem in a patient. But treatment for psychological problems is a different story: The analyst's own attitudes, values, and emotional conflicts can seriously interfere with understanding and helping the patient.

In this regard, the concerns of some careerist patients and the orientation of the therapist often seem made for each other. For example, some patients desperately want to get rid of their symptoms and conflicts quickly and painlessly, without having to look at themselves too deeply, or deal with their values or hidden motives which might be a source of their symptoms. As though guided by a finely-tuned antenna homing in on a target, such patients often gravitate toward therapists whose views of social adjustment are congruent with this mission. And there are such therapists waiting for them. They will, in effect, encourage their patients to adapt even more, and not explore the reality of the situation at home or work, and how it might relate to their emotional attitudes.

Guided by the unquestioned assumption that the patients' troubles are due to childhood trauma which, once uncovered, will resolve their conflicts and enable them to better adjust to their situations, these therapists probe and wait. They fail to recognize that, while this assumption is accurate for many troubled people, there is a range of feelings, thoughts, and conflicts about present, adult reality that can be repressed as well, and which can result in serious emotional conflict. Too many therapists encourage the patient to seek "health" through more adjustment to the status quo. They therefore dismiss out-of-hand any criticisms the patient may raise about the external environment, like work, or even social and political issues, as an "acting-out" of Oedipal problems. So what happens is that both therapist and patient avoid touching on any hot issues which would arouse conflict over adult morals, values, or motives, such as the price of having devoted too much of one's purpose in life to getting power, or to self-indulgence.

Some patients, searching for something that will work for them, strive to become more "comfortable" with their work and their relationships. "Comfort," here, is usually a code word for maintaining a protective, invisible shield around themselves, walling themselves off from any strong emotions or thoughts which might be disruptive, such as having compromised too many of their principles or having sacrificed too much of their personal lives while scaling the mountain of power and influence. So they become comfort junkies. Too much of that kind of comfort, though, deadens the careerist's capacity to be fully awake and conscious of reality, which typically includes valid self-criticisms of one's decisions, values, the organization, even of society. The person ignores them, does not take them seriously, and they remain unconscious. Particularly when the therapist ignores them too. But then, some therapists are comfort junkies, themselves.

We also find some patients who are drawn to therapists who seem more hip, because they have an entertaining shtick about loving everybody, becoming yourself, or having it all. Patients attracted to these practitioners want a guru-type therapist, who can inspire them to feel good about themselves, despite their anxieties and guilt. Unfortunately, therapists who cultivate a charismatic image and want to create a following advocate, in essence, more self-indulgence, hedonism, and selfishness, or teach looking out for "No. 1," or some other self-centered strategy of pursuing "growth" at others' expense. And while this may appeal to the negative, reactive motives of the new careerist, the end result is destructive: a confusion of emotional spontaneity and freedom with impulsiveness and immature selfishness.

Even more destructive is evidence that the disturbances of therapists themselves are often acted out upon the patient. A study by psychoanalyst Robert Langs of patients who had been in treatment with therapists of a variety of orientations has found that in most cases, the pathology of the therapist had significantly harmed their patients. When some patients tried to deal with this, the therapist often used his role to intimidate or convince the patient that he or she was distorting reality.[15]

Aside from this kind of extremely damaging behavior by pathological therapists, I find that often, underneath all the forays into blind alleys, new careerist patients usually know when they are betraying themselves by the conduct of their lives and the values they have absorbed—which, they privately acknowledge, they don't really believe in. They know what is alienating to them. Often it is not deeply repressed. And it frequently appears in symbolized form, in dreams. For example, Larry, an Ivy League-trained economist with a large consulting firm, told me about a dream which he found disturbing: "There was myself, and some other people in a house, and we were all bugs or cockroaches, though we were still ourselves, too. Suddenly I notice about four or five giant-looking men—maybe they just looked big because we were small—they were marching across the backyard toward the house. They had on gas masks and were carrying those pressure tanks with hoses. They were exterminators, coming to wipe us out. They began spraying the stuff all over. There was no escape. Then I woke up."

Larry's associations to his dream revealed that the people and the house represented his career world. He had become increasingly critical of the contract work he was doing. Much of it was hackwork, he said, chosen simply because it was lucrative. He felt that he was selling himself out more and more, and betraying his talents and his interest in more substantive issues worthier of research. Larry didn't have deep neurotic problems, but did need help to face his conflict. Once he did, he began to look seriously at how he might develop some alternatives within his career that could provide him with more dignity and fulfillment, without sacrificing his success. Larry's dilemma illustrates the point that unless the patient is helped to see and emotionally respond to the actual conflict, he or she may end up intensifying the problem through rationalizations, or more devotion to power, money, position, or using people. All in the hope of ridding themselves of guilt over self-betrayal. These are the kinds of attempted solutions that cause people to join the ranks of the Working Wounded, as we saw in Chapter 4. And they may find therapists who unwittingly support all this by encouraging them to develop better "coping mechanisms," which constitute a harder shell around one's heart and sense of truth.

All this is further complicated by the fact that the conflicts that are part of the New Normalcy lead many career professionals to look upon therapy as a new "product" to be bought and consumed to get rid of unpleasant conflict and suffering. The therapist sells it and the patient consumes to get happiness and symptom relief. And all with a minimum of effort from the patient.

Of course the desire for symptom relief is natural and should be a goal of any therapy. But one can maintain illusions about how it can be obtained. And one can confuse immediate symptom relief which is short-lived with that which is longer lasting. The latter is hard to obtain simply or quickly. It is not like taking some new headache remedy advertised on TV, or punching some data into the computer. In fact, it is difficult to analyze how one's childhood or one's adult motives and values contribute to one's problems. But contemporary patients, reflecting our instant-everything culture, understandably tend to resent this, even if they have a therapist who is willing to help them explore it all. Consequently we find people who don't want to examine themselves or even change at all. They just want to get rid of troublesome feelings and symptoms, and seek a quick fix or tune-up for their emotional engine: an emotional additive that will let them function more smoothly and have fun, but without having to change anything very central to their conduct of life.

Sometimes, if the troubled person thinks a quick fix can be obtained if they play what they think is the psychoanalytic "game," they may react like Linda, a stockbroker and self-described workaholic who entered therapy because of depression. When I began to raise questions about her work, she suddenly lashed out at me, "Why are you asking me all these questions about my career? You should know that has nothing to do with my problem. You're a shrink, aren't you? So why aren't you asking me about my childhood, my father, my mother? That's what I thought I came here for." For some patients like Linda, talking about childhood can be used as an escape from facing present reality about one's motives and attitudes. There are also patients who seem to passively wait around for some form of manipulation or trick to be performed on them, which often mirrors their experience of everyday life in their organizations. A colleague told me about David, a 42-year-old research physician who complained about no "spark" in his life, but who had difficulty accepting his own responsibility for his development. He said, at one point, "Look, I come on time to my sessions, I pay my bill promptly, I fill the whole hour with talk. So how come I haven't changed yet? Why aren't you doing something to make me feel better? Frankly, I'm beginning to question your competence."

But many patients don't fall into these traps. They know they are troubled inside, need help, and that they must bear the responsibility for change. Some are insightful regarding problems that can be caused by the dark side of their normal adjustment. For example, there are patients who tell their therapists that they would like to become less wrapped up in their careers, to reduce their enchantment with money or power. They don't necessarily want or need major personality change. In fact, they look like they are "resisting treatment" to analysts who try to draw them into intensive work. Many of them openly express a desire for more personal development and fulfillment in their emotional life, family relations, and interests outside of career. In effect, they are seeking to develop more fully the positive traits of the New Normalcy.

As we will see in the next chapter, such people can be helped. But they require therapists who can understand how normalcy differs from both sickness and health. And, as we will also see, therapists who are open to considering all possible sources of their emotional troubles, including repressed childhood conflicts, problems of brain biochemistry, and career-related adult conflicts that affect development. The problem is that many practitioners don't look at things this way; nor are they trained to do so. William Faulkner wrote, "A man sees farther looking from the dark into the light, than looking from light into the dark." Professional training, in combination with the character of therapists, tends to lock them into a fixed way of understanding and dealing with people's problems. This limits the practitioner's vision and ability to critically examine the person in the context of what he or she has adapted to, what choices have been made in life, and whether this is bringing out the best or the worst in the person's life orientation. Without exploring this, one cannot fully understand the extent to which emotional troubles may originate in actual internal sickness or in the reaction of a normal person struggling to survive in the New Age.

BUYING HELP: WHAT WORKS AND WHAT DOESN'T

8

God did not will that the way of cultivation should be easy.

— Virgil

When career professionals today consider therapy they tend to choose between two types: the psychoanalytically-oriented approach, and the non-talking, biologically-oriented. The latter, which I discuss later in the chapter, uses medication to treat problems which the practitioner believes are caused by faulty brain biochemistry, circuitry, or hormonal problems.

Among the talking psychotherapies, all of whose origins are in the psychoanalytic point of view, there has been an explosion in variety over the last 15 years. Emerging from it is a broad resurgence of interest in the psychoanalytic method within the general educated public. There is clearly a renewed confidence in analysis as the most relevant and substantive form of help for people in our times. In addition to helping troubled people, the psychoanalytic point of view is being increasingly applied to the understanding and resolution of issues in organization and business management, and is receiving increased attention from research scientists in related fields.[1] For example, recent research in the field of cognitive science has found evidence of the tendency to repress painful or unpleasant information in ways that lead to self-deception, evidence which is congruent with the clinical observations of patients in analysis.[2]

Yet at the same time the psychoanalytic mainstream fails to understand and respond to the kinds of problems experienced by troubled careerists, who form the bulk of patients seeking help today in the larger urban centers. As we saw in the previous chapter, the training, theories, and interpretations of the therapeutic mainstream all fit a disappearing age. At a time when psychoanalysis needs to be enlightened and expanded by new knowledge about the world of organizations and the emotional impact of work and career, it has retrenched and withdrawn into increasingly irrelevant theoretical postures and misleading clinical interpretations.[3]

In addition to the problems I described in the previous chapter, mental health practitioners tend to become wedded to a singular view of emotional problems, a lens through which all evidence is filtered and interpreted. The orthodox analyst believes that cure is achieved by bringing into emotional awareness the childhood conflicts which are assumed to underlie all adult problems. The biologically-oriented ideologue sees faulty brain chemistry or some form of brain disturbance underlying all symptoms, and will slap some pills into the hand of the patient. All with the authoritative aura of providing "real" treatment because it is biological.

In my view, the best practitioners are always open to all possible sources of a person's problems—repressed childhood conflict, situations at work, as well as physical conditions within the brain. But any of these potential sources of problems can be elevated into a quasi-religion; an ideological belief system subscribed to by the practitioner and forced upon the clinical material provided by the patient. This often has damaging results. The upshot of this is that the prospective patient has to become an educated consumer of treatment in order to find the right kind of help.

Psychoanalysis can help the career professional who is in the broad normal range, yet is troubled, one who suffers from the negative side of normalcy. But analysis must become both enlightened and expanded—enlightened by the knowledge of how adaptation to organizational life and careers can affect people emotionally, apart from childhood or biochemical problems, and expanded to bring squarely into treatment the person's values, morals, choices, and overall life orientation. These are shaped and molded both by childhood development and by adaptation to the career culture and the organization. Focus on either without the other is inadequate, something which many disillusioned patients eventually recognize, but which the practitioner often does not.

An expanded and enlightened psychoanalysis helps the troubled careerist by exploring, as a first step, the roots of disturbed attitudes and feelings, including what may have stimulated them in the past and what feeds them in the present. Any evidence for a biologically-based problem, which is more likely in cases of severe depression and the psychoses, also needs to be carefully evaluated. True psychopathology, as contrasted with situationally-generated psychological problems, is developmentally based. It was best defined by Freud: a state of domination by unconscious, irrational passions, rooted in infantile and childhood conflict, such as deep dependency, extreme self-centeredness, and destructive hatred of life. As we saw in Chapter 3, such irrationality can nevertheless be highly adaptive to the work environment. When narcissistic or sadomasochistic pathology is "required" by the role or organizational culture in order to function effectively or successfully, the sick person is well-adjusted, and no symptoms appear.

TROUBLED PEOPLE AND THE CULTURE OF WORK

Some people are so disturbed that they cannot adapt very well to any situation, or else their particular conflicts are not adaptive to their work environments and therefore erupt on the job and interfere with it. For them, increased adaptation and better adjustment to the norm is the best goal. But even for these people the culture of work and management can play an important role in the course and severity of their problems. Most can be better helped by taking into account how their work and management may play a role in the perpetuation of their disturbance and may strengthen their defenses against feelings of, for example, rage or helplessness.

The psychological role of work is gaining more recognition in the working world, if not in analysts' offices. For example, workers around the country have been filing and winning compensation awards for emotional problems they claim were caused by their jobs. Fifteen states now make disability payments in cases in which severe anxiety, depression, or other emotional problems have been ruled to be caused or aggravated by work. Some have successfully argued that their manager or the work itself placed extreme demands on them which triggered or exacerbated emotional problems. For example, a woman claimed that her manager constantly criticized her and made her hysterical. She was awarded a disability. Other rulings found that cases of anxiety neurosis were contributed to by the work, and totally disabled the worker.

Such cases suggest that work can trigger or make worse an emotional problem that was there to begin with. People whose inner disturbance is not adaptive to the work situation, unlike those who develop the "surface sanity" described in Chapter 3, tend to show psychiatric problems on the job. In general, the healthier the work environment, the more likely it is that disturbance within the person will surface on the job.

Also, differences in severity of disturbance can affect what becomes noticeable on the job. And the work environment, in turn, can affect how visible a person's disturbance may become at work. For example, some people have major emotional problems that have interfered with their basic relationships and ability to work throughout most of their lives. Often they have been hospitalized one or more times and have long histories of psychotic disturbances like schizophrenia or manic-depression. They show gross distortions of reality, an inability to comprehend or execute work responsibilities, bizarre behavior, or severely impaired relations with co-workers.

Although most of these people do not rise very high up in the hierarchy, some do, particularly if they are very talented in an area important to the work of the organization. And even for these people, who are deeply disturbed for reasons that have nothing to do with work, the severity of their problems and symptoms is nevertheless strongly affected by their work, especially by how they are managed. Often the stress of their career, combined with the reactions of co-workers or managers, trigger new psychotic episodes or reinforce their existing sickness.

One reason for this is that the managers of psychotic or severely neurotic careerists often fear them. They try to avoid confronting the reality that the person is very disturbed, which doesn't help either the person or the organization. Managers are afraid for various reasons, many of them understandable. Some fear being slapped with a lawsuit or grievance. Others don't want to risk looking bad. Or, since most lack the proper training, they fear that if they say the wrong thing to the person, he or she will jump out the window or become violent. And that happens enough times to justify the fear. Sometimes the disturbed worker knows this. For example, a woman alcoholic took advantage of her superiors' fear of asking her to get help or to point out that she was in danger of losing her job. They were afraid she would kill herself. Actually, she had convinced them of this, played it to the hilt to keep them off her back, and had bragged about it to another alcoholic employee.

As a result, managers often try the ostrich solution—hide one's head and try to ignore the employee's emotional problems completely, even if some assistance is available from the human resources staff or the employee health office. As one manager said to me, "I wouldn't touch that problem with a ten-foot pole, not even if you paid me." The irony escaped him: that's what he *was* being paid for—to manage his subordinates.

What usually happens is that the employee gets worse, may become afraid of cracking up, and then becomes openly irrational. His friends and family start telling him his behavior is deteriorating. By then it is often too late and the person has to be hospitalized. Of course, some managers are more sensitive than others. In one case, a person who was psychotic had a supportive boss, who quietly put her on administrative leave while she was getting help.

On the other hand, there are managers who not only don't know how to deal with overtly disturbed subordinates but don't care. They want to put the problem out of sight and out of mind by "shelving" the employees; putting them in a part of the organization where they can ignore them. Some do this by creating a "turkey farm," a special ad hoc unit of the organization in which they put everyone who they think is disturbed, incompetent, or both, an organizational "ship of fools." One manager in a large data-processing firm tried to persuade me to interview a group of people he had listed and then give him some justification to lump them together in a new organizational unit he would create, to get them out of his hair. "I want to put all the nuts and losers together," he told me, "to get them the hell out of the way."

Other managers try to ignore the problem by reassigning the employee's work to others, and allowing the disturbed person to continue drawing his or her paycheck. Or the manager continuously reassigns the individual from one supervisor to another, or to other parts of the organization, sloughing the problem person off somewhere else. This "solution" is often found when the organization has employees who are very sick—psychotics, usually schizophrenic or manic-depressive. Rather than deal with the problem in a way which balances concern for the person with the needs of the organization, the manager often keeps transferring the person around, perhaps out of fear, or from lack of knowledge about what would really help. These employees become known as "floaters," organizational lepers, who have serious difficulties for whomever, and wherever, they work.

Grace, a heavy-set woman in her late 50s, was one. She had worked in the same organization for about 30 years, moving from clerical/secretarial work to being a competent research assistant. She had been diagnosed many years earlier as paranoid schizophrenic, and had been hospitalized numerous times, usually when she stopped taking her anti-psychotic medication and began deteriorating. This happened while she was working for her most recent supervisor. She began to accuse people in her office of stealing things and frequently had angry outbursts. Her supervisor told me that at the time he was scared that she might attack someone—namely himself, because one time she had thrown a cup of coffee at him—or try to kill herself.

Over time, she became increasingly paranoid about what she thought was a conspiracy to deny her a deserved promotion to a top executive level. Management responded by shifting her from one supervisor to another, and humored her about her prospects for promotion. They thought that given enough time, she would "settle down." Of course, she didn't. She became increasingly disturbed on the job, and eventually had to be hospitalized again. This might have been avoided if management had had the courage to face the reality of her disturbance, and encouraged her to get some help.

In contrast to deeply disturbed people like Grace, and in greater numbers, are people who are also disturbed but not psychotic. People with neurotic personalities also have symptoms on the job when their conflicts are non-adaptive to their work environment. They often have clear talents and capacities, which have contributed to their career success. But they consciously suffer from anxiety, depression, alienation, destructive impulses, obsessions, compulsions, impotence, and other symptoms which are debilitating and cause tremendous emotional pain and unhappiness in their lives.

There are others who are also disturbed by internal conflict, but to a lesser degree. Their inner conflicts cause suffering, limit their ability to enjoy life, and may result in their being less able to adjust in certain areas of life than most other people. For example, they may chronically misinterpret the actions and intentions of others, feel rejected or superior without justification, project unwanted feelings onto others, alienate themselves from others, and display a lack of sufficient self-esteem.

Whatever the degree of severity of neurotic impairment, it differs from Surface Sanity, in which one is dominated by sado-masochistic power-lusting and grandiose passions which are more adaptive to the environments. The openly conflicted careerists often have more passive-aggressive, independently obstinate, and obsessive tendencies. The passions which underlie their symptoms often limit, rather than aid, their rising very far. Their problems interfere with getting ahead in most organizations. For these people, intensive psychoanalysis can be very helpful to uncovering and resolving the roots of their neurotic problems.

Some, however, are able to seek out or create a kind of protective umbrella of security and protection in their organization; a niche which actually allows the acting-out of their neurotic problems in the daily work environment, with little negative consequence. For example, they may experience few demands for the kind or amount of work that they might find impossible to perform because of their problems. Of course, this is not only a loss to the organization, but it also keeps the person immobilized with respect to experiencing the reality of his or her problem, without which there is little hope for change.

Because many practitioners never examine the role that the patient's work may play in keeping problems immobilized, the result is often what one patient described, when talking about his previous analyst. "I know I have a lot of problems, but I also know that my work is all tied up with my problems. But all [he] wanted me to talk about was my parents. I learned a lot about my relationship with them, and how this has affected me and my relationships with people, but I'm still having severe problems. He would always accuse me of acting out or resisting if I tried to bring up problems from work."

This was the situation with Harold. After getting a graduate degree he was hired by a large corporation that had a reputation for being a sluggish bureaucracy. An only child of a harsh, demanding, ambitious mother and a weak father, Harold experiences the typical narcissistic duality of extreme, grandiose self-evaluation on the one hand, and feelings of deep inferiority and worthlessness on the other.

He finds reality disappointing and painful. Especially rejection by women, which happens a lot, because he views them as objects of conquest and acquisition, which he thinks they don't notice. He looks for total devotion and instant love from whomever he dates. As compensation for the disappointments in his love life, Harold has developed a Walter Mitty–like fantasy world, in which he imagines himself to be an internationally known financier, a Romeo playboy, jet-setting around the world with his harem in tow, or a popular rock star, applauded by thousands while he performs.

At work, he doesn't have to do a whole lot to get by. This leaves ample time for fantasizing. He also spends a good portion of the workday talking with friends, calling up women for dates, and reading the paper. Others have passed him by with promotions, but that is the trade-off he has made. At home, he frequently listens to live recordings of rock music and pretends that he is the star receiving the applause. He spends long hours sleeping and masturbating, the latter often while talking on the phone to women he is dating.

Consciously, Harold wants to be more productive and develop more realistic expectations and greater mutuality in his relationships. But unconsciously, he is filled with rage toward his mother, against whom he rebels by being passive-aggressive, withholding, and inactive in his work. This, he knows, infuriates her. Yet he fears loss of her love, domination, and of her affirmation of his greatness. He feels empty and frightened inside, without any real powers of his own. He is afraid to face it all because of the terror and rage it would unleash within him.

And there is a lot within him. His Rorschach test responses contain symbols of impotent rage and magical escape: exploding volcanoes and magical-looking lands of bliss. Similar themes are also revealed by some of his dreams, such as one in which he is screaming at his mother, then feels terrified and finds himself floating up in the air, above her, and flying away.

Interestingly, for all his inner conflict, Harold shows a more developed heart than many other people who are less troubled. For example, he can be compassionate and cooperative with others, within the limits of his illness. He enjoys socializing, and has a well-developed sense of humor about himself. And when work assignments become important, or if there is pressure to get something done quickly, he turns out good-quality work. Because of this we must ask whether Harold might become more motivated to change if his work were more stimulating and challenging; whether a more positive work environment could help him face and deal with his serious emotional problems.

His case shows how a person's neurotic personality can combine with the career environment to make it very difficult to struggle against pathological passions and develop oneself any further. When I interviewed him he had already spent several years in analysis without any progress. The role of work in supporting his problems was never analyzed. It is virtually impossible for a person to struggle seriously with deep problems until he develops sufficient courage, with the help of the analyst, to face the truth. Not only about the inner conflicts, but also about the ways his work and career situation may be locking him into his emotional conflicts. Facing this might require a radical change of work or require greater courage and activeness in dealing with it for there to be any hope for healthier development.

For people whose conflicts originate in childhood, the roots can be very deep. Typical neurotic problems usually originate in the Oedipal period, from around three to five, which gives rise to adult issues of, for example, dependency, competition, rivalry, rebelliousness, incomplete identity formation, and the kinds of symptoms discussed above. But recent research on infancy shows that a complex emotional, physical, and intellectual life exists at a much earlier age. Infants are born with different temperaments and coping capacities, so there can be a good or poor fit between the infant and his or her mother's temperament. A mother might be insensitive or ignorant of this and stimulate the development of later psychological problems. The parent may respond only when the baby is active, or not respond at all. All of this affects emotional health as the child grows.

In fact, the more severe problems in people—the psychoses, narcissism, and "borderline" conditions,[4] which lie somewhere between psychosis and neurosis in severity—are believed rooted in this early phase of life, which is so critical for the formation of an integrated sense of self and the capacity to perceive the outer world realistically, with minimal distortion by our own needs and wishes. For people whose problems originate in this pre-Oedipal period, traditional analysis is often too stressful. Their sense of reality may be damaged or they may become too overwhelmed by unleashed rage or guilt. They are better helped by therapy which is more structured and active.

FACING THE PSYCHOTHERAPY MARKETPLACE

Helping a troubled person with problems that are rooted in childhood and infancy, or in the negative side of normalcy, requires that the therapist understand how these two sources of problems differ from each other and how they interact, and make a part of treatment an examination of the patient's work situation and value orientation, in terms of whether they support positive development or lead to self-betrayal and immobilization. Even troubled people who suffer from internal pathology which limits the ability to enjoy life more fully or interferes with relationships, frequently complain of a gnawing sense that something is wrong or missing from their lives, or find that successful adjustment has brought with it stress, alienation, or physical symptoms on top of whatever internal conflicts they may have had to begin with. One patient who was treated with medication for serious depression said that he still wanted therapy because, while he was no longer debilitated by depression, he was still having conflicts over his career values, and needed help to deal with that.

As we saw in Chapters 4 and 5, the organizational situation and culture can nurture latent irrational attitudes which might have otherwise remained dormant. And those who are within the normal range and have only minor irrational tendencies can nevertheless develop psychiatric symptoms because of overadaptation, values conflict, and the emotional impact of molding themselves into salable commodities to achieve career advancement. Too much adaptation, compromise, and trade-off lay the foundation for emotional problems.

When looking for professional help to deal with and understand all this, the troubled careerist is faced with a bewildering array of treatments in the marketplace. One product of the New Normalcy, in fact, has been an explosion of new treatments for emotional conflicts. These include not only the orthodox psychoanalytic and other analytically-oriented therapies, but also a variety of family and group therapies, and a host of other therapies which focus on more specific, situational problems. And there are the behavior therapies, the quasi-therapy group experiences like est and Lifespring, and others.

Our 30-second-news-break culture makes it tempting to embrace any form of help that looks quick and not too costly. But eventually, the superficiality and short life span of these methods have become clear. For example, behavior therapy, which was in vogue for a time, has declined in its appeal to career professionals who want help to change. Its superficial attempt to "reinforce new behaviors" was based on wishful thinking: that one can avoid dealing with the reality of emotional passions and attitudes which underlie problems and which generate tremendous resistance to our conscious desire to change. Advocates of this form of help believe that change occurs from "trying on new behaviors," like slipping into a new set of clothing, in which, presumably, the person can present a newly packaged self to gain a better foothold in the competitive world. No need to experience or struggle with powerful passions which underlie neurotic behavior. That's too messy. But disappointed consumers have found that will power is not enough. We resist acting rationally, in accordance with our conscious desires, because of unconscious desires and attitudes which work against our conscious goals. If you have three wheels turning one way, and the fourth moving the opposite direction, you won't get very far. In essence, the behavior therapist advocates a kind of self-bribery, which, at best, redirects some outward activity while changing nothing regarding motives and conflicts.

Nationwide, for a time, upwardly mobile careerists who felt they had been rendered too passive and deadened by their work, or secretly perceived themselves to be losers, were enticed by alternatives to mainstream therapy and analysis: the group-oriented "growth experiences" like est, Lifespring, and other post-counterculture programs for "actualizing" the self. Recently, the latter have coalesced into the so-called New Age movement, which reflects a yearning, though misguided and ultimately unproductive, for more spiritual fulfillment in life. Alumni and devotees of these quasi-therapies whom I interviewed often reminded me of racing cars that pull over in the pit for a rapid-fire tire or oil change during the race, and then burn rubber pulling back out to join the pack. Participants in the quasi-therapies feel good about themselves while participating in the experience. They often feel more alive and inspired to do something more with their lives. But the glow quickly fades when they return to the reality of their daily lives and of themselves, and find that nothing has really changed in either realm.

Many people, desperate to become winners and acquire a feeling of control in their lives, especially in the midst of our recent economic climate, became attracted to the relief promised by these experiences and the aura of positive thinking they create. All developed their own following and still appeal to certain segments of the public. And all, of course, provide handsome fees for their "facilitators" and "consultants." To be fair, most of the quasi-therapies address real problems and conflicts that concern mostly career-ambitious urbanites who have become deadened, angry, passive, frustrated, or guilty while trying to achieve success and power, and who don't know a way out. They are receptive to someone who will shake them by the shoulders, kick them in the rear, and shout in their faces that they can be in charge of their lives and be winners without feeling guilty or troubled. But often they are receiving a pop philosophy which rationalizes, rather than examines, their values and life choices under the guise of "personal growth."

The quasi-therapies became appealing also because they exploited one aspect of the emerging New Normalcy, in which knowledge of passions and motives is seen as too difficult, too time-consuming, with little to show for it in the end. Inspirational techniques and positive thinking for dealing with life are promoted as a product that is neatly packaged and could be quickly consumed. Not only is little accomplished by these techniques; sometimes they are actually destructive, by encouraging regression and supporting narcissistic attitudes.[5] They have actually triggered serious emotional disturbance in some participants.

The bottom line is that the quasi-therapies can't deal with why people are troubled to start with, and what keeps feeding it. They provide illusory gimmicks and bags of tricks, the mental health equivalent of supply-side economics. They teach how to become more hardened, how to tough it out and "get yours" before it is too late. In short, they fail to help the person develop self-awareness of his or her motives and passions, which then remain hidden yet continue to steer the person, as though on automatic pilot, into a life of more misery and self-deception.

Other, more traditional, varieties of therapy have emerged in recent years that try to be more relevant to the concerns of the Working Wounded and those suffering from the traumas of the New Age. These therapies tend to offer specific help for relatively circumscribed problems like situational anxiety and depression. Or they are specific, problem-focused programs like stress management, burnout control, and assertiveness training. These short-term programs and treatments deal with specific concrete crises, whether in the realm of work, family, or marriage, which the practitioners see as a product of ordinary life changes. The most positive benefit of these approaches is that they deal with the real world, outside the practitioner's office. They focus on concrete and immediate problems that concern many of the Working Wounded. But they are limited and partial solutions as well. They lack a framework of understanding how career- and work-related problems differ from internally-based problems, and how this affects what helps and what doesn't. The treatment is often a mishmash of practical advice, based on conventional values, blended with some analysis of childhood, whether or not it is relevant, and some inspirational encouragement to get tougher.

Some of these techniques can be helpful, however, when they serve as an adjunct to therapy, especially the techniques that aid the physical aspects of stress through relaxation techniques, meditation, or biofeedback technology. Learning and practicing these techniques can help a person gain greater conscious control over heart rate, blood pressure, and brain waves, all of which can help in dealing with stress and anxiety. Similar results can be obtained for most people through practicing disciplined meditation, breathing and relaxation exercises, or yoga.

There is value to learning coping strategies or relaxation techniques when organizing our busy and pressured lives. Many of us need help in recognizing when we are getting overloaded and learning how to establish priorities and take time for relaxation in order to "recharge." But none of these kinds of help deal with the more important sources of stress, burnout, and the deeper problems of anxiety and depression: what we are adapting to and becoming successful at in the first place; the values and attitudes we acquire through our career development and how they affect us; what the costs are, morally, emotionally, and

spiritually, of being successful in our times; and, what our own responsibilities are in overcoming our emotional and value conflicts that result.

Many stress- and burnout-management experts who lack this perspective teach, in effect, that there is something wrong within the person
who feels stress to begin with—that, by definition, the well-functioning
person does not experience stress or burnout. Few analyze the work
situation and environment as a source of stress for normal people. The
implication is that a "normal," well-adjusted person has an arsenal of
coping mechanisms at his or her disposal to whip out and fend off
whatever attack is imminent. Moreover, most stress- and burnout-
management experts fail to recognize how the larger situations in the
economic and social realm can be a source of problems, too. Yet, as we
saw in Chapter 5, this regularly happens when rapid change or instability
develops in the larger environment that affects work. Then, some people suddenly develop problems because they have adapted to values
and attitudes which make them less able to deal with whatever change
or pressures develop, less flexible in responding to it, but not because
of a neurotic personality or internal defect.

In fact, the stress- and burnout-management people mystify this
issue by creating the illusion that the problem and solution lie in specific,
small anxieties that can be "controlled." For example, Herbert Freudenberger, the psychologist who first popularized the term "burnout"
in his book of the same name, later replaced it on the top-40 list of
mental health problems with "situational anxiety."[6] He argues that our
worries about large issues like war and the economy get channeled into
many little anxieties. This particularly affects affluent careerists striving
to stay on top of it all who end up feeling overwhelmed. His explanation
is that a "quest for perfection" leads to burnout, beneath which is situational anxiety, and that common triggers are loneliness, job anxiety,
concerns about aging, body image, and appearance. His prescription
for overcoming it consists mainly of trying to control it and playing
games with yourself not to give in to it.

Unlike many practitioners who completely ignore the outer world
when dealing with situationally- or socially-generated symptoms, Freudenberger accurately describes the stresses and strains many of the new
careerists deal with and tries to relate them to the outer world. But
there is a basic contradiction in his thinking. If the root of these anxieties
lies in the big issues facing everyone in our times, then trying to deal
with the small substitute anxieties is misleading and superficial. Moreover, when he describes the anxieties of some people as rooted in concerns about maintaining youth, staying affluent, and maintaining career
success, he is really talking about values. These must be understood in
terms of how and why they develop, in order to deal with problems
that are generated by them. What is missing from the stress- and
burnout-management treatments is the distinction between ordinary

stress from outside demands and pressures and the negative side of careerist values and ambitions, which generate many of the symptoms people have.

Stress, anxiety, and burnout became the mental health buzzwords during the '80s. Therapists and organizational consultants have jumped onto the bandwagon by offering a myriad of treatments for these modern maladies. Most offer help in the form of a packaged product that, because of the above limitations, is very limited at best, and illusory and misleading at worst. For example, the human body does not respond generally and uniformly to stress. Our bodies may cope with different kinds of stressors in different ways, each of which involves particular neurochemical pathways. There is evidence that early life stress may be triggered again and relived later in life. The anxiety associated with that experience may make the hypothalamus chronically overactive to stress, secreting a neurohormone which triggers the release of the hormones of "fight-flight," the experience of stress.

There is also evidence that, after heart attacks, men at lower levels in their organizations are four times as likely to die as upper level managers, even though the latter may be dealing with more overall stress.[7] The reason may be that the upper-level executives have more recourse in terms of action which can vent anger, release frustration, or do something productive about the source of the stress, whereas the middle-level careerist has fewer options for productive action, and keeps the resultant stress bottled up. There is no evidence that the so-called Type A personality is more likely to die from a heart attack, either. Prevention and treatment for stress and burnout conditions are highly limited—even off the mark—unless they begin to take into account the relationship between the individual's value orientation, emotional attitudes, and the situation at work to which he or she adapts.

THE BIOCHEMICAL QUESTION

Any discussion of what helps people deal with contemporary emotional conflicts must address the rising popularity of biochemical theories and treatments for emotional problems. Earlier in this chapter I pointed out that the psychoanalytic and the biochemical points of view are emerging as the most preferred by consumers of the mental health industry. The popularity of the biochemical explanation of problems has been aided by recent evidence that at least some varieties of manic-depressive psychosis, schizophrenia, and severe depression are probably biologically-based, caused by a defect in brain biochemistry, which can be helped by specific drugs like lithium. But the relevance of this evidence to the broad range of problems in personal relationships and values, particularly those resulting from adaptation to work, have been distorted and misunderstood, both by the general public and some practitioners. Some of the latter became pill-pushers because of the discomfort of feeling responsible for how they relate to people or the values they live by. And some patients want the assuring promise of a drug which can elevate their depressed mood, quell their anxieties, or numb their guilt, with only a gulp of water a few times a day. No need to deal with whatever it is about their values and life orientation that creates their troubles to begin with.

Drug treatments, which now involve tens of millions of people, include such categories as tricyclic antidepressants, monoamine oxidase inhibitors, and lithium for manic-depressive psychosis; other major tranquilizers for schizophrenia and thought disorders; and Valium for garden-variety anxiety. Medication treatments generally appeal to people who, for whatever reason, want to believe that there is a biological "cause" of problems, especially depression, which, by a conservative estimate, affects about 20% of the population.[8]

But the danger, here, is to mix what is correlative with what is causative. That is, the human being is one organism, in which the brain and body are intertwined. The experience of reality affects brain biochemistry and the entire body; and internal malfunction or defects of hormones, brain circuitry, and genetic material affect personality and behavior. In certain cases, dramatic events outside the person can affect the inside; and vice versa. But in other cases, emotional experience and brain chemistry correlate without either "causing" the other.

Drugs must be recognized as an important and useful source of help, particularly to deeply disturbed people whose acute suffering and symptoms call for immediate relief. The best practitioners will be open to exploring all possible sources of a patient's problems, and to all possible forms of help. But too often drugs are either prescribed or ruled out for ideological reasons. For example, I consulted to the case of a prominent physician who developed manic-depressive psychosis. He was hospitalized while in a manic state in a psychoanalytic institution, in which no medication was used. The man became more grossly disturbed. His partner in the practice left, and persuaded most of the patients to follow him, explaining that their former doctor was hopelessly insane. Finally, through the efforts of friends, the man was transferred to another institution, and to another psychiatrist, who immediately placed him on lithium, which is highly effective for treating this psychosis. He responded quickly. But the story didn't end there. After recovering, he successfully sued both his former partner, the psychiatrists, and the hospital at which he had been first treated.

But misapplication of drug treatment can cut both ways: there are many cases of improper use, in which drugs are used as an easier form of treatment, often because the practitioner doesn't find the patient interesting enough to work with in verbal therapy. This particularly

affects troubled people from the blue-collar working class, who historically have received more drug treatments for emotional problems than
the white-collar and career professional class. Inappropriate use of
drug treatment simply trades off symptoms of emotional disturbance
for symptoms of being drugged and numbed to one's emotional experience. This, in essence, is a value choice: one can numb anxiety with
a tranquilizer or artificially elevate depression with an antidepressant
more efficiently than with therapy, but then one is making the choice
not to face or struggle with what is making one anxious or depressed
to begin with. It is a question of values. Does the person place greater
value on struggling with painful reality and truth for the sake of further
growth and development within, or on numbing the pain in exchange
for remaining static and never dealing with that part of reality that has
been numbed? A manic-depressive person once told me that he had
made the decision to stop taking lithium and struggle with his illness,
because he no longer wanted the trade-off of feeling drugged in exchange for emotional stability. He felt it wasn't worth it, and preferred
to struggle for sanity on his own.

Sometimes the biochemical theories serve an ideological cause more
than the patient. Examples are seen in proposed biochemical causes
and solutions for conditions which are linked with the values and conflicts of contemporary society. For example, a recent theory holds that
women who become depressed about love relationships that fail suffer
from a defect in brain chemistry.[9] Such women, who are described as
often attractive, intelligent, and charming, are able to attract men but
the relationships fail because they are suffering from a new brain disease: "hysteroid dysphoria." It is a chemical imbalance which, it is claimed,
can be relieved by a particular category of anti-depressant drugs. Some
of the symptoms are feelings of elation when the woman meets a new
man, then depression when the relationship ends. Or feeling high when
admired and low when rejected. Using these "symptoms" as criteria, a
majority of single heterosexual women must be suffering from this brain
disease.

And what about men? Certainly they must suffer from some form
of this brain disease too, don't they? Guess again. The psychiatrists who
invented this theory find that men don't suffer from it because, the
psychiatrists say, men can always have a few drinks or find a new woman.
These "outlets" apparently alter the brain biochemistry of the male.
Now there is a clinical pattern of some women whose self-esteem is so
low that they fear being rejected, and may actually help undermine a
new relationship. But there are also men who fit a similar picture.
Moreover, this theory ignores the fact that some of these women may
be reacting to some features of the men that are available potential
partners in their milieu, in which case their depressive reaction, while
painful, may be normal, not a brain disease.

Anxiety is also frequently treated as a biochemical disorder. One

estimate is that about one-third of all cases of anxiety actually benefit
from drugs, usually those involving panic attacks,[10] although the percentage who are prescribed drugs for their anxiety is probably much
higher. And drug treatments are also being used for the condition of
joylessness, in which some people seem unable to be happy. They show
an inability to have fun or enjoy pleasure. This condition differs from
depression in that the victims experience no joy, but not all of them
suffer from the deep sadness or sleeping and eating disturbances that
mark depression. Some describe a bored feeling that sets in if they aren't
constantly engaging in some new source of stimulation.

The biochemical theory that has been proposed is that there is a
shortage of brain chemicals that are normally released during the experience of pleasure. Two substances produced in the brain, norepi-
nephrine and dopamine, are neurotransmitters that carry messages between brain cells. Chemically they both resemble amphetamines. Another
region of the brain produces opiumlike substances, endorphins, which
produce the so-called "runner's high." It is not known if the lowered
levels of these chemicals is caused by damage from other drugs and
alcohol, or if it is the norm for these people. But the explanation of
this and other conditions illustrates how an area of research investigation
can evolve into an ideology. Any emotional state has biochemical cor-
relates. Some of the conditions of anxiety, depression, or joylessness
may, in fact, reflect a defect of brain chemistry. But anxiety, depression,
and joylessness are also pervasive in our society, particularly among
careerists struggling to remain winners and have fun under the shadow
of economic downturn and the Bomb. The practitioner who ignores
such realities when explaining and treating symptoms does a disservice
to the patient and to the mental health profession, rendering the latter
an apologist for destructive social conditions. And this is independent
of the danger of tranquilizers and antidepressant drugs themselves.
For example, there is evidence that mood-altering drugs can cause mental and emotional disorders that are unrelated to the original disorder.
Peter Breggin, a psychiatrist who has studied the use of drugs on psychiatric patients, argues that the evidence is overwhelming that psychiatrists have effectively lobotomized millions of patients with chemicals
that are toxic to the brain.[11]

A BROADENED VIEW OF MIND AND BODY

A more balanced view of the relationship between brain chemistry and
life experience is found in the mounting evidence of the linkage between
mind and body as it affects illness and health, both physical and emotional. Unfortunately, this evidence is ignored by practitioner ideologues

within both the psychoanalytic and the biological points of view, who argue positions which are based on partial views of people.

It is becoming clear that emotions influence nearly every human disorder. Studies show that, for example, human emotions affect immune responses. The hypothalamus in the brain, when stimulated by emotions, causes the autonomic nervous system to set off a chain of reactions that alter the functions of the organs and glands. Catecholamines from the adrenal medulla cause kidneys to raise blood pressure. The pituitary gland, when stimulated by stress, triggers the release of beta endorphin, which can reduce pain. It also triggers the release of corticosteroids, which suppress the immune response to infection and foreign tissue.

The range of human emotions can influence the onset and course of disease. Emotions can suppress or stimulate disease-fighting white blood cells and trigger the release of adrenal-gland hormones and neurotransmitters, which affect many body processes. Because of this, researchers are recognizing that emotions are really a necessary component in the cause and treatment of most all illness. This has particular relevance to stress. In our earlier discussion of stress and burnout, we saw that our conventional concept of stress is too broad. What is stressful to one person is stimulating to another. The real question is how the person responds to various events and situations. This is what determines susceptibility to disease. Failure to cope with stress can impair ability to fight off illness. It is even possible that coping with a high-stress life reflects a hardiness that helps protect the person.

It is known that those who report a high level of perceived stress have a reduced immune response, lower levels of a natural killer-cell activity. A decline in white blood cell function has also been found after the death of a spouse. Also animal studies show that the immunological response to stress varies with the duration and frequency of stress, whether the animal is able to do something about it or not. If no underlying disease is present, stress will have no effect on the development of disease.

Other studies have found that those oriented to power and domination are less resistant to disease when under stress.[12] They were found to have lower levels of an antibody-secretory immunoglobulin-A (IGA). The experience of stress in some people lowers resistance by inhibiting parts of the immune response. Epinephrine can inhibit immune reaction. Inhibition of the immune response is mediated through the release of hormones like epinephrine. What emerges from these studies is that a person's orientation to life, including values and attitudes, makes a difference in terms of the response of the immunological system. They can affect the development of physical illness.

Similarly, other studies have found a drop in the effectiveness of the immune system of dental students when they were under considerable stress.[13] Their personalities were identified as significant factors in how their immune system responded to stress. The evidence is that people who cope better with job, school, and emotional challenges are less likely to show lowered levels of IGA, a substance important to warding off illness. This antibody, found in human secretions, rose and fell relative to the degree of stress students experienced. Its presence fights viruses and bacteria causing tooth decay, colds, bronchitis, and so on. Individuals who were more competitive tended to show lower levels of IGA. Personality determines how one interprets what is stressful.

It has also been found that stress from which one perceives no escape harms the immune system. People who feel unable to escape stress or cope with it are more likely to develop cancer. Studies of rats who couldn't escape shock developed a weakened immune system. Another group who could shut it off remained normal. The element of control affected the outcome. The key is one's perception of what is stressful, which seems determined by whether the person can control it or cope with it. Other studies show that the brain can exercise direct control over the immune defense system, and that some brain chemicals have specific effects on immune cells.[14] There is evidence that the brain can be trained to activate the immune system.

All of this research points to the effects of life experience, attitudes, and values upon the broad spectrum of disease and well-being. Consistent with this new knowledge, methods of Eastern psychology are gaining new respectability in the West. These include healing the body through mental concentration, visualization therapy, and integration of Buddhist psychology with psychoanalysis, all of which are congruent with the goals and practice of optimal health and point to the importance of understanding the role of adaptation to work and career situations and values when helping a troubled careerist.

THE EDUCATED CONSUMER OF THERAPY

We have examined the kinds of help offered the troubled careerist today, as well as some directions an enlightened and expanded psychoanalysis might take to better help the career professional deal with work-related conflicts and disturbance. On the other side of the coin, a person considering professional help can become a more educated consumer, to aid the evaluation and selection of a therapist. Below are some questions one may ask of a prospective practitioner, explicitly or by observation, together with some guidelines for evaluating the response:

1. *If someone wants help because of, for example, anxiety or depression, what kinds of reasons would you look for as possible causes?*

    A good therapist will consider all possible sources of your problems. Childhood conflicts are the most obvious, but the therapist should also include possible biochemical disorders, personal values, and external situations of work and love. A therapist who ignores or dismisses any of these is to be avoided.

2. *What are your personal values and attitudes about work, love, money, and life in general?*

    This not only helps you learn something about the therapist as a person, but also gives you some information to consider regarding how his or her own outlook and values could affect the treatment. Does the therapist seem to enjoy his or her work, or sound bored and depressed? Be wary of therapists who sound extreme, either overly idealistic or overly self-centered. Does he or she seem interested in life in general, or strike you as a joyless, narrowly focused technician?

3. *What is your experience with or understanding of large organizations and bureaucracies and how they may affect people's problems?*

    The therapist should show some recognition of the realities of careers in big organizations, in which most of us work. Be wary if the therapist indicates that such understanding is irrelevant to your problems or the treatment.

There are also some questions that are useful to ask yourself:

1. *Do I feel sufficiently challenged by this therapist to look at myself, without feeling attacked or treated with disrespect?*

2. *Do I think he or she is capable of understanding me?*

3. *Do I think that he or she is sincerely interested in helping me, or views me as just a diagnostic category? Or as a big dollar sign?*

Being human, we all resist facing and exploring unpleasant truths. We can rationalize our resistance as simply our response to a "bad" therapist. So one must struggle to be open, use one's intuition and judgment and not hesitate to discuss these questions—and one's own conclusions about the answers about them—with the therapist. One should keep in mind, however, that it is part of the experience of treatment to develop feelings toward the therapist that comprise a microcosm of how one relates to the outside world. This must be weighed against one's response to the above questions.

Therapists and patients alike would do well to become aware that the values of normal adjustment, when uncritically embraced, inevitably lead to suffering and conflict. Realizing this is made more difficult by practitioners who don't try to develop their own hearts more fully, and by intellectualized, detached analysts who search for the precise technique to apply—the proper word-magic. They fail to properly understand the troubled careerist's life and emotional reality. Most sobering is that there are limits to what therapy can do, because there are problems and conditions that can only be alleviated by change in our institutions, organizations, and leadership, as we will see in the next chapter—change which affects our perception of normalcy and success.

BEYOND SUCCESS

9

I believe that man will not merely endure: he will
prevail ... because he has a soul, a spirit capable
of compassion and sacrifice and endurance.
— William Faulkner

Among the many obstacles to positive change for the career professional
is the presence of the "cover story" and "hidden plot" in people's lives.[1]
The cover story is the explanation one gives oneself and communicates
to the world; a plausible rationale for one's behavior and motives. Beneath it lies a hidden plot, as in a Shakespearean drama: the true story,
sometimes unconscious and often the opposite of the cover story. It, in
fact, directs and motivates the person's thoughts and actions. People
often tinker around with the cover story here and there; make it
smoother here, more persuasive there. The unconscious or semiconscious aim is to avoid exposing and confronting the hidden plot for fear
that facing it would cause too much disruption, or would be too demanding of rectification. When the cover story is firmly entrenched,
no change may be possible, unless a crisis occurs or the person gets
professional help.

Careerists cannot afford to ignore the cover stories and secret plots
in their lives. For truth, if emotionally experienced and exposed with
compassion and respect, has the power to awaken and heal. Writing
about this, Freud said that even the "harshest truths" are eventually
heard and recognized, after one's feelings of injury and the demanding
passions within us have "exhausted their fury." He recognized that the
capacity for emotional problems to exist at all requires ongoing distortion and lack of recognition of one's true motives and needs: one's
hidden plot. He said that exposing the truth is something like what
happens in some fairy tales in which the power of the evil spirits is
broken as soon as you can tell them their name.

In this chapter we look at what people can do on their own to
support positive change within their lives, as they face their personal
hidden plots. It is helpful, here, to think of adulthood as something

one practices, like an art form. One's practice must embody a vision of life; a framework which provides meaning, purpose, and direction through conscious efforts to cultivate positive values, strengths, and resources.

Viewing life as a "practice" is, of course, alien to most urban careerists, who experience increasing disconnection and separation from the world—beyond that which supports simply going for quick satisfaction of important "needs." But looking beyond these things can provide a greater sense of meaning and purpose for people within the urban career culture. A first step toward developing a broader vision involves analyzing one's adult values, as reflected in one's pattern of decisions, actions, and choices in terms of how they contribute to or hinder one's development and the resolution of conflict.

To do this one must have a framework of what human development is and is not to begin with, in order to identify and practice values consistent with, rather than contradictory to it. For example, a person who tries to develop a more compassionate heart while engaging in deceit or exploitation in his or her career or personal life engages in a daily contradiction. If three wheels are turning one way and the fourth another, one will not get very far. Sometimes the contradiction drives the person into insanity or into unconsciously motivated behavior which results in being exposed. Some of the Wall Street inside traders were probably motivated by this contradiction, given their pattern of behavior, which made their exposure probable.

The struggle for personal development can be aided by the cultivation of competencies and talents outside of one's career that don't produce money but are sources of fulfillment and pleasure that help balance what the career cannot provide. In the career environment it can be aided by changing the trade-off equation through development of new skills, competencies, abilities, and more meaningful work. Much of this can occur within the context of a person's existing career. Change and transformation are essential, but do not necessarily require a radical alteration of one's career and life: few want to drop out in the 1980s.

Another potential source of help is found in the significant changes under way in the larger realm of leadership and the organization of work. These, when combined with a personal effort to create positive change, can help curb the tendency to twist the twin desires for success and fulfillment into their perverted counterparts: material greed and escapism, such as through drugs or other short-term pleasures.

AN ALTERNATIVE VIEW OF HEALTH AND SUCCESS

Whenever we embark on a journey of change—or at least feel the yearning for it—we are guided by certain underlying values or principles, although we may not be fully conscious of them. For example, "change," as commonly defined by the mental health mainstream, is based on the value of adjustment. It equates adjustment with health and success, and uncritically accepts the conventional standards of health and success as mature and desirable. In the larger culture, the self-help, how-to books written by psychologists, social scientists, organizational consultants, and others teach the same thing: fine-tuning one's attitudes, behavior, and desires, as one would an automobile engine, to produce a more efficient performer in the career race. The assumption, here, is that embracing such norms and goals as money, prestige, and power is equivalent to maturity and health. What these self-help experts don't recognize is that this contributes to the problems of the Working Wounded, and sets the stage for perversions of the drive for success and fulfillment.

There is an alternative, more holistic view of "success" and mature adulthood, which values ongoing development and integration of the individual—emotionally, spiritually, mentally, physically, and creatively. It contains a different, broadened meaning of success, including, of course, seeking traditional career achievement and material reward. But it goes beyond this to include the development of a deeper sense of meaning, fulfillment, and integrity, from work and life in general. Within this alternative view, "development" of the individual means strengthening, through practice, emotional, intellectual, spiritual, and physical capacities that are typically unsupported by, or unrelated to work. For example, it means an active search for opportunities for developing new skills and competencies which have meaning and substance, and which occur in a context of participation and integration with a team. The thrust, here, is the principle of integration of aspects of personality and character which a person may recognize but experience as disconnected or hopelessly isolated from each other, something like people who see each other from their adjacent apartment windows but who never meet.

For the troubled career professional who is relatively healthy and well-adapted, what does such "integration" mean? And how can this alternative point of view help people deal with conflicts and the creation of productive alternatives? One thing it means is viewing development as movement in the direction of a kind of optimal state. A person can strive toward it, but can never reach it. (In a deeper sense, of course, there is no "it"; there is no state to reach, something which the person who seriously undertakes the journey eventually realizes). An analogy would be the ideal of optimal physical health. This, most would agree, results from a combination of proper nutrition, exercise, weight, sleep, stress level, and so on. No one can reach a fully optimal physical state, but this does not mean that most people are diseased. Instead, most are within a normal, average range, which carries with it certain advantages and limitations. A person may become diseased, however, either through neglect or overaccentuation of any one of the components of optimal health. Most of us might be capable of greater physical health if we really worked at it, but it would take a great deal of motivation, discipline, and sacrifice. No one can predict in advance what the upper limit might be for any given individual because it depends upon a mix of personal will and overall physical and genetic limitations.

Working toward optimal personal development involves a similar struggle. An example would be working in the practice of daily life to strengthen independence, mutuality, love, social concern, courage, and creative spontaneity. It also requires recognizing that failure to practice these capacities cripples us in some way. It takes effort in our culture to see oneself with a minimum of illusion and deception, and to struggle against attitudes, passions, or external conditions that enslave or pervert the spirit, regardless of how adaptive or "normal" they are.

While no one can reach full development, one can continue to develop as long as one lives. Though no one lives or works in an ideal world, one can use this point of view as a practical guidepost or framework with which to evaluate how one lives: whether one's choices, decisions, and behavior support development or hinder it. It also provides an alternative view of success that is more fulfilling because it is more consistent with the dual goals of achievement and meaning that emerge as a significant driving force for the person who reaches the level of career success that commonly occurs during one's 30s and 40s.

This combination of fulfillment and achievement, a broadened definition of "success" that reflects the strivings of younger careerists, expresses the positive values of the New Normalcy. A life journey in this direction provides the person with greater feelings of inner strength and clarity of focus, as opposed to self-centeredness or narcissism, with which they are sometimes confused. It also provides greater capacity to see and face reality, particularly when it is painful, disappointing, or lacking security. It provides resources for openness, creative spontaneity, and humor; the capacity for mutual love and the experience of the strong emotions, both good and bad, that are a part of a developed life.

This point of view is consistent with a tradition linking the major civilizations throughout history that views misery and suffering as a product of how we live: an inevitable product of a life dominated by greed, self-centeredness, childish resentment, dependency, and the like. All of us are faced with the struggle to moderate, limit, or transform such passions, which requires both self-knowledge and action. This theme is found in the major works of Western literature, such as the writings of Shakespeare, Balzac, Ibsen, and others. It is also expressed in the major religious writings of Eastern and Western civilizations, including the Bible, the Koran, the Bhagavad Gita, the teachings of the Buddha, and the Tao Te Ching. This theme is also consistent with psychoanalytic truth, but stands in sharp contrast to some of today's popular conceptions of "humanism" or "self-actualization," which are offerings of the pleasure merchants of today who rationalize greed, self-indulgence, and exploitation.

Dealing with the Values Gap.   We know that some people develop emotional troubles because of the stress of living or working in an emotionally unhealthy environment. Sometimes people can resist such stress and pressure, rather than buckle in the face of it, but it is hard to contain it all. Often people develop psychiatric problems or unexplained physical symptoms. The urban careerist, who is swamped with situations and attitudes which keep one underdeveloped, though adaptive, requires self-knowledge, a strong heart, and tolerance of the fact that one suffers when experiencing unhealthy or destructive situations, in which case it is normal to feel troubled.

We have seen that the central failing of the psychotherapeutic mainstream is its inability to deal with the questions of meaning and purpose in life, which underlie much of the malaise and psychiatric problems associated with the New Normalcy. I pointed out in a previous chapter that in Freud's time it took tremendous courage to open up the issues of repressed sexuality. In today's world of uncertain economic conditions, shifting social attitudes, and the constant explosion of new technology, similar courage is needed to work on integrating success with fulfillment in life. The task here is to develop a framework of values that transcends the immediate moment, the new electronic gadget, and the comfort-seeking and self-indulgent transitory pleasures that have practically become addictions. That is, the task is one of developing a value base that reduces the gap between what one believes and how one actually lives each day; of practicing values that make sense and provide deeper and longer-lasting meaning and fulfillment than those, for example, that lie behind the "need" to beat out the guy in the adjoining office for the next promotion, or stretch financially to afford membership in that upscale racquet club.

To work toward this creates an understandable dilemma for the successful but troubled careerist. It is difficult to analyze the values, satisfactions, and meaning one has developed in one's life to date, particularly their effects upon oneself, both good and bad. It is hard, for example, for a person to face honestly the effects of having chosen an easy and rewarding path by developing talents in an area in which he or she had no real interest. It is hard to face the consequences of having betrayed one's principles or talents for short-term gain, or cheating and using people—even people one claims to love.

To develop such awareness and apply it in a way that leads to positive change may require outside help, but not necessarily. In any case, the struggle must be one's own. What makes it more difficult is that change doesn't proceed automatically from insight. Awareness of the truth is merely a beginning. It provides the opportunity to struggle with doing something about it.

A talented journalist I interviewed had continuously let herself be drawn into the aura and glamour of the journalistic arena, and had no goals beyond the next assignment, the next trip to somewhere exciting, the next award she might get. As she pointed out, at her paper you were only as good as your next story. Inside, she felt she was squandering her life, selling out for perks and image that ultimately were empty. She had no overall sense of what she was doing with her life, or why. For her to explore goals, values and attitudes more consistent with mature ideals, a positive spirit, and a more active orientation to life would not be easy. Our culture has a frozen—and increasingly obsolete—view of what healthy, successful adjustment is. And the career-oriented person may not want to engage in too much sacrifice, but some may be necessary to develop more balanced values. By exploring the possibility of change, even on a small scale, as a test, the person usually finds that it is not as difficult as one might think.

Change requires conscious effort to develop other commitments and values that aid personal fulfillment and pleasure in less material ways, ways that fulfill the spirit more than the stock portfolio. This was the case with Art, a highly successful businessman who resigned his position at the peak of his career, because, he said, he began to realize that his position required so much of him that he had to sacrifice any meaningful relationship with his wife and children. And he decided it was no longer worth it, given the brevity of life. He was able to develop an alternative, starting up a smaller-scale business, because of his financial security. Most careerists, particularly those at the mid-levels or on the way up, are not going to drop out, but most identify with the feelings that motivated Art to do so. And there is often much room for change short of dropping out, both in work and in one's personal life.

To change old values, the person must work at developing new values; for example, developing a warmer, more generous heart. This requires struggle and action, perhaps in the concrete form of volunteering to help, teach, or contribute direct service to others, or working on some social/political issue, in order to struggle against cynicism and isolation. For example, Joe, the dissatisfied lawyer I described in a previous chapter, found that teaching illiterates how to read provided a source of meaning and fulfillment that had been missing from his work.

Sometimes hardship can be an agent of change. Executives and managers who have been asked about what contributed to their careers have cited significant hardships—failure, mistakes, and misfortunes—as central to their progress. By discovering what was really important to them, how to cope with the difficulty, how to rely on others, they experienced greater personal development. In particular, negative experiences like demotion into boring jobs or a sense of personal failure motivated them to examine and clarify their values. They had to face themselves, their goals, and direction in life at such moments and come up with a solution they could live with. Self-delusion or rationalization wouldn't work. From this process often emerged new value orientations and new desires.[2] I have seen this confirmed in the experience of fired executives who have been helped to view the crisis as a new opportunity to examine the values embedded in the lives they have been living and to explore what they really want in life and career at this juncture.

There is no simple formula or shortcut. Change is not easy for anyone, especially if one has made a conscious decision at some point in life to harden oneself, to opt for money and power as compensation for the lack of fulfillment and meaning in one's work. And change requires treating oneself with understanding and compassion to start with.

CHANGING THE TRADE-OFF EQUATION

Some people find that they can develop new values or strengthen others which were weak but important to them by taking a stand on principles at work. This often takes the form of resisting the system in some way, either to maintain a principle which they believe the organization has violated, even at the expense of their career, or to maintain their sanity within what they perceive to be an insane environment.

These resisters fight the system, either through conventional or guerrilla warfare. Some are individual commandos; others join together to form networks of non-cooperation. Their battles may result in victory, defeat, or quitting the system. Of course for some, this serves a neurotic purpose, best seen in some cases in which the fight becomes the end in itself and almost a second career. Some hunker down into a long-term guerrilla warfare of lawsuits, grievances, memo and letter writing to company, union, or public officials; of attempts to undermine the "enemy"; and so on, which can go on indefinitely. But most are acting upon values which have become central to their lives.

I have found more of these resisters within government organizations—local, state, federal, and international—probably because such bureaucracies, at their worst, tend to be more deadening to the career professional than private-sector organizations and are more likely to stimulate underground resistance among some of their members. A well-known example of a resister who won the battle is Earnest Fitzgerald, a Pentagon whistle-blower who was harassed and fired from the Air Force for revealing multibillion-dollar cost overruns. After a 13-year legal battle for reinstatement, he finally won, in 1982. For the second time. In 1973, four years after he was fired, the Civil Service

Commission had ordered him reinstated with back pay. But Fitzgerald sued, claiming that the job he was given was not the same as the one he had held in 1969, before he exposed the overruns over the purchase of military transports. He did not romanticize his battle; he acknowledged that his 13-year exile was very difficult to endure, and that he has questioned whether it was worth it.

Others form networks of resisters. For example, an Alabama aerospace engineer formed a national network for whistle-blowers who phone or write him from all over the nation, and he provides legal information or simply moral support. Such communities provide a rational and effective strategy to fight unfairness within the system which violates personal values. For example, a Public Employees Roundtable was formed to combat the jokes and slurs that affect worker morale and drive out talented careerists from government. Members of the Senior Executive Service, the top category of federal government executives, formed an association soon after the formation of the Service, into which top executives must go if they want higher promotion, because they felt they were being cheated and treated shabbily by Congress. They became furious over cutbacks on the bonuses that were offered to them to join the SES in the first place. For some, the fight ceased to be worth it after a point. For example, over 40% of those who joined the SES when it was created by the Carter administration subsequently left the government, a much higher rate than for other government employees. The most frequent reason they cite for leaving is a broken promise of eligibility for bonuses, awards, and other benefits. They decided they wouldn't stand for it anymore.

There is often sacrifice involved in acting upon important values. Resistance requires a different kind of trade-off, in effect. For example, one man won a 30-month-long battle to regain his federal job, but said if he had it to do over again, he would not have fought. He had revealed that his boss and several co-workers had pocketed travel advances for trips they never took. He was fired, and eventually he won on appeal. But he felt that back pay and reinstatement couldn't compensate for the turmoil.[3]

A resister who acts from an unconscious need for martyrdom would probably not acknowledge doubts as to whether fighting for principle was worth the personal toll. Nor is he or she likely to abandon the effort if the compromises are too massive. An example of a resister who quit the system is the case of a Deputy Associate Solicitor for Employment and Training in the U.S. Department of Labor who abruptly resigned during the first Reagan administration, saying, "I do not want to work another day amidst the unproductive destructiveness which now pervades much of the Department." He blamed the leadership of the Labor Department, took a public stand about it, and left. Similarly, a man who came to Washington during the Reagan administration was serving as an ombudsman for the International Communications Agency, under whose umbrella was the Voice of America and other international information and cultural functions. But only six months after he began, at which time he had been heralded by the Reagan White House as the kind of injection from the business world that government needed, he resigned.

He emphasized that he saw himself as a patriot and an expert in management who had looked forward to doing public service. But it had become clear to him, he said, that President Reagan's call for volunteers was "a sham," because the agency was "overmanned, wasteful of resources, and so poorly run that allegations of corruption were constantly raised but rarely corrected." When he took the constant complaints of nepotism, cronyism, and sexual misconduct to agency investigators, he was told that upper-level officials wanted to kill any unpleasant findings. An employee union newsletter said that every time he pointed out a management problem or a legitimate employee concern he was ignored. So he left.[1]

Most careerists do not find themselves in situations in which they must face whether to fight for a principle in the form of resistance. For most, however, changing the trade-off equation can result from action in three areas: developing new talents of discipline; practicing more balanced values; and learning sane self-marketing skills. Developing talents of discipline, by which I mean non-career competencies which have no monetary compensation and don't provide career "mileage," can help balance devotion to careerism as the sole source of fulfillment in life. A better balance of values results in more productive trade-offs and less debilitating compromises in one's work and career goals. Because both of these require taking more responsibility for one's own development and taking action which requires some risk and courage, it is necessary to learn how to engage in honest marketing of oneself, which recognizes the competitive realities of the '80s but is grounded in honesty and realistic self-appraisal rather than in image building or résumé-padding or by pretending that the problem can be solved by the right packaging, which just leads to another form of self-betrayal and values conflict.

For any of these three steps to occur one must accept responsibility for one's own development, tempered by understanding how hard it can be to do this when one has been accustomed to waiting for something to happen—a door to open, a lucky break to occur. Or when one has habitually indulged in complaints about the impossibility of change or development on the job. In both organizational consultation and treatment of patients I repeatedly discover that the person who complains the most vigorously about the barriers to change at the office or in the career has also made few attempts to actually create any change. Yet the person is convinced that it is impossible. In some cases this is due to unconscious resistance to improving the situation, perhaps based on fear of authority, which must be first resolved. But I have also found that for others it is part of a passive orientation of responding to whatever comes one's way, but with little initiation. This is often compounded by a lack of actual knowledge about or experience in creating and testing out strategies of change that are in one's own self-interest.

Talents of Discipline.   The troubled careerist is likely to remain in conflict as long as he or she tries to obtain fulfillment solely or primarily from career. Organizations as presently structured and managed do not provide enough opportunity for participation, development of new skills, or meaning derived from work that is integrated with organizational goals, though there are some positive signs of change, as I will discuss later in this chapter. The retreat into grabbing onto and maximizing perks, material rewards, and position-acquisition which many career professionals engage in is an understandable response, in the absence of an alternative. But it is also a ticket on the express train to the land of the Working Wounded. The careerist must look outside of work for greater balance, through the development of competencies, skills, and sources of pleasure and fulfillment outside of career, especially those which do not provide the monetary, glamour, and power compensations of the job.

What form this takes varies widely, of course. For one person it may involve pursuing an intellectual interest in some subject; for another, some craft or artistic or musical skill or interest. The important point here is that for non-career sources of fulfillment to work, in the sense of helping bring a life back into balance, seriousness of purpose, study, commitment, and practice through discipline are needed. Talents of discipline are not the same as "hobbies," which tend to be dabbled in and trivialized.

Some people try to turn talents of discipline into substitutes for career. In this sense they have given up, not necessarily in that they become burned-out casualties, but rather in that they abandon hope that work and career may ever provide meaning or a sense of fulfillment, or that the conditions of work which caused them emotional and values conflict can ever be improved. Their solution is to develop alternatives outside of work as a substitute for it. This is different from the passivity and hopelessness into which some careerists sink, which cripples their spirit and makes them the butt of jokes about having retired early—on the job. These abandoners, in contrast, are actively seeking enjoyment and more fulfillment from sources completely outside their career. But this works only to a limited extent at best, because of the central role work plays in everyone's life.

For example, a vice president of a large financial institution abandoned his career because he had become "disgusted with the power plays and internal politics." He said, "I repeatedly saw cover-ups . . . managers vomiting into trash cans. I risked my career to improve an unhealthy and dishonest situation in my office. I succeeded in part, but it was too pervasive, so I finally maneuvered events so I could retire early." During that time, before he retired, he developed a hobby of old-time photography, using tin plates. "This became my therapy," he quipped. "It kept me sane. But," he added, "it's not the same as doing productive, intellectually challenging work, and being part of an achievement-oriented group. I really miss that."

A black woman who won a discrimination lawsuit against her managers said, "If I only had financial security, I might have tried developing a different career. Unfortunately, I was widowed at an early age, had a handicapped son, and was held down fast to my career. But the work situation didn't destroy my creativity in my private life. What was within me came out and provided me with a life away from the work situation. I bought an inexpensive, old house which was near the point of being condemned. I rebuilt it from the ground up, and redecorated it. I also developed interest in gourmet cooking, interior decoration, and organic gardening. These activities were very therapeutic for the daily trauma I faced in my workday situation. Exercising these qualities in my private life gave me a sense of fulfillment. If I had been weak-minded and with no other interests in life, I would have become a disaster."

Ultimately, the abandoner's solution is too limited and unfulfilling to be a productive alternative for most people. The role of work in our lives is too important to give up entirely as a source of meaning and satisfaction in life.

More Balanced Values.   Rob was a person with nearly twenty years of experience with a prestigious law firm. Highly respected in his work, he originally sought treatment for depression. One issue that emerged was that he felt his life was dribbling away, because he had become less and less enchanted with his career. His work was boring and empty. He saw no alternatives; certainly none within law. He thought of radical alternatives, which he talked about semi-seriously, mostly semi. He enjoyed his comfortable life-style, his BMW and his SAAB, the beach house he and his wife had had designed by a prominent architect. But he didn't get to enjoy these things too much, because of the demands of his work. And when he did, they didn't turn him on the way they had. A turning point for him was when he was walking to lunch one day and overheard a couple of people talking about a beautiful flowering tree which had been in blossom a few weeks before. Rob suddenly realized that although the route to and from his office took him past that tree, he had never noticed that its blooming had come and gone. It was his own personal version, he joked, about not having stopped to smell the roses.

My evaluation of Rob, including analysis of his Rorschach test, indicated that he was relatively healthy, with considerable intellectual energy that was not being used. While he had some tendency to control anger to avoid getting in trouble, he was emotionally open, highly creative, and had a loving relationship with his wife.

Through his treatment, he began to discover that one reason he maintained a passive view about the possibility of change, and masked it with charming humor, was that he knew that his career was a successive series of trade-offs. He had chosen it that way, telling himself at each step that this is what a man has to get used to in life, this is reality, and so on. What really mattered was the money and what it could buy. All along he knew it wasn't enough, but with each small trade-off and self-betrayal, he found himself sinking deeper into a pit. And now he was flat on his back, on the bottom.

But as Rob began to face his feeling about all this, and explore the roots of his hopelessness in his own decisions and actions, he began to take his dissatisfactions and criticisms of his career more seriously, rather than languish in them. Not surprisingly he began to have ideas about alternatives, concerning how he could develop some expertise in another area of law that he had greater interest in but had not previously considered a viable alternative. He also decided to do some teaching at a local law school, something which had always intrigued him, but which he had not acted on. None of this was ideal (his fantasy was being a corporate entrepreneur) and there would have to be some financial sacrifice, but he found that a more productive trade-off was, in fact, possible for him.

Issues affecting women provide another arena for developing more balanced values. In fact, women have undertaken some of the most difficult and courageous attempts to create more productive career trade-offs. This is for several reasons. The broadest is that women careerists seeking greater fulfillment do so in a culture that is still largely patriarchal and oppressive toward women and not at all supportive of mutuality or equality, despite the gains women have made in being "accepted" by men in the workplace. In the context of career experiences, women on the fast track find it hard to balance having children and careers, because most companies and male managers are reluctant to create flexible hours and work schedules, including the opportunity for part-time careers, that would make such balance more feasible. Yet more and more women want to have both careers and children. They have been willing to make sacrifices for both, but increasingly resent the lack of accommodation to the situation and needs of women career professionals, and the necessity of having to keep their lives in two separate compartments to stay on a fast track. As a result, women have tremendous difficulty developing a better balance of values within the existing structure of careers and organizations. And too much awareness that these limitations are rooted in a male-dominated career culture—in which most men fail to recognize that women's development is a trans-gender issue, in that both men and women would benefit from a culture of mutual support—can lead the woman careerist to develop anger, anxiety, depression, and a sense of being an "impostor," which masks one's semi-conscious critique of the values of power and domination which characterize the career culture.

Consequently, women careerists increasingly question whether the trade-offs are worth dealing with at all. For example, having to compromise the quality of their lives by trying to reconcile a full-time career and motherhood. Those who have attempted this usually find that it degenerates into a juggling act which falls primarily on them and not on the male. Husbands, even those among the younger careerists, find it difficult to actively support or facilitate their wives' careers. As a result, the juggling takes a toll of everything—women's career development, their marriages, and their relationships with their children. Many are beginning to reevaluate their goals and conclude that it is not really possible or desirable to do it all.

Because of the difficulty of practicing more balanced values, some drop out, a loss to the organization and to themselves. For example, many women who became lawyers or got MBAs have been dropping out after they become mothers. They are fed up feeling torn between motherhood and career desires, and dealing with the resultant stress, anxiety, and lowered productivity. Therefore many conclude that combining career and motherhood is impossible, and they no longer want to try.

Some women abandon their careers in frustration; others have tried to alter their work schedules. But it's not easy. The main barrier to more productive trade-offs for women is the reluctance of companies to agree to part-time careers, which would allow the woman to contribute her talents and competencies, but not at the sacrifice of motherhood. Part of the problem is that men continue to believe that women with children are only temporary and not committed to career. So part-time careers and flexible schedules remain rare in most companies. The woman careerist has to prove, in effect, that having children won't interfere with her career.

Most companies show little willingness to accommodate the growing desire for part-time employment or flexible schedules, particularly among the growing number of career women who are having children for the first time in their 30s, and who want to resume their career after a period of time. One woman in a dual-career marriage observed that, while some companies may have an appreciation of dual-career family problems, such as conflicts over transfer or equal career opportunities, "I don't see any move to lessen the pressures on the job."[5] But organizations are fighting a losing battle, and one that works against their own self-interest. The pressures toward part-time careers and flexible work schedules will increase, and organizations will be forced into realizing that it is to their benefit to recognize that women can pursue careers and make contributions to the organization without having to devote their lives to their careers.

While some women deal with this situation by reassessing and altering their own values—concluding, for example, that they don't need traditional "success" as much as they once thought—others have tried to turn the situation around. Some women, faced with the reluctance of companies to support part-time work, create other alternatives. For example, one woman who quit her career began part-time consulting, and eventually formed her own consulting firm, made up of other part-time mothers with business and professional training. A common theme heard from women in these situations is that they suffer a period of lower productivity, frustration, anger, and stress, while trying to make the transition, particularly in the face of male management showing little understanding of the pressures. They feel guilt over not doing enough, anxiety over their career, and having to cope with all the pressures from both ends. This is heightened by the fact that women who don't have children until their 30s, when they are well established in their careers, are more deeply invested in both career and family than younger women. When it comes to developing more productive career trade-offs, to overcome the emotional conflicts career women must deal with, the woman careerist is playing with a stacked deck.

People who are able to create more productive trade-offs in response to a demoralizing or disturbing work experience do so through action which is based on a mixture of realistic self-appraisal, sacrifice and risk, and some self-marketing, in order to adapt themselves to a different environment. For example, a mechanic attempted to cope better with what was, for him, a dead-end job market that only fostered low self-esteem. He began studying to become a computer repairman. A high school drop-out, he experienced tremendous emotional and financial strain while making the effort, calling it "the biggest challenge I've ever had." Another man, an unemployed steelworker, switched to a white-collar job as a computer programmer. He said he felt like a refugee trying to adjust to a new country. Although he got all A's in the 14-month training course, he, like the former mechanic, found the transition to his new career very difficult. Both felt lower than their better-educated new yuppie colleagues.[6]

Another person changed careers outright by opening a small business with her husband. Previously she had been in such conflict over her work that she had sought therapy for depression. But her depression remained pretty constant until she made the decision to take a risk to improve her feelings about work. At the same time, her husband said "Why am I coming here each day? No one is holding a gun to my head." While dealing with the usual problems of trying to make a small business work, they both feel they have achieved a better trade-off than before.

Another said, "I finally came to the conclusion that I can be of greater service to the world doing work I enjoy. I then had to begin taking responsibility for myself in such a way that would allow me to do such work. Since I began to define what I wanted to do, the outer circumstances have been gradually changing and improving, not because of luck, but because of my inner changes."

Still another, a real estate development executive who left to study engineering, said, "I have come to believe that people get exactly what they want on a subconscious basis, and that each of us had therefore be very clear about what our main goals are. Even our mistakes can be used to refine our values and increase our awareness of ourselves, our environment, and other people's feelings. People are slowly struggling toward the realization of their own value and worth. When we recognize that we deserve better than what we've been giving ourselves, maybe we'll change from power systems based on dominance and from environmental degradation to something more humanistic and whole."

Overall, the career professionals who experiment with developing different value orientations and creating more satisfying career trade-offs, tend to share a strong belief in commitment to what they are doing, a perception of having taken more control over their own lives, and a feeling of stimulation by the challenge and the risk of what they are attempting. They also show a high level of awareness of their positive strengths and weaknesses, and are careful to limit their identification with their work, and not make it the sole or most important reason for being alive.

Self-Marketing. Whether one seeks more productive trade-offs or attempts to develop more balanced values as a way of striving to overcome conflict and reaching for that mixture of success and fulfillment, one must deal with the need for being able to market oneself to some degree in today's career world. The marketing of self is actually a part of the contemporary orientation of career professionals; a version of what Erich Fromm called the "marketing orientation" in modern, consumer-oriented society. He first described this in post-World War II America as an orientation "rooted in the experience of oneself as a commodity and of one's value as exchange value . . ."[7] Part of this is being dependent for success on personal acceptance by those who need their services or who employ them. In a competitive marketplace, he said, self-esteem depends on conditions beyond one's control. One's value is primarily determined by one's success in the competitive market, and therefore, in a changing market one's self-esteem is shaky and in constant need of affirmation from others. The danger is that one can become driven to strive relentlessly for success, and any setback is a severe threat to self-esteem. Helplessness, insecurity, and feelings of inferiority are the result.

The more developed person derives identity from experience of self as agent who is one with his powers. But part of the New Normalcy of today involves a version of this marketing orientation, which most people in our culture share to some degree; it is a feature of today's career world. Given this, the task for individuals striving to combine success and fulfillment and to avoid the emotional land mines along the way is to learn how, in our highly competitive economic and career marketplace, one can market oneself while avoiding the negative extreme of viewing oneself as nothing but a commodity and feeling alienated from one's powers.

There is a place for responsible marketing of oneself and one's talents, based on a recognition that the world we live in is intensely competitive, but balanced by practicing values and attitudes which help keep one in touch with one's active powers and worth independent of their market value at the moment. The cornerstones of this balance for the careerist are sophistication about the vagaries of the market as they affect one's own work; study and learning about what one must know to better position one's talents, skills, and experience in the changing workplace, so as to aid one's career or the kind of work one wants to do in the future; and skillful "packaging" of all this in a way that will help one be successful, while maintaining honesty and integrity by not taking the image too seriously or confusing salesmanship with substance. That is, to know that what one is "selling" about oneself has substance and is integrated with one's vision of life.

Although the focus of this book is on the individual, there is an important link between individual development and new directions in leadership and organization. There are currently winds of change in organizations that affect emotional conflict and healthy development: new models of management, leadership, restructuring of work; and increased participation, decentralization, and teamwork. All of this actually aids effective business strategy by supporting the positive strivings of the new careerist, and therefore minimizes the conditions and values which feed the problems of both Surface Sanity and of the Working Wounded.

THE DOUBLE HELIX OF DEVELOPMENT

This chapter has focused on strategies of help for careerists who are troubled, and preventive strategies for others that can minimize the potential for developing conflicts during career adaptation. But this emphasis on the individual is only part of the picture. The sea change in the world of work and in the values and motives of the new-breed careerist requires us to think in terms of separate but intertwined strategies at both the level of the person and the level of the organization: a *double helix of development*.

Contrary to the individually-based views of the mental-health mainstream and the current pop-psychology ideologies, some problems can only be solved through action on the level of the organization, institution, or society; the level of policy and politics. Moreover, we have seen throughout this book that the work-related conflicts new careerists develop today, whether problems of surface sanity or problems rooted in the negative side of normalcy, are strongly affected by the larger realm—the organization, its work content, management, and leadership.

We have seen that help on the personal level requires an enlightened and expanded psychoanalysis which understands the effect of career adaptation upon the person's emotional development. And that this, in turn, requires a view of normalcy and success which better fits changing historical realities. But interwoven with individual therapeutic help for troubled people is the need for new models of work organization, management, and leadership. Both are needed to mitigate the negative side of normalcy, and help prevent the development of emotional conflicts over careerism. The new-breed careerists require work which provides a greater sense of meaning; expanded opportunities for autonomy, participation, and entrepreneurial-style innovation within large organizations; teamwork, with fewer layers of bureaucracy; integration of technology; greater linkage between work and the mission of the organization; and leadership which incorporates the values that best support all of this.

Strategies based on such a holistic perspective support not only the economic viability and market competitiveness of organizations, but also greater commitment and more positive development from the new careerist. But most organizations have not yet developed in ways which sufficiently recognize these business realities and accommodate the values and motivations of the new breed of careerist, as well.

Our thinking regarding development of the individual and of organizational efficiency is fragmented and unintegrated. Programs designed to aid the worker on the organizational level tend to be focused on the "troubled employee," that is, the person with alcohol or drug problems, or with work-related supervisory/behavior problems. More recently, companies have begun developing programs of stress management and health promotion, which recognize, at least implicitly, the link between disturbance and career adaptation.

Programs of Help Within the Organization. There are programs designed to help the troubled employee address alcohol, drug, and employee-behavior problems through "employee assistance programs" or similar counseling by human-resource staff, or staff of employee health units. The employee may be referred by his or her manager, or may be a self-referral. Many organizations offer a variety of approaches to helping the employee with alcohol or drug problems, through counseling, psychiatric referral, information dissemination, self-help groups, and other means.

Too often, however, the manager of such employees doesn't know how to refer the person for treatment, or fears doing so, even when, for example, the employee comes to work drunk and disrupts the office, shouting or becoming violent. Managers often prefer to try to deal with an employee who functions minimally, at best, fire the person, or try to transfer him or her to someone else, much as they do with emotionally disturbed employees. Nevertheless, organizations are increasingly recognizing the economic efficiency, if nothing else, of trying to salvage the employee.

Other programs, which offer counseling to employees with work-related behavior or superior-subordinate problems, help not only the employee, but also the manager, who has the first responsibility. Managers need to be able to examine themselves in relation to the employee, in terms of, for example, assumptions they may hold about personal problems and stress which may not be correct. The manager may have personal feelings about the employee, positive or negative, which can affect how he or she deals with the problem. I have found that managers are often in a quandary regarding how to deal with conflicts of their subordinates, in part because it is hard to be of help without also playing therapist. It is difficult to focus on performance problems but not on personal problems or motivation, when they are so often intertwined. It is also difficult not to look at the personal side, but just the deterioration of work performance, confront the employee about it, set schedules for improvement, and so on.

All of this is further compounded, of course, if the manager is contributing to the employee's problem as well, in any of the various ways we have seen in previous chapters, such as poor communication, management which frustrates the motives of the careerist, or by being disturbed himself or herself.

There are also programs of stress management, and quasi-forms of help like wellness programs, recreation, career diversions, and so on, offered by increasing numbers of companies. Some of these programs deal not only with job-related stress, but also try to encourage the development of more productive trade-offs and greater self-expression on the job. For example, 51% of companies in the United States either now have or are considering offering anti-stress plans. Most are based on the conviction that keeping workers healthy lowers health-care costs. Eighty percent of the big companies, 73% of the medium-sized, and

61% of the small say they have developed specific strategies to cope with stress.[8] The most common is physical exercise, sometimes in combination with biofeedback or massage.

Some companies now give sabbaticals to help employees develop perspective on their lives and careers, to "recharge" and renew creative energy. Similarly, some organizations, like IBM, have developed the concept of an alternative career path for employees who do not want to move up in management. IBM calls the position an IBM fellow. Outside of the work itself, companies, particularly in high-tech areas which tend to attract the new-breed careerist, offer adjunct health- and recreation-oriented benefits like recreation centers, tennis courts, and swimming pools. Also, increasing numbers of resorts and fitness centers are sponsoring escapes called mental-health breaks, which provide information about stress management, balancing roles and career choices, and women's issues. They focus on ways to cope with stress and set new goals. They encourage reflection about one's values, relationships, career orientation, and exploration of creative and more fulfilling alternatives. Many corporations also offer lunch-hour diversions, such as exercise classes, dance classes, and courses or lectures by college professors. Such extra-career offerings also include efforts by companies to support greater overall interest in health and disease prevention. The assumption is that the expense of such programs pays off in the long run by reducing costs of absenteeism and treatment of disease. Typical programs involve a mixture of exercise, nutritional information, and stress-management education. There is implicit recognition in such programs that the healthy balance for the modern careerist consists of involvement in non-career competencies and sources of stimulation, as we saw earlier in this chapter. The programs support reexamining one's priorities regarding career, family, friendships, and outside activities.

Based on my work with organizations, I am critical of the usefulness of such programs, though there is much that is good and useful about many of them. For example, programs of employee assistance do address concrete problems and provide significant help to many troubled people. Efforts to help careerists deal with work-related problems—or prevent them—are based on the growing recognition that an employee's personal and family life have an impact on productivity and effectiveness and the recognition that it is more cost-efficient to help troubled employees overcome their problems than to train someone new to step into their position.

But these programs are also limited by the "Big Brother" context in which they exist. Many troubled careerists have told me that they would never talk to the employee-assistance counselor about their conflicts, for fear that it would be used against them. They realize that the counselor or company psychiatrist works for the organization, after all, which compromises the objectivity of the practitioner and limits confidentiality. Moreover, the career professional often questions, rightly or wrongly, the competence of counselors or psychiatrists who work in these settings to begin with. And the programs of help for troubled employees are also marred by an image problem: they are perceived by managerial and professional workers as being primarily for lower-level workers. Employee assistance programs also tend to remove the responsibility for dealing with subordinates' problems from the level of the manager, where it belongs. The bottom-line role of the manager is the development of his or her subordinates. Learning how to deal with problems which interfere with development is a legitimate part of that role.

More broadly, these programs also fail to perceive or address problems on the organizational level that, as we have seen with cases of both Surface Sanity and the Working Wounded, underlie many conflicts to begin with. In this sense, such programs mystify and ultimately mislead the careerist regarding the source and resolution of conflicts.

Techniques are not enough. Counseling programs, stress management, and wellness programs are ultimately limited to helping the person cope with the situation. They can effectively help the person deal with a circumscribed, specific problem, and can provide a useful adjunct to developing better trade-offs at work. But at best, they are an organizational Band-Aid. They exist in isolation from the larger context of understanding how the symptoms are linked to more systemic issues which require holistic strategies of change and development involving increased participation, building a team orientation, diminishing bureaucratic layers, and increasing the experience of meaning in the work.

Holistic Strategies Are Good for Business.   American careerists are in a squeeze. Most feel motivated to do high-quality work, but their desire to do so is undermined by management practices. A study of attitudes of careerists found that managerial practices blunt rather than stimulate and reinforce people's desire to work productively.[9] Careerists' experience a distinction between what would make jobs more satisfying versus what would make them more motivating. They want more motivation, from potential for advancement, a chance to develop their abilities, to job challenges; the range of desires that are characteristic of the New Normalcy. But most are not convinced that employers really even want high-quality or optimum performance.

Similarly, in studies of executives about what should be emphasized in business school education, one finds increasing recognition of the need for adaptability to changing economic, technological, and social conditions that affect the workplace and the marketplace. More and more, they see the need for enhanced marketing skill, computer literacy, and increasing motivation through participation and opportunities for development. While managers have traditionally been engaged in complex financial gymnastics, many now recognize that this absorption has caused them to lose touch with the realities of social and technological change. In fact, one study found that successful executives consider unimportant the various "new management" techniques like the capital-asset-pricing model, the probabilistic decision tree, beta coefficients, linear programming, econometric and technological forecasting, and the like.[10] Increased value is being placed on a broad-based liberal arts education as the best preparation for the vision, thinking, and understanding necessary to bring companies into the twenty-first century.

Opportunities are needed within organizations for development on the job, new skills, participation, decentralization, the creation of meaningful work in the job market that taps into the high level of motivation, ambition, and education of the new careerist; that taps the positive motives rather than inhibits, thereby strengthening the negative.

This is particularly essential in view of the fact that, as we have seen, work today is too often insufficiently meaningful for the new breed of careerists. They are not sufficiently motivated by traditional economic and social incentives. More holistic strategies take into account technology, organizational culture, the values of workers, prevailing ideology, and national policies. No one factor is sufficient, by itself, to bring about positive change. Michael Maccoby's several-year study of the value orientations and motives of careerists within service-oriented organizations portrays the transformation taking place and the holistic strategies it requires in this way: "Technology and international competition are transforming the dominant mode of production in the U.S. and the other industrialized countries. The emerging post-industrial mode of production is called technoservice. This implies not only the use of computer technology to produce information, but also using this information to solve problems for customers and clients. In contrast to the fragmented jobs of industrial bureaucracy, the technoservice mode requires teams and networks which respond to customer demands that are not fully predictable. Teams require knowledge of the business, its goals and values, and skill in interpersonal relations to share information. This mode thus requires changes in organization, attitude, skills, knowledge and leadership."[11]

The point is that the traditional structure and management systems of industrial bureaucracy no longer fit a world of changing technology and intensified competition. Thinking of overall organizational development in a holistic way means developing ways to adapt to the needs of customers and clients, manage new technology, and engage the positive drives and values of the new breed of careerist. That is, new technology, intense competition, and the changing values of workers seeking self-development require new thinking. Previously successful concepts of work productivity, motivation, organization and authority fit a disappearing industrial-bureaucratic system. In the new technoservice economy, the fragmented roles of the bureaucratic office and factory must be integrated into participative, service-oriented teams.[12] There has been insufficient awareness of how programs like quality circles, employee involvement, or participatory management must be integrated into organizations; or how effective innovation requires all participants to develop a shared understanding of strategy, roles, and relationships.

This new thrust, which reflects the organizational strand of the double helix of development, has roots in the concept of the "sociotechnical" system developed by E. L. Trist and his colleagues at the Tavistock Institute in England, during the early 1950s. They tried to take account of both the technical-production system, and the accompanying social-psychological system of work organization that surrounds the work being performed. Using this concept, the Tavistock researchers demonstrated that productivity in certain work settings was increased by greater participation of workers. For example, the use of particular technology required a minimum of hierarchy for the organization to function most efficiently and productively.

Evolving from this early work, a new approach in the United States, based on a Scandinavian model—which in many ways provides a better model for the U.S. culture than the Japanese—has been evolving. Its roots go back to 1972, when a joint labor-management project, the first in the United States, was begun by Harman International Industries and the United Auto Workers, at an auto-parts factory in Bolivar, Tennessee. Subsequent to this, similar projects were developed in business, government, and factories, to develop new ways of looking at productivity and technology in relation to principles of human development. The goal of these projects was to improve both the quality of working life and organizational effectiveness. The programs have been based on the assumption that the satisfaction of workers can be improved and positive motivation can be increased, by involving teams of workers in problem-solving groups.[13] As a result, product quality increases, administrative costs decline, and workers seem to adapt more cooperatively to new technology, since they are involved in modifying their jobs.

Maccoby's research and projects he has developed with business and union leaders show that intense competition requires the technoservice industries to replace rule-oriented hierarchies with flexible teams, which can be more responsive to customers. This shift has reverberations in other areas, including organizational structure, performance-evaluation systems, training, and management style. While old-style industrial bureaucracies could be run by administrative experts, technoservice teams require more leaders who focus on defining business goals and creating a climate of trust essential to participation, delegation of authority, and exchange of information. The industrial bureaucracies, composed of segmented roles and discrete specialties, all coordinated by a hierarchy of bosses, is no longer effective. Computerized technology and changing markets demand delegation and interdependency, in which people cooperate out of self-interest, learning to solve problems and make decisions together.

There is also evidence from these studies and projects that the younger, new-breed careerists see their work in terms of opportunities for self-fulfillment. Reflecting the traits and attitudes of the New Normalcy, these careerists are less hierarchical, more flexible, and more readily adaptive to teamwork and the new technology. Yet many, particularly those who become troubled and conflicted, feel torn between the values of this new orientation and those of the individualist-expert orientation, which lends itself to seeking approval of higher authority, continued movement up the career ladder, and adapting well to the old-style hierarchical, bureaucratic organization.[14]

In line with these new directions, management roles shift and evolve. For example, human resources management requires an expanded role in order to improve productivity. In the most productive companies human resource managers work closely with top management on strategic planning, locating problem areas, suggesting new initiatives, planning for future personnel needs during both growth and recession periods, and motivating the highly skilled new-breed careerist. Participative management is another essential to contributing to productivity through supporting opportunities for further development among careerists. Studies of the relation between participation and productivity show that the old methods of labor-management relations are no longer economically viable. Participation is necessary in order to stay competitive.

A growing number of corporate chiefs are trying to learn firsthand what is occurring within their companies, and are breaking with the tradition of being aloof, getting information indirectly from committee reports, financial statements, or from lower managers. At the same time, organizations are recognizing that the shift to new methods requires broader-based skills among mid- and upper-level managers. The new thrust is toward giving managers an understanding of how the entire company functions, in response to the recognition that these managers have traditionally viewed the company too narrowly. Japanese companies have dealt with this by rotating managers into new jobs at intervals, to develop broader generalists. This contrasts with the traditional tendency of American managers to develop the orientation of a specialized expert in, for example, sales, engineering, accounting, and other areas.

The twin requirements of the market and the values of the new careerist also lead to increasing flexibility in such areas as corporate planning and asset management. The aim is a heightened focus on the overall direction of the business, anticipation of how changing events might impact it, and an understanding of how to manage invested capital to maximize productivity in a world of changing and intensified competition.

Even with successful adaptation to these changes, the careerist has to live with a level of uncertainty that, as we saw in Chapter 6, is part of the New Normalcy today. And there are inevitable conflicts that arise from the transformation itself that is under way. A person may be well prepared, both personally and professionally, for success in the New Age of work, and capable of dealing with uncertainty, yet be suddenly and adversely affected by shifting market forces. Job security has almost vanished for professionals and middle managers. The trend toward mid-level dismissals means the end of the tradition that career professionals could count on job security.

The leader is central to developing effective, holistic strategies of change. Attempts at teamwork or quality circles fail when employees don't trust leadership. They end up feeling manipulated. Top leadership must demonstrate values which support development. In fact, evidence is mounting that managers who fail to develop subordinates and articulate relevant values end up with less productive businesses.

The emotional effects of successful career development occur within a context of rapid social and economic change. The careerist culture provides many positive and understandably desirable rewards. But it also demands a price in one's emotional life and values. It generates compromises, trade-offs, simmering anger, acute emotional conflict, and other symptoms—psychological, behavioral, and physical. These all affect normal, relatively healthy individuals. In depressing circumstances, normal people feel depressed; conflict or self-betrayal cause normal people to feel anxious. "Normal" adjustment in our culture, reflected in the attitudes, behavior, and life goals that are more or less shared, deadens the heart and causes suffering and conflict when we embrace them uncritically and fail to recognize the negative side they generate for our emotions and values.

Yet our passions motivate; we cannot hide from them. Solutions to the negative side of success will not be found in blind belief that all conflict is simply a legacy from childhood; or that one can graft on "new behaviors" as easily as slipping a new software program into the computer; or that biochemical defects in the brain are the cause of all our conflicts; or, at the opposite extreme, that all troubles are caused by bad situations or the "wrong" management techniques.

The struggle to change is especially difficult when the work environment and overall career culture support and reinforce unhealthy or destructive attitudes while at the same time providing certain pleasures. Then it is normal to feel troubled and conflicted. Successful lives today stimulate, for many, emotional conflict, resentment, depression, and physical illness. This has become an inevitable part of life in modern society. It can only be altered by change which supports the cultivation of a more integrated vision of success and fulfillment, in which the definition of "success" moves away from a narrow one, focused on career, to a broader definition, based on a view of successful life, in which career is a central part, but not its sole component. Such a vision can support, our most positive yearnings and impulses and help us develop more balanced, creative, and fulfilling lives.

APPENDIX

The research method I used in studying the emotional lives of careerists is called social–psychoanalysis. This method does not involve psychoanalyzing individual people (unless they are patients to begin with), but rather applies psychoanalytic interpretation to a combination of material. This includes intensive interviews; interpretation of dreams, particularly those relating to work; study of the person's history and culture of work; and analysis of Rorschach tests, which facilitate understanding of unconscious attitudes and passions; the person's inner life and style of thought.

The method combines some features of anthropological study of the culture of work and context of the person's life with psychoanalytic interpretation of the individual's conscious and unconscious motives and orientation. A central feature of it is the process of participant study. This involves a dialogue in which the individuals studied are expected to benefit from the process of study, not just the researcher, through feedback and discussion.

The interview portion takes a minimum of two hours for each person, often longer. The interview consists of questions which tap into the person's work history; personal values; perceptions of self; life goals; significant experiences in personal development and in career choices; responses to different kinds of work environments and management; philosophy of life; religious orientation; view of love; views of significant problems facing society; and other related areas. The questions do not constitute a survey instrument, but rather, serve as a guide to discussion.[1]

A main part of the research method was my interpretation of the Rorschach test, which consists of ten inkblots printed on separate white cards, about 7 × 10″ large. Some are in shades of black and white (Cards I, IV, V, VI, and VII), while some have, in addition, portions of red (Cards II and III), and others are multicolored (Cards VIII, IX, and X).

The person is handed each card and asked to describe what they look like—everything they see in them. The card may be looked at in any way the person wishes, and there are no time limits. After the responses are obtained, the person is asked questions about the location and other aspects of the inkblot he or she utilized in a particular perception.

Interpretation requires both experience and training in combining both the "formal" aspects of responses (use of space, color, shading, etc.) with symbolic meaning of content, movement, and color. In this way we can clarify and uncover unconscious impulses, needs, fears, tendencies toward pathology, modes of relatedness, and so on. The sequence of perceptions reveals how certain attitudes or wishes may provoke anxiety, guilt, rage, etc. The traditional interpretation, developed by Rorschach,[2] Klopfer et al.,[3] and Beck et al.,[4] is based on analyzing the form, color, shape, shading, and movement of the person's responses, and their perceptual accuracy. Others, such as Schafer,[5] Schachtel,[6] and Brown,[7] worked on developing character interpretation from the Rorschach in terms of psychoanalytic theory.

Interpreting the Rorschach is experiential, in that it requires seeing things through the eyes of the individual: feeling what determines his or her response. What a person sees on the cards are projections of the individual's own character attitudes and orientation. For example, whether a person sees something in the whole inkblot versus a small detail may indicate how he or she deals with new information.[8] Can the person integrate a set of information into a dynamic whole, or are unrelated data simply collected together? Does the person stick to tiny details and avoid the larger picture? How accurately does he or she perceive complex reality? Do the person's needs distort perceptions so that what he or she sees makes no sense to anyone else? If he or she does see reality accurately, is this achieved at the expense of ignoring emotional stimuli, represented by colors and shading?

Can the person integrate thought and feeling into more vivid perceptions? Or do strong colors, especially reds, suggest passions that break through the person's controls and upset his or her intellectual effectiveness? Does he or she inject movement and life into what is seen? Does the movement show active identification with human activity? Is it a projection of animal strivings, not fully integrated with conscious values? Or does the person empathize with creative work, dance, or sports? Does he or she feel comfortable with spontaneous impulses? Or does the movement express natural forces experienced as totally beyond control? Is the person afraid to see anything different from the conventional, or does he or she have the imagination and daring to perceive with originality?

The symbolic content of responses is determined, in part, by the shapes and colors of the different blots. Although the possibilities for response are limitless, the inkblots tend to suggest different themes:

Card I suggests a common winged creature like a butterfly or bat, but it may stimulate expressions of inner conflicts (the side figures struggling). Sometimes a person expresses a central theme of self-image, such as grandiosity, self-contempt, or mask-like self-concealment.

Card II suggests two figures touching, with common themes of intimacy, passion (the red portion), play, or lively celebration. It may stimulate themes of performing for others, with repressed negativism and feelings of humiliation and anger.

Card III presents two figures in some type of relation to each other, and to objects. It stimulates themes about work or structured-play relationships, such as cooking, waiting on tables, dancing, etc.

Card IV presents a bulky figure that is often seen like a child's view of a looming authority figure. Responses sometimes indicate how a person handles authority: directly, by going around it, and so on. The shading suggests texture and may stimulate attitudes about affection.

Card V, another winglike figure, tends to evoke themes of birds, or feelings of tension, reflecting the two halves that may appear to buttress each other.

Card VI, with its phallic, totemic top and furry shading below, stimulates for men symbols of sexuality and potency, and attitudes about them. Women sometimes express attitudes toward male sexuality. (For example, worshipful, castrating.)

Card VII has a cloudy, soft, and fluffy texture and often evokes the individual's attitude toward women, femininity, or the mother; for example, graceful dancers versus stuffed animals versus pet dogs versus gossipy old women. Some who are threatened by softness turn the figures into rocks.

Card VIII, with its many colors, seems to stimulate themes of self-image, in part because of the two animal-like figures on the sides which appear to be standing or moving from one area to another.

Card IX, with its misty colors, presents a certain sense of the spiritual or supernatural, which produces total rejection or inability to respond from some people who lack a sense of self. For others it is a stimulus to express their deepest values and purposes, their frame of orientation and devotion, or sense of ultimate meaning.

Card X, with its many small, colorful figures, evokes in some symbols of undisciplined appetite, underdeveloped emotions, or an intellectual challenge to integrate seemingly unrelated events. How this is done expresses a sense of the world as alive versus dead, hopeful versus threatening, and so on.

The social–psychoanalytic method was developed over a period of years by Fromm and Maccoby, and has been used in a number of studies of people and organizations both in the U.S. and other countries. Its roots lie in an early version that Fromm developed in the early 1930s in Germany, before fleeing Hitler. Directing a group of researchers at the Frankfort Institute, he explored whether the German masses would support Nazism, should Hitler come to power. By applying psychoanalytic understanding to society and groups he was able to probe beneath the level usually allowed by conventional public opinion surveys or social psychology research.[9] For example, opinion surveys usually tap just into surface opinion which can easily change with circumstances or fashion.

Using an open-ended interpretive questionnaire which he developed, Fromm examined the more deeply rooted attitudes and strivings of the German working class in relation to unconscious yearnings to submit to authority, the influence of child-rearing practices in the culture, resentment toward the middle class, and so on. About thirty years later

Maccoby joined Fromm in Mexico, where they further developed the methodology to a project of understanding how social and technological change affected peasant villagers' deeply-held attitudes and passions, including those that were unconscious and repressed. They set out to study the villagers under the impact of new technology and the social forces accompanying industrialization and modernization: who did and did not adapt successfully to these changes, and what the consequences were for the peasants as individuals, for the village culture, and the larger society. Using this method, they explored the relationships between character structure and work, farming methods, and family relations. And they analyzed the process by which certain types were better adapted to new agricultural technology and the developing economy; and at what cost, both to themselves and to other types who were less able to adapt. They related this to the emergence of certain negative character traits and behavior, like alcoholism and violence. Their findings were published in a 1970 book, *Social Character in a Mexican Village*.

Maccoby further developed and utilized this method in his studies of corporate and government managers and executives, *The Gamesman* and *The Leader*, and it is also the basis of a major study of workers in the technoservice industries, now in preparation.[10]

Using this method of research for *Modern Madness*, I interpreted significant themes based on the combination of material from the interview, Rorschach test, dreams, and any other available material. Consistent with the principle of participant research, these themes were discussed with the individual whenever possible, to stimulate a dialogue about self. When I presented my interpretations, the person was able to further confirm, clarify, challenge, or modify them. In some cases, discussion of themes occurred in the context of clinical evaluation or treatment of the person, which allowed particular themes to be further verified by clinical evidence.

NOTES

PREFACE

1. Erich Fromm and Michael Maccoby, *Social Character in a Mexican Village*, Prentice-Hall, 1970.
2. Michael Maccoby, *The Gamesman*, Simon & Schuster, 1976.
3. I later published some of these early findings: "Uncle Sam's Working Wounded," *The Washington Post Magazine*, February 17, 1980; "Emotional Disturbance in the Federal Government," *Administration and Society*, 1983, 14:403–448; and "Bureaucracy and Psychopathology," *Political Psychology*, 1983, 4:223–243.

CHAPTER 1

1. *The Gamesman*, op. cit.
2. This point of view builds upon earlier works of Fromm and Maccoby, such as Fromm, *The Sane Society*, Rinehart, 1955; Fromm and Maccoby, *Social Character in a Mexican Village*, Prentice-Hall, 1970; and Maccoby, "Work and Human Development," *Professional Psychology*, 1980, 11:509–518.
3. Typical examples: An upper-level manager in a retail firm, brain-damaged in an auto accident, could no longer perform executive-level work. His boss felt sympathetic, and attempted to shift his duties and responsibilities to others, as much as possible. Compassionate but soft-hearted, this strategy did not last very long. The man was eventually retired by higher management, and his boss got into serious difficulty for attempting to help in the way he did. Another person, a brilliant economic analyst, was paranoid schizophrenic, with delusions about foreign trade with visitors from other planets. The latter were humored by superiors as a strategy to reap the benefit of his expertise, but

233

everyone around him suffered: some worried about him, and others were frightened. Grossly disturbed people usually don't rise very high up the career ladder, but some do, particularly if their professional or technical expertise is needed by the organization and relatively untouched by their sickness.

4. Bureau of Labor Statistics.

5. This has occurred in companies like Apple Computer and MCI.

6. Evidence for this is presented in Michael Maccoby's *Why Work: Leading the New Generation,* Simon & Schuster, 1988.

7. Opinion Research Corp., 1984.

8. National Institute of Mental Health, 1984.

9. Cited in *Corporate Commentary: Worksite Health Evaluation Report,* Washington Business Group on Health, March 1985.

10. Dorothy Lang, "Preconditions of Three Types of Alienation in Young Managers and Professionals," *Journal of Occupational Behaviour,* 1985, 6:171–182.

11. Michael Maccoby, personal communication.

12. Thomas Mann, "Tonio Kröger" (1903), in *Stories of Three Decades,* Alfred A. Knopf, 1936.

13. For example, in fiction: D. M. Thomas, *The White Hotel;* Morris West, *The World Is Made of Glass;* Judith Rossner, *August;* and nonfiction examinations of psychoanalysis: Janet Malcolm, *Psychoanalysis: The Impossible Profession;* and Jeffrey Masson, *Assault on the Truth.* Most were widely read, if not best-sellers.

14. For example, Aristotle wrote about moral character, including the human "virtues" and "vices" which describe human passions; the poet Ovid wrote around 8 A.D. in the *Metamorphoses* about passions that rule human beings, and how humans are impelled and often destroyed by passions they barely comprehend; and modern writers such as William Faulkner and Isaac Bashevis Singer, among others, have also dealt with the role of passions in human lives.

15. Though dealing with different issues, some of these writings nevertheless contained precursors of the present theme. For example, T. S. Eliot's depiction of the spiritual decay of post–World War I man in "The Wasteland"; Malcolm Lowry's classic 1947 novel *Under the Volcano,* about the spiritual dissolution and alienation of modern man; and other writers who have portrayed similar themes, such as Henry Miller, Norman Mailer, William Burroughs, Allen Ginsberg, and Jack Kerouac.

16. Much of this malaise has been captured in the fiction of some contemporary writers, particularly Ann Beattie, as well as Mary Robison, Raymond Carver, and others. The characters they write about are often more extreme, spaced-out casualties of the '60s who have degenerated into passive alienation, who feel unconnected and paralyzed by impotent anger, and are living flat, attenuated lives.

CHAPTER 2

1. For an analysis of the careerist work ethic in the context of previous work ethics in American society, see Michael Maccoby, *The Leader,* Simon & Schuster, 1981, 23–38.

2. Edgar H. Schein, "Career Theory and Research: Some Issues for the Future," and Donald M. Wolfe and David A. Kolb, "Beyond Specialization: The Quest for Integration in Midcareer," both in C. Brooklyn Derr, ed., *Work, Family, and the Career,* Praeger, 1980. Also, Michael Driver, "Career Concepts—A New Approach to Career Research," in J. Paap, ed., *New Dimensions in Human Resource Management,* Prentice-Hall, 1981.

3. Edgar H. Schein, *Career Dynamics,* Addison-Wesley, 1978.

4. Ibid.

5. *The Wall Street Journal,* December 20, 1982.

6. Paul Evans and Fernando Bartolome, "Professional Life and Private Life: Three Stages in the Lives of Managers," *Organizational Dynamics,* Spring 1979.

7. Rage at the office also takes a heavy toll on other employees, as well, regardless of whether the person's rage is the product of emotional disturbance. For example a colleague of one person whose rage became increasingly noticeable said, "Half the employees around him were popping valium all day long, yet *he* was the one who was nuts."

8. Carol Tavris, *Anger: The Misunderstood Emotion*, Simon & Schuster, 1983.

9. Center for Industry and Health Care, Boston University, August 1983.

10. Survey conducted by the 800-Cocaine Helpline, a national drug treatment service based at Fair Oaks Hospital, Summit, New Jersey.

11. The quotes regarding loneliness were reported in *The New York Times Magazine*, August 15, 1982.

12. Thomas J. Peters and Robert H. Waterman, *In Search of Excellence*, Warner Books, 1982.

13. *The New York Times Magazine*, op. cit.

14. *The Washington Post Magazine*, September 19, 1982.

15. Opinion Research Corporation, 1983.

16. *The Wall Street Journal*, November 2, 1983.

17. Op-ed column by Ralph Nader and Mark Green, *The Wall Street Journal*, March 12, 1976.

18. Earl Shorris, *The Oppressed Middle*, Doubleday/Anchor, 1981.

19. Joseph Heller, *Something Happened*, Alfred A. Knopf, 1974.

20. See, for example, Morton Feinberg, *Corporate Bigamy*, William Morrow, 1981.

21. Opinion Research Corporation, 1984.

22. *Putting the Work Ethic to Work: A Public Agenda Report on Restoring America's Competitive Vitality*, Public Agenda Foundation, 1983.

23. Paul Solman and Thomas Friedman, *Life and Death on the Corporate Battlefield*, Simon & Schuster, 1983.

24. *The Gamesman*, op. cit.

CHAPTER 3

1. Albert O. Hirschman, *The Passions and the Interests*, Princeton University Press, 1977.

2. D.H. Lawrence, *Sons and Lovers*, Viking, 1913.

3. Similar situations were described by Arthur Koestler in his 1941 novel *Darkness at Noon*, about the Stalinist purge trials during the 1930s. He described the willingness with which many midlevel communist careerists degraded themselves and subordinated their achievements, their careers, and dignity to the interests of the Party.

4. *The Wall Street Journal*, July 1, 1982.

5. Norman Mailer, *The Naked and the Dead*, Rinehart, 1948.

6. Also, a senator once publicly praised an outgoing head of a major federal agency as someone "who knows how to kick ass and take names."

7. *Fortune*, January 29, 1979.

8. See *The Gamesman*, op. cit., pp. 76–85.

9. For example, Lawrence Stone, "Madness," *The New York Review of Books*, December 16, 1982.

10. Thomas C. Schelling, *Choice and Consequence*, Harvard University Press, 1983.

11. This and the following quotes are from *The New York Times*, January 19, 1982.

12. See also Anatole France's well-known quote, "When a man is endowed with power, it is hard for him not to misuse it;" Henry Adams' classic novel of 1880 about power-lust in Washington, *Democracy;* and Louis Auchincloss' contemporary novels about power, morality, and arrogance.

13. Richard Sennett, *Authority*, Knopf, 1980.

14. John Kenneth Galbraith, *The Anatomy of Power*, Houghton Mifflin, 1983.

CHAPTER 4

1. *Playboy*, December 1980.

2. Melvin L. Kohn and Carmi Schooler, *Work and Personality: An Inquiry into the Impact of Social Stratification*, Ablex Publishing Corp., 1983.

3. Erich Fromm, *Man for Himself*, Rinehart, 1947.

4. Benedict de Spinoza, *Ethics*, in *Works of Spinoza*, Vol. 2, Dover, 1955.

5. Srully Blotnick, *The Corporate Steeplechase*, Facts on File, 1984.

6. See also *The New York Times Magazine*, May 22, 1983, regarding conflicts among law students.

7. American Bar Association survey.

8. *The New York Times*, March 9, 1984.

9. The quotes are from *The New York Times*, March 22, 1985, and August 19, 1984, respectively.

10. *The New York Times*, December 27, 1982.

11. *The Wall Street Journal*, June 1, 1983.

12. *The Wall Street Journal*, March 12, 1982.

13. *The Washington Post*, June 10, 1980, and *The Wall Street Journal*, August 16, 1983.

14. The quotes and data are from *The Wall Street Journal*, December 15, 16, and 17, 1981.

CHAPTER 5

1. John Naisbitt, *Megatrends*, Warner Books, 1982.

2. Alvin Toffler, *The Third Wave*, Morrow, 1980.

3. For example, the World Center for Computers and Human Resources in Paris is engaged in such projects as putting medical knowledge in computers to enable workers with minimum training to diagnose and treat illnesses in remote areas and Third World countries where no doctors are available.

4. In Greenock, Scotland, in which high-tech industries have sprung up, tensions have arisen between older people and others who are unable to embrace and adapt to the new wave of change, and those who are. Women are promoted into management and young careerists travel regularly, unlike their parental generation. Also, the automation of factories sometimes has unforeseen effects for cultural reasons, such as in the episodes of mass hysteria in Malaysia. Spirits are believed to be possessing people, usually young women who work in the new semiconductor factories, and factories are often closed for a week or more as a result. "Possession" seems to be a symptom of the rapid movement from a traditional culture into intense modernization, in which people are moving from the sixteenth century into the New Age without a chance to make adjustments. There are no outlets, particularly for women in the Malay culture. Healers and goat sacrifices are used by factory managers. There, valium won't work.

5. Interview in the Brussels newsmagazine *Pourquoi Pas?*, June 3, 1982.

6. *The Washington Post*, January 23, 1983.

7. Bureau of Labor Statistics.

8. *The Wall Street Journal*, April 12, 1983.

9. When Blue Shield of Massachusetts became highly automated, using video display terminals for workers to transfer data from claim forms to the company's computer system, a variety of problems quickly developed. Claims processors began calling the office a modern sweat shop, and personnel staff found that the workers couldn't last more than two years at it. Much of the criticism that computerized technology has created the electronic equivalent of the moving assembly line concerns the negative side of automating routine office jobs, without changing the organization and management of the work.

10. U.S. Public Health Service report, cited in *The Wall Street Journal*, May 6, 1983.

11. *The Wall Street Journal*, June 19, 1984.

12. The study of angina pain among VDT operators was conducted by the University of North Carolina School of Public Health, 1983–1984. The findings about eye strain and other stress were reported in a 1983 study by the National Academy of Sciences. For related evidence see *Science News*, July 16, 1983, and *The Washington Post*, March 13, 1985. In recent years I have consulted to cases of workers who sought medical disability on the grounds that working in front of the VDT was driving them crazy and causing extreme anguish.

13. This study, "The Human Side of Robotics: How Workers React to a Robot," was conducted by Linda Argote, Paul S. Goodman, and David Schkade, of Carnegie-Mellon University, and published in *Sloan Management Review*, Spring 1983. There are many examples of similar themes: Studies of insurance and utility companies in New England found many worker complaints based on the fact that VDT operators were expected to enter material into computers without change, even though they could see errors. They were not expected to be able to know or decide if the information was correct. And studies by the National Institute for Occupational Safety have concluded that the key issue is not computerized technology or robotics per se, but the context of work organization and management in which they are employed.

14. Bureau of Labor Statistics.

15. *The Wall Street Journal*, March 7, 1983.

16. *The Wall Street Journal*, January 12, 1983.

17. *The Wall Street Journal*, December 16, 1983.

18. *The New York Times*, April 7, 1982.

19. 1981 survey of career employees in the Senior Executive Service, conducted by the General Accounting Office.

20. Poll conducted by *The Washington Post*, reported April 26, 1983.

21. *The Wall Street Journal*, July 19, 1982.

22. Bureau of Labor Statistics.

23. 1982 survey by Korn/Ferrey International, an executive search firm.

24. The example and quote that follow were reported in *The Wall Street Journal*, September 22, 1982.

25. AT&T survey, 1982.

26. *The Wall Street Journal*, July 19, 1982.

27. 1981 survey by Booz, Allen & Hamilton Inc.

28. AT&T survey, 1982.

29. *Business Week*, April 25, 1983.

30. International Labor Organization report, 1983.

31. Personal communication. Also, *The Washington Post*, June 28, 1983.

32. A lawyer quoted in *The New York Times* (January 16, 1983) about this issue said, "I think of myself as an excellent trial lawyer. I was not educated to manage a firm and I'm not sure I'm temperamentally suited for this."

33. Paul Johnson, *Modern Times*, Harper & Row, 1983.

34. Erich Fromm, *The Anatomy of Human Destructiveness*. Holt, Rinehart & Winston, 1973.

35. This theme has been most strikingly portrayed in literature, such as Orwell's *1984* and *Animal Farm*, Huxley's *Brave New World*, and Kafka's tragicomic portrayals of bureaucratic mentality, imprisonment, and alienation in *The Trial* and *The Castle*.

36. *Escape From Freedom*, Farrar & Rinehart, 1941; *The Sane Society*, Rinehart & Company, 1955; *The Art of Loving*, Harper & Row, 1956; *The Anatomy of Human Destructiveness*, op. cit.

37. Some literati enjoy subscribing to a vision of "state, sadism, and individual helplessness," as novelist E. L. Doctorow put it in *Playboy*, January 1984, as representing the sum total of the twentieth century.

38. This is discussed by David Burnham in *The Rise of the Computer State*, Random House, 1983.

39. Seymour Martin Lipset and William Schneider, *The Confidence Gap*, The Free Press, 1983.

40. Column in *The Washington Post*, November 8, 1983.

41. The survey was conducted by Donald Kanter, University of Southern California, for Campbell-Ewald International.

42. For example, sixty signatures are needed before a company can begin producing iron. A Soviet economist wrote that 90% of the documents generated (800 billion per year) contribute only to making administration more cumbersome and inflexible. Other officials are openly advocating greater involvement of workers in management and more decentralization, in order to improve efficiency. A magazine read by Soviet managers has criticized planning and production methods, and has excerpted articles from U.S. business publications, to illustrate Western industrial efficiency and work styles. A Soviet journalist wrote about buying a pair of shoes that immediately fell apart. He visited the factory, where he learned that no one had instructed the operator of the machine that attaches the soles to the shoes how long to keep them under it. The factory director said it didn't matter, as long as production quotas were met.

43. Milovan Djilas, *The New Class*, Praeger, 1957. His comments about Yugoslavia are from an op-ed column he wrote in *The Wall Street Journal*, November 23, 1983.

44. Bureau of Labor Statistics.

45. 1983 survey conducted by *Fortune* magazine.

46. 1981 poll by Catalyst, a New York resource center for professional women.

47. *The Gamesman*, op. cit.

48. For example, a 1982 survey by Korn/Ferry International, an executive search firm, and the UCLA Graduate School of Management.

49. Fran Worden Henry, *Toughing It Out at Harvard*, Putnam, 1983.

50. Personal communication.

51. 1982 *Wall Street Journal*/Gallup Survey.

CHAPTER 6

1. Alexis de Tocqueville, *Democracy in America*, Vintage, 1958.

2. This argument is based on Maccoby's analysis of the work ethic in *The Leader*, op. cit.

3. Joseph Heller, *Catch-22*, Simon & Schuster, 1961.

4. Bureau of Labor Statistics.

5. Co-sponsored by the Association of American Colleges and the National Endowment for the Humanities.

6. *The New York Times*, July 19, 1982.

7. Some have started their own companies, marked by informal and individualistic styles of management. One, who gave up the security of lifetime employment in a major corporation to start his own company said, "To be a part of a big company is like being a component in a big machine." He hires reformed juvenile delinquents because, he says, he wants people who think in unusual ways, whose curiosity runs away with them (reported in *The New York Times*, March 8, 1983).

8. AT&T survey, 1982.

9. *New York Times* poll, December 4, 1983.

10. Even when entire companies relocate, the new careerist may not. For example, when the 600 employees of Georgia Pacific Corporation, a forest products company, were asked to move from Oregon to Atlanta in 1982, half said they wouldn't, despite generous offers of help to purchase new homes, expense-paid trips, and other deal-sweeteners. The reasons cited were the quality of life and desire to stay rooted, even at the expense of career.

11. Quoted in *The Wall Street Journal,* May 16, 1985.

12. Survey and marketing campaign conducted by Advertising for Women, an advertising agency, in 1983.

13. Daniel Yankelovich, *New Rules,* Random House, 1981.

14. For example, the Dalai Lama has frequently written about the connection between personal values and social concerns, pointing out the commonality among different spiritual systems regarding exploitation, injustice, and corruption.

15. Quoted in *The New York Times,* December 4, 1983. Also, some advertising campaigns target the self-fulfillment theme among women. For example, the Revlon company changed its focus in the mid-80s away from the unattached, independent woman to one who is interested in more personal fulfillment, a more whole life.

16. Some women writers have addressed this theme. See, for example, Germaine Greer's argument in *Sex and Destiny* that permissiveness has led to women still being manipulated by men, and that motherhood should be reinforced because it is a degraded, lonely occupation. Similarly, Ingrid Bengis concludes in *Combat in the Erogenous Zone* that ideologies about "nonpossessiveness" were destructive to intimacy.

17. Both men and women to whom career is important tend to marry later. One survey found that 60% of the women said that supportiveness of their career is a man's most important quality.

18. For some, this leads to an actual career change to religious work. The ministry is now attracting more professionals who are dropping out of other careers in search of more fulfillment. This has contributed to a sharp increase in enrollment at theological seminaries in recent years.

19. These previous examples and quotes are from *The Wall Street Journal,* November 22, 1982, and June 9, 1983; and *The New York Times,* May 20, 1982.

20. Notable examples, here, are the works of playwright Sam Shepard, whose characters are often getting lost or crippled by the struggle for success, and the search for more solidity, in the context of the family; and of multimedia performance artist Laurie Anderson, whose themes are emptiness and meaninglessness within a high-tech, commercial world.

21. Study conducted by the Urban Institute, Washington, D.C.

22. The study of executives' children was reported in *The Wall Street Journal,* March 19 and 20, 1985; the survey of college freshmen, "The American Freshman: National Norms for Fall 1984," was conducted jointly by UCLA and the American Council on Education.

23. The quotes that follow are from *The Washington Post,* December 2, 1983.

24. Data from the Seven College Study, based at Radcliffe College, a study of men and women students from the classes of 1981–1985.

25. Article by Mark Sanders in *The Washington Post,* December 30, 1984. See also the 1981 series on changing values and concerns of American youth by *Washington Post* writer Dan Morgan. His in-depth interviews confirm the theme of desire for achievement mixed with hope for expression of positive ideals.

26. The motives of profit and power among the rebelling colonialists have been overlooked as a factor in the development of the American Revolution. But the American experiment was motivated by ideals, not just by the prospect of getting rich. It was concerned with issues of freedom, corruption, the right to dissent, and the denial of representation.

27. Albert Hirschman, *The Passions and the Interests,* op. cit.

28. Fernand Braudel, *Civilization and Capitalism, 15th–18th Century,* Vol. 1, *The Structures of Everyday Life;* Vol. 2, *The Wheels of Commerce;* Vol. 3, *The Perspective of the World,* translated by Sian Reynolds, Harper & Row, 1981, 1982, 1984.

29. *The Leader,* op. cit., 23–55.

30. Cases of Richard Napier, collected and discussed in Michael MacDonald, *Mystical Bedlam,* Cambridge University Press, 1981.

31. Lawrence Stone quotes MacDonald's description of the "hatred, fear, and violence endemic in rural England before the Industrial Revolution," and adds that it was a world of suspicion, intrigue, petty jealousy, sudden brawls, and vindictive revenges for assumed slights or injuries (*New York Review of Books,* December 16, 1982).

32. It was first used by William Cullen, a Scottish doctor, in a 1777 book, *First Lines of the Practice of Physic.*

33. George Drinka traces this evolution in *The Birth of Neurosis,* Simon & Schuster, 1984.

34. "Psychological Gossip," *Asylum Journal of Mental Science,* 2, 1856.

35. Daniel H. Tuke, *Insanity in Ancient and Modern Life,* Macmillan (London), 1878.

36. J.E. Esquirol, *Mental Maladies, A Treatise on Insanity,* translated by E.K. Hunt, Lea & Blanchard, 1845.

37. For example, Daniel H. Tuke, *The Insane in the United States and Canada,* H.K. Lewis (London), 1885; G.M. Beard, *American Nervousness, Its Causes and Consequences,* Putnam, 1891; G.M. Beard, *A Practical Treatise on Nervous Exhaustion,* Wood, 1880; S. Weir Mitchell, "The Evolution of the Rest Treatment," *Journal of Nervous & Mental Disorders,* 31, 1904; E.H. Van Deusen, "Observations on a Form of Nervous Prostration (Neurasthenia) Culminating in Insanity," *Journal of Insanity,* April 1869; see also, *One Hundred Years of American Psychiatry,* American Psychiatric Association and Columbia University Press, 1944.

38. Listed in Daniel H. Tuke, 1885, op. cit.

39. Sigmund Freud, "The Neuro-Psychoses of Defense" (1894), in *The Standard Edition of the Complete Psychological Works of Sigmund Freud,* Vol. 1, ed. James Strachey, The Hogarth Press (London), 1966, 43–61.

40. Erich Fromm, "Freud's Model of Man and Its Social Determinants," and "The Oedipus Complex: Comments on the Case of Little Hans," both in *The Crisis of Psychoanalysis,* Holt, Rinehart & Winston, 1970.

41. This is discussed by Maccoby in *The Leader,* op. cit.

42. *The New York Times,* March 25, 1984.

43. Jean-Paul Sartre, *Being and Nothingness,* Philosophical Library, 1956, pp. 47–70. See also his novel, *The Reprieve,* translated by Eric Sutton, Alfred A. Knopf, 1947.

44. See, for example, the writing of Gena Berriault, a novelist and short-story writer, who has portrayed the kinds of lives that touch each other without intimacy; Raymond Carver, whose characters are typically alienated and bland, living out passive lives, devoid of hope; Mark Stevens, whose novel, *Summer in the City,* is about fast-track New York narcissists, given to extreme pursuit of passive pleasures. Similarly, the short stories of Lynne Sharon Schwartz, collected in her volume *Acquainted With the Night,* portray themes of personal betrayal and overall spiritual malaise. In David Leavitt's *Family Dancing* everyone tends to feel unconnected or emotionally damaged in the search for love and meaning. Other writers like Mark Strand, in *Mr. and Mrs. Baby and Other Stories,* satirize lives of extreme self-absorption, in which the trivial is treated as significant, and people's daily lives are filled with boring emptiness. Also, Richard Yates' *Young Hearts Crying* describes the sense of emptiness and meaninglessness many experience in their lives today, having lost or given up hope for fulfillment, and remaining stuck and trapped where they are. And Bret Easton Ellis' *Less Than Zero* gives, perhaps, the most devastating portrayal of all of the vacant souls at the younger end of the spectrum drowning in the emptiness of their own lives, wasted by riches and indulgence. Other writers, like Bobbie Ann Mason, Mary Robison, and Russell Banks portray the general theme of blunted, adrift lives, in which people hate how they live, but feel trapped and passive over unfulfilled dreams and possibilities. They feel so knocked around by the New Normalcy that they are filled with doubt about everything and can't pursue anything that has meaning.

CHAPTER 7

1. Sigmund Freud, "Future Prospects of Psychoanalytic Therapy," (1910) in *The Standard Edition of the Complete Psychological Works of Sigmund Freud*, Vol. 11, ed. James Strachey, Hogarth Press (London), 1957, 150.

2. Similar themes were the subject of Vance Packard's *The Status Seekers*, David Riesman's *The Lonely Crowd*, and such films as *The Young Philadelphians* and *A Thousand Clowns*.

3. See Erich Fromm's collection of essays, *The Crisis of Psychoanalysis*, op. cit., for an in-depth discussion of this issue, as well as Russell Jacoby's *The Repression of Psychoanalysis*, Basic Books, 1983.

4. Janet Malcolm, *Psychoanalysis: The Impossible Profession*, Alfred A. Knopf, 1981.

5. For example, a Houston hospital found that residents and interns missed at least one important symptom or made significant errors in two-thirds of their patients, and missed important findings that affected serious medical conditions. And periodically, physician researchers are found to have engaged in fraud to promote their career. For example, in 1983 the *New England Journal of Medicine* had to retract two fraudulent heart studies after it found that no records were kept, and that the collaborators the author listed were fictitious people.

6. Lewis Thomas, *The Youngest Science: Notes of a Medicine-Watcher*, Viking, 1983.

7. C.P. Snow, *The Masters*, Scribner, 1960.

8. Truman Capote, *Music for Chameleons*, Random House, 1980.

9. Several studies revealing essentially the same findings were reported in *The New York Times*, March 13, 1984.

10. Jerome Kagan, *The Nature of the Child*, Basic Books, 1985.

11. It has become the current vogue to perceive narcissism and "borderline" pathology beneath the conflicts of patients. This is primarily based on the work of the late Heinz Kohut and of Otto Kernberg, though their views differ in certain key areas. Normally, the child internalizes love from the parents, which becomes the basis of self-worth. The narcissist is one who has failed to develop a sufficiently independent sense of self-worth, and tries to obtain it through affirmations of worth from others. Although superficially charming, the narcissist has severe difficulty forming intimate or lasting relationships and, in fact, views others with contempt or indifference. Coupled with the need for admiration is an underlying feeling of worthlessness. Kohut argued that narcissistic disorders are being generated by changing family relationships and society and change in the quality of family life; that the narcissist is a new kind of patient reflecting today's world. He looked at thwarted developmental needs; that the "self" was not supported or confirmed by parents. Therefore the narcissist uses people and when they are gone is left with a feeling of incompleteness because the sense of self is inadequate. However, his analysis was limited to child rearing, and his claim that children are too unstimulated and isolated was unaccompanied by any analysis of why this is. Also, he ignored the angry and aggressive dimension of narcissism. Kernberg, also a prominent analyst, argues, in contrast to Kohut, that sexual and aggressive drives that are related to the Oedipal period are critical in helping narcissists. In addition to the narcissist, Kernberg has analyzed the "borderline" personality, which is also seen as a new kind of patient. The borderline individual is more disturbed than the neurotic, but lacks the delusions of the psychotic. The person tends to be manipulative, self-destructive, and unstable. Some practitioners claim that this diagnosis characterizes as much as 10% of the population and 25% of all patients, and that the borderline's disturbances in identity and in maintaining stable relationships reflect the fragmentation of contemporary society. While typical neurotic problems concerning the Oedipal

and later stages concern, for example, jealousy, guilt, and anxiety, "object relations" theorists like Kernberg focus on earlier stages, in which awareness of the distinction between self and external world first emerges. It is believed that the origins of borderline, narcissistic, and psychotic lie here. The borderline has failed to integrate good and bad aspects of others and oneself, a phenomenon known as "splitting." The distinction between borderline and narcissistic problems is that the borderlines do not have the sense of exaggerated self-importance, superiority, and uniqueness that characterizes the narcissist. They have very negative and indistinct sense of selves and their relations are less stable. Narcissistic personalities do not have the borderline's tendency toward disorganization of thought nor the intolerance of frustration. Kernberg believes that the lack of structure in society with ambiguous role expectations may be difficult for borderlines. See Otto Kernberg, *Object Relations Theory and Clinical Psychoanalysis*, Jason Aronson, 1976; *Borderline Conditions and Pathological Narcissism*, Jason Aronson, 1975; Heinz Kohut, *The Analysis of the Self*, International Universities Press, 1971; *The Restoration of the Self*, International Universities Press, 1977.

12. There are many examples of executives who commit suicide after business reversal, or who undermine their success in subtle or overt ways, often noticeable to everyone but themselves, who illustrate the acting out of unconscious conflict.

13. Mickey Mantle discussed his dreams in an interview in *Baseball Digest*, February 1982.

14. *The New York Times*, November 7, 1982.

15. Robert Langs, *Madness and Cure*, Newconcept Press, 1985.

CHAPTER 8

1. For example, there is now an annual Symposium on Psychoanalytic Studies on Organizational Behavior and Experience, sponsored by the New York State School of Industrial and Labor Relations, Cornell University; and a collection of research papers on psychoanalytic applications to management and organization was recently published: *The Irrational Executive: Psychoanalytic Studies in Management*, ed. Manfred F. R. Kets de Vries, International Universities Press, 1984.

2. See the work of Daniel Goleman, *Vital Lies, Simple Truths*, Simon & Schuster, 1985.

3. For evaluations of the psychotherapeutic spectrum see, for example, G. L. Klerman and P. London, "Evaluating Psychotherapy," *American Journal of Psychiatry*, 1982, 139: 709–717; Morris B. Parloff, "Psychotherapy and Research: An Anaclitic Depression," *Psychiatry*, 1980, 43:279–293; A. L. Cochrane, *Effectiveness and Efficiency*, Nuffield Hospital Trust and Webb, Son, & Co. (London), 1972.

4. See Note 11, Chap. 7, for distinction between these conditions.

5. This was found, for example, in the research of Janice Haaken and Richard Adams, "Pathology as 'Personal Growth': A Participant-Observation Study of Lifespring Training," *Psychiatry*, 1983, 46:270–280.

6. Herbert Freudenberger, *Situational Anxiety*, Anchor Press, 1983.

7. See Meyer Friedman and Diane Ulmer, *Treating Type A Behavior—And Your Heart*, Alfred A. Knopf, 1984.

8. National Institute of Mental Health report, 1984.

9. Formulated by psychiatrists Donald F. Klein and Michael R. Liebowitz of Columbia University.

10. The Anxiety Disorders Clinic, New York State Psychiatric Institute, Columbia-Presbyterian Medical Center, New York.

11. Quoted in *Science News*, October 1, 1983. Breggin maintains that the chemical damage to the frontal lobes accomplishes the same thing as psychosurgery. See also his book, *Psychiatric Drugs: Hazards to the Brain*.

12. For example, a report by John B. Jemmott III, et al., in *Lancet*, June 25, 1983, documents that stress affects the human immune system, and that how one deals with stress is significant with regard to its effect on the immune system.

13. Ibid. Also, related work has been conducted by the psychoimmunity research project at Beth Israel Hospital, Boston, and Mount Sinai Medical Center, New York. See also *Psychoneuroimmunology,* ed. Robert Ader, Academic Press, 1981.

14. For example, research conducted at the University of Alabama Medical School, and undertaken by the National Institute of Neurological and Communicative Disorders and Stroke. Related research was reported at the First International Workshop on Neuroimmunomodulation, at the National Institutes of Health, Bethesda, Maryland, December 1984.

CHAPTER 9

1. The concept of "cover story" and "hidden plot" in psychoanalysis was originated by Erich Fromm and further elaborated by Michael Maccoby in an address to the William Alanson White Psychoanalytic Society, New York City, December 1972.

2. Findings from an ongoing study of top executives in large organizations conducted by the Center for Creative Leadership, Greensboro, North Carolina.

3. *The Washington Post,* March 5, 1984.

4. *The New York Times,* May 19, 1982.

5. From a 1981 report, "Corporations and Two-Career Families: Directions for the Future." issued by Catalyst, a New York-based resource center for professional women.

6. These cases were reported in *The Wall Street Journal,* May 31, 1983, and June 1, 1983.

7. Erich Fromm, *Man for Himself,* Rinehart, 1947.

8. Gallup survey, published in *The Wall Street Journal,* September 29, 1982.

9. Opinion Research Corporation survey, 1984.

10. Survey of executives conducted by Jeffry Timmons, Babson College, and Howard Stevenson, Harvard Business School, 1983.

11. Michael Maccoby, *Why Work: Leading the New Generation,* Simon & Schuster, 1988.

12. Ibid.

13. Reports on the Bolivar Project (a joint project of the United Auto Workers and Harman International Industries), and projects at the U.S. Dept. of Commerce, Dept. of State, and ACTION, were published as part of the Discussion Paper Series, John F. Kennedy School of Government, Harvard University. They and others are also available from the Project on Technology, Work, and Character, Washington, D.C.

14. See Maccoby, *Why Work,* op. cit., for an analysis of this evolution and its implications, some of which are summarized in the paragraphs that follow.

APPENDIX

1. The interview represents a modification of that originally developed by Fromm and Maccoby (op. cit.) and by Maccoby (1976, 1981). Its full version is in Maccoby, 1976, 247–274.

2. Rorschach, Hermann, *Psychodiagnostics: A Diagnostic Test Based on Perception,* Hans Huber (Berne), 1942.

3. Bruno Klopfer, et al., *Developments in the Rorschach Technique,* Harcourt, Brace, & World, 1954.

4. Samuel J. Beck, et al., *Rorschach's Test,* Grune & Stratton, 1961.

5. Roy Schafer, *Psychoanalytic Interpretation in Rorschach Testing,* Grune & Stratton, 1954.

6. Ernest G. Schachtel, *Experiential Foundations of Rorschach's Test,* Basic Books, 1966

7. Fred Brown, "An Exploratory Study of Dynamic Factors in the Content of the Rorschach Protocol," *Journal of Projective Techniques,* 1953, 17:251–279. Reprinted in *A*

Rorschach Reader, Murray H. Sherman, ed., International Universities Press, 1960, 354–392.

8. The following discussion of the Rorschach, including description of the cards, is adapted from Maccoby, 1981, op. cit. Reprinted, in modified form, with permission.

9. This initial version of the research method was not published in English until recently: Erich Fromm, *The Working Class in Weimar Germany*, translated by Barbara Weinberger, Harvard University Press, 1984.

10. Erich Fromm and Michael Maccoby, op. cit.; Maccoby, 1976, 1981, 1987.

INDEX

247

Printed in the United States
45182LVS00004B/53